effect, the book embodies an original way of understanding major intellectual and artistic movements, employing the Baroque as a theoretical tool to analyse contemporary works of art and the so-called modern condition.

The author

Gilles Deleuze is Professor of Philosophy at the University of Paris. His other works include *Nietzsche and Philosophy* (Athlone 1983), *Kant's Critical Philosophy* (Athlone 1984), *Cinema I* (1986), *Cinema II* (Athlone 1989) and *Logic of Sense* (Athlone 1990).

Also from The Athlone Press

Cinema I: The Movement-Image
GILLES DELEUZE
1986 0 485 11281 7 (hbk) 0 485 12081 X (pbk)

Cinema II: The Time-Image
GILLES DELEUZE
1989 0 485 11359 7 (hbk) 0 485 12070 4 (pbk)

Logic of Sense
GILLES DELEUZE
1990 0 485 30063 X

Nietzsche and Philosophy
GILLES DELEUZE
1983 0 485 12053 4 (pbk)

Anti-Oedipus: Capitalism and Schizophrenia
GILLES DELEUZE and FELIX GUATTARI
Preface by Michel Foucault
1984 0 485 30018 4 (pbk)

A Thousand Plateaus
GILLES DELEUZE and FELIX GUATTARI
1988 0 485 11335 X (hbk) 0 485 12058 5 (pbk)

Difference and Repetition
GILLES DELEUZE
1993 0 485 11360 0

Foucault
GILLES DELEUZE
1988 0 485 11345 7

Kant's Critical Philosophy
GILLES DELEUZE
1984 0 485 11249 3

Dialogues
GILLES DELEUZE and CLAIRE PARNET
1987 0 485 11333 3

The Fold

Leibniz and the Baroque

Gilles Deleuze

Foreword and translation by Tom Conley

THE ATHLONE PRESS
London

First published in Great Britain 1993 by
The Athlone Press Ltd
1 Park Drive
London NW11 7SG

First published in France as
Le Pli: Leibnitz et le Baroque

A catalogue record for this book is available from the
British Library

ISBN 0 485 11421 6 (hbk)
0 485 12087 9 (pbk)

Printed in the United States of America

Contents

II. Inclusions

III. Having a Body

Translator's Foreword
A Plea for Leibniz

Soon after finishing what would bear the title of *The Art of the West,* an esthetic history of the High Middle Ages, Henri Focillon theorized the experience of his research in *Vie des formes.*[1] Reflecting on the emergence of the Romanesque and Gothic styles, Focillon confronts dilemmas facing all historians of the Middle Ages and *ancien régime.* How do styles develop, and why do they differ so markedly? Do they succeed one another or share pertinent traits? Do esthetic styles convey, in a broader sense, the notion of particular "manners of thinking"? Can styles be periodized and, if so, what are the ideological motivations betraying the historical schemes that also tend to produce them?

In the context of French literary and esthestic history in the aftermath of the First World War, Focillon departs from traditions of esthetic and literary botany that date to Sainte-Beuve and Auguste Comte. For them, tables, categories, genealogical trees, and lines of phyla could map out great mnemonic systems. They would soon program the ways the French nation would construct its patrimony. Students of these paradigms would forever recall the grids, fill them with appropriate facts and traits, and thus be "informed" by schemes of knowledge.[2] To the contrary, Focillon notes that the Romanesque and Gothic, two dominant and contrastive styles, often inflect each other. They crisscross and sometimes fold vastly different sensibilities into each other. The historian is obliged to investigate how the two worlds work through each other at different speeds and, in turn, how they chart various trajectories on the surface of the European continent.

In *Vie des formes,* Focillon rethought the logic of evolution that had been bequeathed to the twentieth century. On the one hand, a remarkably firm tradition of inquiry, observation, and historicization came with positivism. Yet, on the other, the really creative positivists of the nineteenth century—Balzac, Hugo, and Proust—built works whose mass, fragmentary totality, and changing effects impugned the tabled symmetries that their scientific counterparts had invented. The history of the Romanesque and Gothic appeared, in the eyes of Focillon, no less massive in its overall effects than the poems and novels of nineteenth-century literary masters.

At certain points, Focillon's overview of the Middle Ages resembles a mix of technical history and organic chemistry. Forms move back and forth, disappear, recur, or bring out new shapes when they are superimposed or interconnected. Gothic maidens at Reims indeed "smile" where Romanesque peasants at Vézelay had been staring, exorbitantly and aghast, at the onslaught of the Second Coming. Both styles experience a Baroque phase. Romanesque buildings, and sculptures on tympana and capitals, with their solemn aura, share features that can be identified best by categories whose descriptives belong to a later period.[3] In a similar vein, the textured effects of "irreality" in the *flamboyant* in the fifteenth century tend to narrate the entire history of the adventure of the ogive, and flow into the life of culture in general.

Through the theory gained from his observations, in *Vie des formes* Focillon calls into question the rationale of periodization. With figures borrowed from biology, he bends many of the schematic lines of positivistic forebears. At the same time, adapting Wilhelm Wörringer's notion of the "Gothic" as what signifies a will for movement running through the entire Middle Ages, Focillon assails the gap that existed, in the *entre-deux-guerres,* between French and German culture. He writes of a history of art composed of differently paced but intermingling phases. An "experimental" beginning seeks solutions to problems that a "classical" moment discovers and exploits. A "radiating" (*rayonnant*) period refines the solutions of the former to a degree of preciosity, while a "Baroque" phase at once sums up, turns upon, contorts, and narrates the formulas of all the others.

The Baroque thus does not comprise what we associate with Bernini, Borromini, or Le Brun. "The Baroque state reveals identical traits existing as constants within the most diverse environments and periods of time. Baroque was not reserved exclusively for the Europe of the last three centuries any more than classicism was the unique privilege of Mediterranean culture."[4] "Baroque" designates a trope that comes from the renewed origins of art and has stylistic evidence that prevails in culture in general. Under its rubric are placed the proliferation of mystical experience, the birth of the novel, intense taste for life that grows and pullulates, and a fragility of infinitely varied patterns of movement. It could be located in the protracted fascination we experience in watching waves heave, tumble, and atomize when they crack along an unfolding line being traced along the expanse of a shoreline; in following the curls and wisps of color that move on the surface and in the infinite depths of a tile of marble; or, as Proust described, when we follow the ramifying and dilating branches of leaves piled in the concavity of the amber depths of a cup of tea.

Gilles Deleuze appears to share these same sensations in his dazzling reading of Leibniz. *The Fold* tells indirectly of the reincarnation of the Franco-German philosopher through the Baroque, as understood by Focillon in its broadest and most influential way, that radiates through different histories, cultures, and worlds of knowledge. Deleuze's work may be the first and most daring venture to take the Baroque, in the specific figure of the fold, through the history of art, science, costume, mathematics, lyric, and philosophy. *The Fold* might also stand as one of the most personal, sensuous, and original of all of Deleuze's writings. At the same time its breadth might also strike readers as difficult and opaque. At first glance, the book is disarming. The implied reader is taken to be as familiar as the author is with atomic theory, differential calculus, classical and contemporary painting and music, and with the history of logic. Yet the pleasure Deleuze affords comes with the confidence he invests in the reader: the work is composed as if spoken to a friend relaxing on a sofa by a window of a small apartment, on a second or third floor, that overlooks a large city. Without pretension Deleuze speaks of marvelously difficult equations in differential calculus, biological and fractal models, of the performance of the music of Pierre Boulez, and of esthetic history. The book's tone flatters us at the same time it dismantles — without posture or grandiloquence — some of the most shopworn beliefs we have inherited about the texture of our physical world. In what remains of this preface I should like to touch on what Deleuze appears to be doing with Leibniz, and how his affiliation with the philosopher affects what we discern about contemporary issues.

Deleuze argues that while the Baroque has been a disputed term in the fine arts, esthetic history, and music, it has not been associated with either a philosophy or a philosopher apt or complex enough to embody and theorize its principles. For Deleuze, Leibniz happens to be *the* philosopher of the Baroque. Leibniz is so contemporary that the ensemble of his research on science and mathematics, or his treatments of contradiction, belief, music, and theology help to explain — or unfold — what we know about the world at the end of the twentieth century.

The experience of the Baroque entails that of the fold. Leibniz is the first great philosopher and mathematician of the pleat, of curves and twisting surfaces. He rethinks the phenomenon of "point of view," of perspective, of conic sections, and of city planning. Included in the category of things folded are draperies, tresses, tesselated fabrics, ornate costumes; dermal surfaces of the body that unfold in the embryo and crease themselves at death; domestic architecture that bends upper and lower levels together while floating in the cosmos;

novels that invaginate their narratives or develop infinite possibilities of serial form; harmonics that orchestrate vastly different rhythms and tempos; philosophies that resolve Cartesian distinctions of mind and body through physical means — without recourse to occasionalism or parallelism — grasped as foldings; styles and iconographies of painting that hide shapely figures in ruffles and billows of fabric, or that lead the eye to confuse different orders of space and surface.

Now in *The Art of the West,* Focillon remarks that the age of the "Baroque Gothic" witnessed the birth of the mystical experience. It is characterized, as other thinkers have since shown in greater detail, by an individual's account of his or her voyage to and from an ineffably universal event, which set the body in a trance, and which has left marks, scars, or other physical evidence that confirm the individual's tale of passage.[5] The mystical venture convinces because no language can be said to represent what it means. It is tantamount, in part, to what Deleuze, by means of Leibniz, Henri Michaux, and Gaëtau Clérambault, might call an *event*: it may not have an empirical or historical basis, but it happens to be the virtual sensation of a somatic moment of totalization and dispersion. In the novel or poetry, it can be felt as a seriality of epiphany. Its scientific analogies might include the thoughts of infinity that come with the view of the world in which all of its visible objects are moving aggregates of infinite numbers of atoms and molecules. In the vision of Alfred North Whitehead, a philosopher inspired by Leibniz, an event can be seen in the duration that produces the site of a pyramid, an avalanche of snow, or the jagged edge of rifts in a block of ice. For Deleuze, an event unfolds from the union of our perception and the duration of a fan — of the kind Mallarmé describes in his occasional verse — that unites and disperses a word (an *event*) and an object (an *éventail*) when it swirls the atmosphere.

These rarefied areas of sensation constitute a mystical and mathematical dimension of the Baroque. Leibniz, declares Deleuze, stands as the first philosopher able to deal with the experience of events and the world of atomic dynamics. Deleuze himself appears to be mystical insofar as much of *The Fold* — especially in the arguments that develop from sufficient reason, incompossibility, perception, and the apportioning of space (in chapters 4 through 8) — develops through absolute identity with Leibniz. A reader often notices an indirect discourse that melds with the movement of the *New Essays on Human Understanding* or the correspondence with Arnauld. Deleuze, whose voice translates better than any the experience of contemporary time, is harmonized with that of the Franco-German philosopher at the threshold of the Enlightenment. As we listen to Deleuze, in the intimacy of the Baroque home in which *The Fold* appears to be taking place (figure 1 in the first chapter), we perceive philosophical and ethical dilemmas on the horizon of our lives.

Reincarnation of Leibniz follows a pattern of force. Deleuze has often identified with philosophers of the past—not always the most renowned—in order to confront political and ethical issues of the present. When he wrote on Nietzsche in the early 1960s, Deleuze *was* Nietzsche: he launched a transvaluation of a culture, mired in existentialism, that had not completely assimilated the effects of its colonial history. He then became Spinoza and Bergson at a time when intellectuals collectively cried for a "return" to Freud. To extend and modify the canon of philosophical writing, he wrote on Kafka, Melville, and, later, Francis Bacon. Yet Leibniz has always been a powerful force in all of Deleuze's writing, and at this stage of the philosopher's career *The Fold* comes as no surprise. The earlier writings (especially *Logique du sens*) often mention Leibniz with admiration, or use the *Monadologie* to recall the complexity of scientific theory in the *ancien régime,* but they never develop into identification with Leibniz's signature.

A truism of French intellectual history states that for national and philosophical reasons every postwar thinker, from Jean Hippolyte to Jacques Derrida, must contend with Hegel. Deleuze had resisted the totalizing effects of the dialectic by aligning himself at once with Cartesian and left-wing political traditions. He made moves that showed how, by way of Spinoza, a more complex, fragmented, and prismatic philosophy antedated Hegel and could not be supplanted by systematic dialectics. In this light the study of Leibniz implies that an extraordinarily delicate filigree of concepts, winding through organic and inorganic worlds, has to be retrieved. Leibniz is thus also a philosopher of habitat and ecology. His myriad connections and series of concepts are not held in a prescribed order or a unifying system. Multiplicity and variety of inflections produce "events," or vibrations, "with an infinity of harmonics or submultiples." Movement of a concept that has bearing upon a subject's impressions of the physical world does not elevate according to a spiral plan, which belongs to philosophy, but radiates or ramifies everywhere in the geography of experience, such that we can imagine movement of light and sound, together, as folds of ethereal matter that waft and waver.

An exquisitely sensuous view of the world is obtained through the curved shapes that Leibniz creates with calculus, and from manifestations of folds that we follow in modern art and poetry. Deleuze implies that if a chronology of the history of philosophy is mapped over the kinds of vibrations and events developed from the Gothic period until now, something goes awry. Leibniz is not merely a chapter in the history of mathematics, cognition, or logic. The relation of monadic thinking to our sense of the world cannot be discounted; the movement of his reasoning shares many common traits with what theorists of science, musicians, and artists are now making of habitat.

Leibniz, he implies, develops a philosophy that bridges the pre-Socratics, Lucretius, and neo-Einsteinian thinkers. In light of earlier work (*Proust et les signes*) and his most recent writing (*Qu'est-ce que la philosophie?* with Félix

Guattari), *The Fold* joins philosophy to the ecology of hypothetical experience. In his study of *In Search of Lost Time,* Deleuze noted that Proust's mission bore a Platonic label. The quest would restore art and lead to an enduring and redemptive idea. But what the text seeks to redeem is riddled from within by a stylistic practice that scatters everything that would comprise a "whole" or a "unity." Yet since the work is finished in its incompletion, "there must be a unity which is the unity *of* that multiple piece, *of* that multiplicity, as in all *of* those fragments."[6] Deleuze's stress on the partitive shows how Proust's great project of a total novel betrays a "communication that would not be posited as a principle, but would result from the play of [textual] machines and their detached pieces, of their unconnected parts" (196). It is Leibniz who inspires this observation, since the seventeenth-century philosopher "first posed the problem of communication resulting from closed units or from what cannot be attached" (196). By means of Leibniz's innovation, which marks the limits of communication, the subject is enveloped in the predicate, just as Proust's intention is folded into his effect. Inclusion of the subject in the predicate implies that the world makes up a chaotic cosmos or *chaosmos*. By way of Leibniz's logic, Deleuze is able to conceive of artworks composed of units that are neither logical nor organic, "that is, neither based upon pieces as a long unity or a fragmented totality; nor formed or prefigured by those units in the course of a logical development or of an organic evolution" (191). As in Focillon's vision of a "life of forms" that mixes biological and serial figures in its description of the Baroque phase, or in the giddy effects of partial things in the novel that betray Proust's intentions, a hierarchy of organic and inorganic things no longer holds. "Life" is invested into brute matter insofar as it, too, is perpetually moving, metamorphosing, or emigrating from one condition to another.

All of a sudden, by way of the relation of atomic theory to that of the monad, an ideology of hierarchies of life begins to totter. When organic and inorganic materials are differentiated not by a wall but by way of a vector (early in chapter 1). There ensues an ethical problem about how we are to apprehend the world. That humans stand as triumphant subjects among inert objects no longer holds. They no longer own things as they had in the world of possessive individualism. Now it must be asked how humans select and designate what they call "living" or "inert." If organic life cannot be easily demarcated from inorganic matter, it behooves subjects to look at all matter from a different angle. Leibniz points toward an ethics that appends the science of ecology. In his turn, Deleuze suggests that an at once abstract and tactile sense of matter must figure at the crux of any social practice.

In more recent work that follows the implications of *The Fold,* Deleuze (and Félix Guattari) promote conceptual activity that will move in the direction of a "geophilosophy." Entailed is a revolution of "absolute deterritorialization."[7] The authors do mean that philosophy advocates the collapse of national boundaries or a return to diversities of economic or ethnic worlds, but that the totalitarian aspect of liberal democracy (spurred by the demise of the Soviet Union and the prospect of the European Economic Community) has to be atomized, at least in one stage, by the labor of conceptual thinking. They suggest that philosophy can acquire agency by the use of a monadic sensibility when it addresses issues of habitat and thinking.

In *Qu'est-ce que la philosophie,* a geopolitics of deterritorialization is advanced. The authors speculate that Greek philosophy is something that originates with migrants who arrive on the Aegean peninsula and, through their example, initiate a collective sense of immanence. Ulysses, not Robinson Crusoe, is the ruseful plebian, the everyman who inhabits urban space, and who gives rise to a conceptual process in which are planted the seeds of its own demise. When it commodifies concepts, marketing seeks to co-opt philosophy. Deterritorialization, and its obverse, reterritorialization, implicitly tie monadic thinking to the art of displacement and transformation. "A stick is, in its turn, a deterritorialized branch" (p. 66). Those who conceive of organic and inorganic matter from this point of view tend to be geophilosophers. Their activity "slides" on the surface of the world, as on a wave. A "surfer," the geophilosopher moves along the crest of turbulence, on the shoulders of waves that envelop mind, energy, and matter, and that diffuse them into the atmosphere.

Allusive as the politics of geophilosophy may be, some of its clearest manifestations are found at the end of *The Fold.* In the final chapter, Deleuze ties Leibniz's concept of "new harmony" to Baroque and contemporary music.[8] He picks up, however, the strands of his discussion on the Baroque home that he had elaborated in the first and third chapters. By virtue of the radiation of musical waves that move in and about monads, the world is made up of "divergent series," and thus resembles an infinity of pleats and creases of unified and dispersed matter. All of a sudden the distinctions that were used to elaborate Leibniz's vision of space—in which the monad is composed of two "floors," including first, an upper, private, intimate area (that would be a stage for a chamber ensemble) and, second, a lower, public level where masses circulate—are no longer sustained. The sentences break off from the music of monadic harmony and decor; they turn to issues of habitat.

The last question that Deleuze poses involves what it means to live in the world. Our experience of a shrinking globe inflects the vision of the monad, since compressions of time and space modify "the difference of inside and outside and of public and private" (p. 137). Thus, contemporary artists and musicians in the line of Leibniz transform *monadology* into *nomadology.* They are emigrant thinkers who deterritorialize accepted notions of space. Like the shift of the opposition of organic and inorganic matter into tonal flow and flux, the movement from an order of ethereal and private space over a teeming public world (or "fishbowl") indicates how the geophilosophy will operate. The two worlds must fold into each other. The political implication is that the "upper floor" of the first world must refuse a distinction with second, third, or fourth worlds by (a) rethinking the difference of organic and inorganic forms and (b) by reducing the speed of its movement to harmonize with that of the "lower" world.

Leibniz had mediated what historians study in terms of social contradiction of the *ancien régime* with an activity that "folds, unfolds, and refolds" matter, space and time. Contemporary artists, also geophilosophers and students of revolutions, are impelled to work in the same fashion. Their activity accounts for the shrinkage of the world, its increased organic mass, and consequent impoverishment of biological variety. Forms, like modes of folding, disappear. The political strategy of *The Fold* continually bends our dilemmas back onto Leibniz's fascination with infinite and curvilinear forms. Leibniz opens a window onto our world: Deleuze appears to use Leibniz's concept of harmonics to advocate the possibility of infinity to be thought within the restricted limits of our habitat. A process without spatial development is implied by the non-Hegelian tenor of the last clause in the book: *plier, déplier, replier.* Thus Deleuze argues for rediscovery of other styles (*manières*) of folding the space of life. If philosophy can theorize the shrinking limits in which we live, Leibniz exemplifies a system that does not flatten nature to a concept or world-picture. The searing irony is that Leibniz refuses simplification so at the very time his work indicates how the technology of capitalism can be developed.[9] By counterexample, the infinity of the fold locates where and how the world has since become compressed. Now if the fold traverses all matter, its movement allows us to conceive ways of inhabiting the world with tactical resourcefulness. Its very abstraction —for what indeed *is* the fold?—allows for elaboration of sensibilities not under the yoke of liberal democracy.

It may be that Deleuze's imagination of the fold harbors an impractical and unfounded optimism in respect to what can be conceived in our history of accelerated compression of time and space. The politics of the fold would seem to be so chimerical that Deleuze and Guattari could be likened to two "spiritual automata," Quixote and Sancho, who venture in an intimate infinity of philosophical space far from the stress that human life and social contradiction impose on the globe. It is licit to wonder if the work withdraws into an interdisciplinary monad.

Seen thus, *The Fold* and *Qu'est-ce que la philosophie* would be hypothetical approaches to problems—population, habitat, displacement, geocide—that require urgent and practical commitment. Habitat, it must be countered, includes conceptual virtue. And since they beg reaction of this kind, these works can also be said to orient philosophy to the future of the planet in ways that pragmatic means have yet to conceptualize. In fact, *The Fold* finds the clearest expression of its politics in the ways that a utopian thought—and by utopia can be meant Leibniz's fancifully lucid invention of the monad—joins the labors of philosophy.

Leibniz is political because he is utopian. His theories of curvature, movement, and point of view cannot be localized. Deleuze and Guattari note that a "utopia is not separated from infinite movement: Utopia designates absolute deterritorialization, yet always at the critical point where the latter is attached to the relatively present milieu, and especially with forces that are the fabric of this milieu."[10] The pleats and hems of the ideal Baroque home thus do not merely refer to a "nowhere," as if prompting a mirror-reading of Samuel Butler's *Erewhon,* but also to a "now-here" that is present whenever and wherever the concept of its space is taken up.

In this sense Leibniz's theories are not specifically "objects" but, in Deleuze's lexicon, Baroque *territories.* They pertain to a nature endowed with forces that Leibniz describes by tracking the motion of infinite folding, or by investigation of the caverns and crannies of porous shapes opened in the twists of stone, fossils, and metamorphic rocks. These are territories of contemplation for the mind, but they are not to be abused while it "lives and thinks in a state of self-contained reflection" (p. 99). A similar politics emerges from Deleuze's comparison of Descartes's and Leibniz's views on extension. For the former, the material world can be mapped out from the axis of the thinking subject, in rectilinear fashion, and can be divided into discrete units. The resulting geography resembles the order and process of the *quincunx,* a two-dimensional system of gridding and squaring that places a center (the ego) at the intersection of the diagonals of a surrounding square. When the self moves into space, it transforms one of the corners of the square or rectangle of its periphery into the site of a new center, around which new extremities are established, and so forth, until space is conquered.[11] For the latter, neither the self nor the world can work so schematically. Everywhere the subject swirls in the midst of forces they exert stress that defines the individual body, its elasticity, and its bending motions in volumes that produce movement in and of extension. The subject lives and reinacts its own embryonic development as a play of folds (endo-, meso-, and ectoderm) rather than as a battleground pitting the self against the world. By way of Leibniz's critique of Cartesian space the author pleads for tact of body and environment.

The Fold makes its sensibility manifest through its turns of style. The sentences are simple, and the transparency of their expression often beguiling. They are built less from the verb or the tension of the subject and predicate than along the path of its logical "seams" on the edges or pleats of each sentence. Many start with what appear to be conversational modes, with *c'est, c'est bien, ce n'est plus, c'est que,* or *c'est qu'il y a. . . .* These beginnings promise less than the philosophically charged incipit, *es gibt,* or the French *il y a,* "there is," "what is . . . is the fact that," etc., that tend to identify the writer with a hidden authority invested with the power to judge and control those who read or listen. Deleuze employs *c'est* as a connector, as a unit that can link concepts into serial chains that attach to any number of other sentences. The construction stages the process—also dear to Leibniz—that conflates subject and predicate. Cast thus, Deleuze's sentences articulate the problem of inclusion and connection of different lexical constructions. Vocables and phrastic units are apt to ramify. The concept itself "becomes a subject" in conformity with each level of grammatical parts and wholes. Leibniz's logic marks a break, Deleuze argues (in "Sufficient Reason," chapter four), with the classical conception of the subject as a rational being. By using terms linked by the copula *to be,* and by varying on *c'est,* Deleuze does not shirk responsibility for elegance of argument or stylistic clarity: following Leibniz, he summons the distinction of subject and predicate that grounds Cartesian reason. The continuity of style in *The Fold* keeps the one—either subject or predicate—from being an attribute of the other.

At the same time, transparency is gained in the apparent simplicity of the sentence. Different and simultaneous movements of logic and style develop within the syntax of each phrastic unit. In this sense, Focillon's description of Baroque "syntax" in medieval art is not without parallel to the style of either Leibniz or Deleuze. Baroque forms, notes the art historian, "live with passionate intensity a life that is entirely their own. . . . They break apart even as they grow; they tend to invade space in every direction, to perforate it, to become as one with all its possibilities."[12] Deleuze's style promotes confusion of form and sign, but paradoxically, in ways such that the overall effect does *not* draw attention to itself. The sentence signifies its content, but the content is seriated to conform to the rhythm of the argument.

With some exception, Deleuze's sentences tend to be short, simple, and pellucid. In their concatenation, they break open and recombine, inviting the reader to isolate given clauses and reconnect them, to produce mobile effects where verbal groups jump into or recur in other clauses. The implied movement mimes what the author finds in the play of fixity and passage in Leibniz's taste for simultaneous mobility and closure of concepts. Once again, the manner confirms what Deleuze observes about the sufficiency of Leibnizian reason: an "extraordinary philosophical activity which consists of the creation of principles," where there are "two poles, one toward which all principles are folding themselves together, the other toward which they are all unfolding, in the opposite way." The double movement betrays what Deleuze calls "the extreme taste for principles," far from favoring division into compartments, that "presides over the passage of beings, of things, and of concepts under all kinds of mobile partitions" (p. 58).

The geometrical shapes of Deleuze's sentences reproduce the serialities of which he writes. Leibniz manifests a vision of the world with consequences that exceed the correlation of philosophy with the beginnings of industrial technology. At the beginning of the eighteenth century, the idea of a stamp (or an impression promoting the effect of individual style) "imposed a law of constancy on the production of objects. With the fold a fluctuation or deviation from a norm replaces the permanence of a law, when the object assumes its place in a continuum of variation." The object acquires a new status when it refers no longer to a spatial conception of molding, but a "temporal modulation" or a "continuous variation of matter" (chapter 2). The object is not withdrawn from the mold that forms it. A "continuous temporal molding" of serialized objects replaces a paradigm of spatiality by another, of temporal order. So, too, is the tenor of Deleuze's style. Deleuze notices that Leibniz's mathematics of continuity and modulation change utterly our ideas about the object and event, but all the while they conform to an order of preformation.

Deleuze's diction tends to replicate this standard for transformation. The sentences do not reflect a law, but vary on their implicit norm. They are declarative; often composed of two or three independent clauses connected by a colon or conjunctions; unlike a classical concept, they do not seek to recall the origin of a signatory stamp. Attention is shunted away from their composition to the logical process that makes their linkage appear as an unfolding of ideas and shapes. Modulation therefore becomes a criterion of style. Consequently, the verbal material does not set forth to tell a narrative, based on Aristotelian poetics (exposition, movement toward a "plot-point," and resolution), that would tend to reach a kernel truth in the story of Leibniz and the Baroque. Nor does Deleuze, as might Jacques Derrida, construct an elaborate system of textual defense that produces a surface of tantalizing involutions, or expressions of foreplay, which defer a gripping conclusion that inverts or twists the exposition. Instead, each chapter establishes a modulated flow, as it were, of concept-sentence-units, which flatten illusion that generally accompanies the rhetoric of argument or narrative. The chapters can be read in any order; their conclusions are enveloped everywhere in the "machinic" manner of the text.

The French edition is composed of long paragraphs that envelop the themes listed serially in the table of contents. Most of the material follows—but not always—the order he places under each chapter-heading. The logic of the argumentation is carefully outlined. If the table of contents is not studied beforehand, the organization of materials can appear dense or chaotic. To attenuate that impression, I have taken the liberty of inserting breaks in the text that roughly follow the themes listed in the summary. I have also divided many of the paragraphs into smaller units. Whereas the specialist of philosophy may have no difficulty following the development of Deleuze's reasoning, readers of different backgrounds may find the added space helpful for pause and reflection. Otherwise, I have stayed as close as possible to the order and rhythm of the arguments.

Wherever possible, I have quoted English translations of Leibniz from standard and available editions. The way that the German, French, and English editions of Leibniz are used in *The Fold* is outlined in the Preface to the Notes.

For this translation I wish to thank Biodun Iginla, of the University of Minnesota Press, who encouraged its undertaking; Brian Massumi for his magnificent example of *A Thousand Plateaus* and timely advice about this project; Ann Klefstad and Mary Byers for their alert reading and emendations; John Aubrey, of the Newberry Library, who solved many bibliographical riddles. Their assistance has been invaluable. The blemishes the reader will find are solely the fault of the translator.

Part I
The Fold

Chapter 1
The Pleats of Matter

The Baroque refers not to an essence but rather to an operative function, to a trait. It endlessly produces folds. It does not invent things: there are all kinds of folds coming from the East, Greek, Roman, Romanesque, Gothic, Classical folds. . . . Yet the Baroque trait twists and turns its folds, pushing them to infinity, fold over fold, one upon the other. The Baroque fold unfurls all the way to infinity. First, the Baroque differentiates its folds in two ways, by moving along two infinities, as if infinity were composed of two stages or floors: the pleats of matter, and the folds in the soul. Below, matter is amassed according to a first type of fold, and then organized according to a second type, to the extent its part constitutes organs that are "differently folded and more or less developed."[1] Above, the soul sings of the glory of God inasmuch as it follows its own folds, but without succeeding in entirely developing them, since "this communication stretches out indefinitely."[2] A labyrinth is said, etymologically, to be multiple because it contains many folds. The multiple is not only what has many parts but also what is folded in many ways. A labyrinth corresponds exactly to each level: the continuous labyrinth in matter and its parts, the labyrinth of freedom in the soul and its predicates.[3] If Descartes did not know how to get through the labyrinth, it was because he sought its secret of continuity in rectilinear tracks, and the secret of liberty in a rectitude of the soul. He knew the inclension of the soul as little as he did the curvature of matter. A "cryptographer" is needed, someone who can at once account for nature and decipher the soul, who can peer into the crannies of matter and read into the folds of the soul.[4]

Clearly the two levels are connected (this being why continuity rises up into the soul). There are souls down below, sensitive, animal; and there even exists a lower level in the souls. The pleats of matter surround and envelop them. When we learn that souls cannot be furnished with windows opening onto the outside, we must first, at the very least, include souls upstairs, reasonable ones, who have ascended to the other level ("elevation"). It is the upper floor that has no windows. It is a dark room or chamber decorated only with a stretched canvas "diversified by folds," as if it were a living dermis. Placed on the opaque canvas, these folds, cords, or springs represent an innate form of knowledge, but when solicited by matter they move into action. Matter triggers "vibrations or oscillations" at the lower extremity of the cords, through the intermediary of "some little openings" that exist on the lower level. Leibniz constructs a great Baroque montage that moves between the lower floor, pierced with windows, and the upper floor, blind and closed, but on the other hand resonating as if it were a musical salon translating the visible movements below into sounds up above.[5]

It could be argued that this text does not express Leibniz's thought, but instead the maximum degree of its possible conciliation with Locke. The text also fashions a way of representing what Leibniz will always affirm: a correspondence and even a communication between the two levels, between the two labyrinths, between the pleats of matter and the folds in the soul. A fold between the two folds? And the same image, that of veins in marble, is applied to the two under different conditions. Sometimes the veins are the pleats of matter that surround living beings held in the mass, such that the marble tile resembles a rippling lake that teems with fish. Sometimes the veins are innate ideas in the soul, like twisted figures or powerful statues caught in the block of marble. Matter is marbled, of two different styles.

Wölfflin noted that the Baroque is marked by a certain number of material traits: horizontal widening of the lower floor, flattening of the pediment, low and curved stairs that push into space; matter handled in masses or aggregates, with the rounding of angles and avoidance of perpendiculars; the circular acanthus replacing the jagged acanthus, use of limestone to produce spongy, cavernous shapes, or to constitute a vortical form always put in motion by renewed turbulence, which ends only in the manner of a horse's mane or the foam of a wave; matter tends to spill over in space, to be reconciled with fluidity at the same time fluids themselves are divided into masses.[6]

Huygens develops a Baroque mathematical physics whose goal is curvilinearity. With Leibniz the curvature of the universe is prolonged according to three other fundamental notions: the fluidity of matter, the elasticity of bodies, and motivating spirit as a mechanism. First, matter would clearly not be extended following a twisting line. Rather, it would follow a tangent.[7] But the universe appears compressed by an active force that endows matter with a curvilinear or

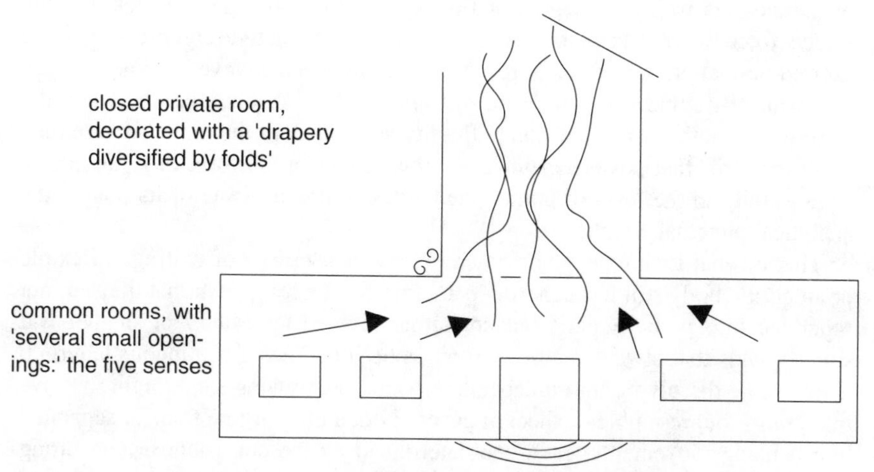

The Baroque House (an allegory)

spinning movement, following an arc that ultimately has no tangent. And the infinite division of matter causes compressive force to return all portions of matter to the surrounding areas, to the neighboring parts that bathe and penetrate the given body, and that determine its curvature. Dividing endlessly, the parts of matter form little vortices in a maelstrom, and in these are found even more vortices, even smaller, and even more are spinning in the concave intervals of the whirls that touch one another.

Matter thus offers an infinitely porous, spongy, or cavernous texture without emptiness, caverns endlessly contained in other caverns: no matter how small, each body contains a world pierced with irregular passages, surrounded and penetrated by an increasingly vaporous fluid, the totality of the universe resembling a "pond of matter in which there exist different flows and waves."[8] From this, however, we would not conclude, in the second place, that even the most refined matter is perfectly fluid and thus loses its texture (according to a thesis that Leibniz imputes to Descartes). Descartes's error probably concerns what is to be found in different areas. He believed that the real distinction between parts entailed separability. What specifically defines an absolute fluid is the absence of coherence or cohesion; that is, the separability of parts, which in fact applies only to a passive and abstract matter.[9] According to Leibniz, two parts of really distinct matter can be inseparable, as shown not only by the action of surrounding forces that determine the curvilinear movement of a body but also by the pressure of surrounding forces that determine its hardness (coherence, cohesion) or the inseparability of its parts. Thus it must be stated that a body has a degree of hardness as well as a degree of fluidity, or that it is essentially elastic, the elastic force of bodies being the expression of the active compressive force exerted on matter. When a boat reaches a certain speed a wave becomes as hard as a wall of marble. The atomistic hypothesis of an absolute hardness and the Cartesian hypothesis of an absolute fluidity are joined all the more because they share the error that posits separable minima, either in the form of finite bodies or in infinity in the form of points (the Cartesian line as a site of its points, the analytical punctual equation).

That is what Leibniz explains in an extraordinary piece of writing: a flexible or an elastic body still has cohering parts that form a fold, such that they are not separated into parts of parts but are rather divided to infinity in smaller and smaller folds that always retain a certain cohesion. Thus a continuous labyrinth is not a line dissolving into independent points, as flowing sand might dissolve into grains, but resembles a sheet of paper divided into infinite folds or separated into bending movements, each one determined by the consistent or conspiring surroundings. "The division of the continuous must not be taken as of sand dividing into grains, but as that of a sheet of paper or of a tunic in folds, in such a way that an infinite number of folds can be produced, some smaller than others, but without the body ever dissolving into points or minima."[10] A fold is always folded within a fold, like a cavern in a cavern. The unit of matter, the smallest element of the labyrinth, is the fold, not the point which is never a part, but a simple extremity of the line. That is why parts of matter are masses or aggregates, as a correlative to elastic compressive force. Unfolding is thus not the contrary of folding, but follows the fold up to the following fold. Particles are "turned into folds," that a "contrary effort changes over and again."[11] Folds of winds, of waters, of fire and earth, and subterranean folds of veins of ore in a mine. In a system of complex interactions, the solid pleats of "natural geography" refer to the effect first of fire, and then of waters and winds on the earth; and the veins of metal in mines resemble the curves of conical forms, sometimes ending in a circle or an ellipse, sometimes stretching into a hyperbola or a parabola.[12] The model for the sciences of matter is the "origami," as the Japanese philosopher might say, or the art of folding paper.

Two consequences result that provide a sense of the affinity of matter with life and organisms. To be sure, organic folds have their own specificity, as fossils demonstrate. But on the one hand, the division of parts in matter does not go without a decomposition of bending movement or of flexions. We see this in the development of the egg, where numerical division is only the condition of morphogenic movements, and of invagination as a pleating. On the other hand, the formation of the organism would remain an improbable mystery, or a miracle, even if matter were to divide infinitely into independent points. But it becomes increasingly probable and natural when an infinity of indeterminate states is given (already folded over each other), each of which includes a cohesion at its level, somewhat like the improbability of forming a word by chance with separate letters, but with far more likelihood with syllables or inflections.[13]

In the third place, it is evident that motivating force becomes the mechanism of matter. If the world is infinitely cavernous, if worlds exist in the tiniest bodies, it is because everywhere there can be found "a spirit in matter," which attests not only to the infinite division of parts but also to progressivity in the gain and loss of movement all the while conservation of force is realized. The matter-fold is a matter-time; its characteristics resemble the continuous discharge of an "infinity of wind-muskets."[14] And there still we can imagine the affinity of matter for life insofar as a muscular conception of matter inspires force in all things. By invoking the propagation of light and the "expulsion into luminosity," by making an elastic, inflammable, and explosive spirit from animal spirits, Leibniz turns his back on Cartesianism. He renews the tradition of Van Helmont and is inspired by Boyle's experimentation.[15] In short, to the extent that folding is not opposed to unfolding, such is also the case in the pairs tension-release and contraction-dilation (but not condensation-rarefaction, which would imply a void).

The lower level or floor is thus also composed of organic matter. An organism is defined by endogenous folds, while inorganic matter has exogenous folds that are always determined from without or by the surrounding environment. Thus, in the case of living beings, an inner formative fold is transformed through evolution, with the organism's development. Whence the necessity of a preformation. Organic matter is not, however, different from inorganic matter (here, the distinction of a first and a second matter is irrelevant). Whether organic or inorganic, matter is all one; but active forces are not the only ones exerted upon it. To be sure, these are perfectly material or mechanical forces, where indeed souls cannot be made to intervene: for the moment, vitalism is a strict organicism. Material forces, which account for the organic fold, have only to be distinguished from the preceding forces, and be added to it; they must suffice, where they are exerted, to transform raw matter into organic matter. In contrast to compressive or elastic forces, Leibniz calls them "plastic forces." They organize masses but, although the latter prepare organisms or make them possible by means of motivating drive, it is impossible to go from masses to organisms, since organs are always based on these plastic forces that preform them, and are distinguished from forces of mass, to the point where every organ is born from a preexisting organ.[16] Even fossils in matter are not explained by our faculty of imagination; when, for example, we see that the head of Christ we fancy in the spots on a wall refers to plastic forces that wind through organisms that already exist.

If plastic forces can be distinguished, it is not because living matter exceeds mechanical processes, but because mechanisms are not sufficient to be machines. A mechanism is faulty not for being too artificial to account for living matter, but for not being mechanical enough, for not being adequately machined. Our mechanisms are in fact organized into parts that are not in themselves machines, while the organism is infinitely machined, a machine whose every part or piece is a machine, but only "transformed by different folds that it receives."[17] Plastic forces are thus more machinelike than they are mechanical, and they allow for the definition of Baroque machines. It might be claimed that mechanisms of inorganic nature already stretch to infinity because the motivating force is of an already infinite composition, or that the fold always refers to other folds. But it requires that each time, an external determination, or the direct action of the surroundings, is needed in order to pass from one level to another; without this we would have to stop, as with our mechanisms. The living organism, on the contrary, by virtue of preformation has an internal destiny that makes it move from fold to fold, or that makes machines from machines all the way to infinity. We might say that between organic and inorganic things there exists a difference of vector, the latter going toward increasingly greater masses in which statistical mechanisms are operating, the former toward increasingly smaller, polarized masses in which the force of an individuating machinery, an internal individuation, is applied. Is this Leibniz's premonition of several aspects that will come true only much later?[18] No doubt, for Leibniz, internal individuation will only be explained at the level of souls: organic interiority is only derivative, and has but one container of coherence or cohesion (not of inherence or of "inhesion"). It is an interiority of space, and not yet of motion; also, an internalization of the outside, an invagination of the outside that could not occur all alone if no true interiorities did not exist *elsewhere*. It remains the case that the organic body thus confers an interior on matter, by which the principle of individuation is applied to it: whence the figure of the leaves of a tree, two never being exactly alike because of their veins or folds.

Folding-unfolding no longer simply means tension-release, contraction-dilation, but enveloping-developing, involution-evolution. The organism is defined by its ability to fold its own parts and to unfold them, not to infinity, but to a degree of development assigned to each species. Thus an organism is enveloped by organisms, one within another (interlocking of germinal matter), like Russian dolls. The first fly contains the seeds of all flies to come, each being called in its turn to unfold its own parts at the right time. And when an organism dies, it does not really vanish, but folds in upon itself, abruptly involuting into the again newly dormant seed by skipping all intermediate stages. The simplest way of stating the point is by saying that to unfold is to increase, to grow;

whereas to fold is to diminish, to reduce, "to withdraw into the recesses of a world."[19] Yet a simple metric change would not account for the difference between the organic and the inorganic, the machine and its motive force. It would fail to show that movement does not simply go from one greater or smaller part to another, but from fold to fold. When a part of a machine is still a machine, the smaller unit is not the same as the whole. When Leibniz invokes Harlequin's layers of clothing, he means that his underwear is not the same as his outer garments. That is why metamorphosis or "metaschematism" pertains to more than mere change of dimension: every animal is double — but as a heterogenous or heteromorphic creature, just as the butterfly is folded into the caterpillar that will soon unfold. The double will even be simultaneous to the degree that the ovule is not a mere envelope but furnishes one part whose other is in the male element.[20] In fact, it is the inorganic that repeats itself, with a difference of proximate dimension, since it is always an exterior site which enters the body; the organism, in contrast, envelops an interior site that contains necessarily *other* species of organisms, those that envelop in their turn the interior sites containing yet other organisms: "Each portion of matter may be conceived as a garden full of plants, and as a pond full of fish. But every branch of each plant, every member of each animal, and every drop of their liquid parts is in itself likewise a similar garden or pond."[21] Thus the inorganic fold happens to be simple and direct, while the organic fold is always composite, alternating, indirect (mediated by an interior site).[22]

Matter is folded twice, once under elastic forces, a second time under plastic forces, but one is not able to move from the first to the second. Thus the universe is neither a great living being, nor is it in itself an Animal: Leibniz rejects this hypothesis as much as he rejects that of a universal Spirit. Organisms retain an irreducible individuality, and organic descendants retain an irreducible plurality. It remains that the two kinds of force, two kinds of folds — masses and organisms — are strictly coextensive. There are no *fewer* living beings than parts of inorganic matter.[23] Clearly an exterior site is not a living being; rather, it is a lake, a pond, or a fish hatchery. Here the figure of the lake or pond acquires a new meaning, since the pond — and the marble tile — no longer refer to elastic waves that swim through them like inorganic folds, but to fish that inhabit them like organic folds. And in life itself the inner sites contained are even more hatcheries full of other fish: a "swarm." Inorganic folds of sites move between two organic folds. For Leibniz, as for the Baroque, the principles of reason are veritable cries: Not everything is fish, but fish are teeming everywhere. . . . Universality does not exist, but living things are ubiquitous.

It might be said that the theory of preformation and duplication, as observations made through the microscope confirm, has long been abandoned. The meaning of development or evolution has turned topsy-turvy, since it now designates *epigenesis* — the appearance of organs and organisms neither preformed nor closed one within the other, but formed from something else that does not resemble them: the organ does not arch back to a preexisting organ, but to a much more general and less differentiated design.[24] Development does not go from smaller to greater things through growth or augmentation, but from the general to the special, through differentiations of an initially undifferentiated field either under the action of exterior surroundings or under the influence of internal forces that are directive, directional, but that remain neither constitutive nor preformative. However, insofar as preformism exceeds simple metric variations, it tends to be aligned with an epigenesis to the extent epigenesis is forced to hold to a kind of virtual or potential preformation. The essential is elsewhere; basically, two conceptions share the common trait of conceiving the organism as a fold, an originary folding or creasing (and biology has never rejected this determination of living matter, as shown nowadays with the fundamental pleating of globular protein). Preformism is the form in which this truth of the seventeenth century is perceived through the first microscopes. It is hardly surprising that from then on the same problems are found in the sense of epigenesis and preformation.

Thus can all types of folding be called modifications or degrees of development of a same Animal in itself? Or are there types of irreducible foldings, as Leibniz believes in a preformist perspective, and as Cuvier and Baër also contend from an epigenic standpoint?[25] Certainly a great opposition subsists between the two points of view. With epigenesis the organic fold is produced, is unearthed, or is pushed up from a relatively smooth and consistent surface. (How could a redoubling, an invagination, or an intubation be prefigured?) Now with preformism an organic fold always ensues from another fold, at least on the inside from a same type of organization: every fold originates from a fold, *plica ex plica*. If Heideggerian terms can be used, we can say that the fold of epigenesis is an *Einfalt,* or that it is the differentiation of an undifferentiated, but that the fold from preformation is a *Zweifalt,* not a fold in two — since every fold can only be thus — but a "fold-of-two," an *entre-deux,* something "between" in the sense that a difference is being differentiated. From this point of view we cannot be sure if preformism does not have a future.

Masses and organisms, masses and living beings thus fill the lower level. Why then is another story needed, since sensitive or animal souls are already there, inseparable from organic bodies? Each soul even seems apt to be localized in its body, this time as a "point" in a droplet, that subsists in a part of the droplet when the latter is divided or diminished in volume: thus, in death the soul remains right where it was, in a part of the body, however reduced it may be.[26] Leibniz states that the point of view is in the body.[27] Surely everything in the body works like a machine, in accord with plastic forces that are material, but these forces explain everything except for the variable *degrees of unity* to which they bring the masses they are organizing (a plant, a worm, a vertebrate . . .). Plastic forces of matter act on masses, but they submit them to real unities that they take for granted. They make an organic synthesis, but assume the soul as the *unity of synthesis,* or as the "immaterial principle of life." Only there does an animism find a connection with organicism, from the standpoint of pure unity or of union, independently of all causal action.[28] It remains that organisms would not on their account have the causal power to be folded to infinity, and of surviving in ashes, without the unity-souls from which they are inseparable, and which are inseparable from them. Here is the great difference that makes Leibniz break away from Malebranche: not only is there a preformation of bodies, but also a preexistence of souls in fertile seeds.[29] Life is not only everywhere, but souls are everywhere in matter. Thus, when an organism is called to unfold its own parts, its animal or sensitive soul is opened onto an entire theater in which it perceives or feels according to its unity, independently of its organism, yet inseparable from it.

But—and here is the whole problem—what happens with bodies, from the time of Adam's seed that envelops them, that are destined to become humans? Juridically, one might say that they carry in a nutshell "a sort of sealed act" that marks their fate. And when the hour comes for them to unfold their parts, to attain a degree of organic development proper to man, or to form cerebral folds, at the same time their animal soul becomes reasonable by gaining a greater degree of unity (mind): "The organized body would receive at the same time the disposition of the human body, and its soul would be raised to the stage of a reasonable soul, but I cannot decide here if it occurs through an ordinary process or an extraordinary work of God."[30] Then in every event this becoming is an elevation, an exaltation: a change of theater, of rule, of level or of floors. The theater of matter gives way to that of spirits or of God. In the Baroque the soul entertains a complex relation with the body. Forever indissociable from the body, it discovers a vertiginous animality that gets it tangled in the pleats of matter, but also an organic or cerebral humanity (the degree of development) that allows it to rise up, and that will make it ascend over all other folds.

The reasonable soul is free, like a Cartesian diver, to fall back down at death and to climb up again at the last judgment. As Leibniz notes, the tension is between the collapse and the elevation or ascension that in different spots is breaching the organized masses. We move from funerary figures of the Basilica of Saint Laurence to the figures on the ceiling of Saint Ignatius. It might be claimed that physical gravity and religious elevation are quite different and do not pertain to the same world. However, these are two vectors that are allotted as such in the distinction of the two levels or floors of a single and same world, or of the single and same house. It is because the body and the soul have no point in being inseparable, for they are not in the least really distinct (we have already seen it for the parts of matter). From this moment on any localization of the soul in an area of the body, no matter how tiny it may be, amounts rather to a *projection* from the top to the bottom, a projection of the soul focalizing on a "point" of the body, in conformity with Desargnes's geometry, that develops from a Baroque perspective. In short, the primary reason for an upper floor is the following: there are souls on the lower floor, some of whom are chosen to become reasonable, thus to change their levels.

Movement, then, cannot be stopped. The reciprocation of the Leibnizian principle holds not only for reasonable souls but also for animal or sensible souls themselves: if two really distinct things can be inseparable, two inseparable things can be really distinct, and belong to two levels, the localization of the one in the other amounting to a projection upon a point ("I do not think that we can consider souls as being in points, perhaps we might say . . . that they are in a place through a connection"). As degrees of unity, animal souls are already on the other floor, everything being accomplished mechanically in the animal itself at the lower level. Plastic or machinic forces are part of the "derivative forces" defined in respect to the matter that they organize. But souls, on the contrary, are "primitive forces" or immaterial principles of life that are defined only in respect to the inside, in the self, and "through analogy with the mind." We can nonetheless remember that these animal souls, with their subjugated organism, exist everywhere in inorganic matter. Thus in its turn inorganic matter reverts to souls whose site is elsewhere, higher up, and that is only projected upon it. In all probability a body—however small—follows a curvilinear trajectory only under the impulsion of the second species of derivative forces, compressive or elastic forces that determine the curve through the mechanical action of the surrounding bodies on the outside: isolated, the body would follow the straight tangent. But still, mechanical laws or extrinsic determinations (collisions) explain everything except the *unity* of a concrete movement, no matter how irregular or variable it may be. Unity of movement is an affair of the soul, and almost of a conscience, as Bergson will later discover. Just as the totality of matter arches back to a curving that can no longer be determined from the outside, the curvilinear course followed by a given body under the impetus of the outside goes back to a "higher," internal and individuating, unity on the other floor, that contains the "law of curvilinearity," the law of folds or changes of direction.[31] The same movement is always determined from the outside, through collisions, insofar as it is related to derivative force, but unified from the inside, to the degree it is related to primitive force. In the first relation, the curve is accidental and derived from the straight line, but in the second it is primary, such that the motive force sometimes is mechanically explained through the action of a subtle surrounding, and sometimes is understood from the inside as the interior of the body, "the cause of movement that is already in the body," and that only awaits the suppression of an obstacle from the outside.[32]

Hence the need for a second floor is everywhere affirmed to be strictly metaphysical. The soul itself is what constitutes the other floor or the inside up above, where there are no windows to allow entry of influence from without. Even in a physical sense we are moving across outer material pleats to inner animated, spontaneous folds. These are what we must now examine, in their nature and in their development. Everything moves as if the pleats of matter possessed no reason in themselves. It is because the Fold is always between two folds, and because the between-two-folds seems to move about everywhere: Is it between inorganic bodies and organisms, between organisms and animal souls, between animal souls and reasonable souls, between bodies and souls in general?

Chapter 2
The Folds in the Soul

Inflection is the ideal genetic element of the variable curve or fold. Inflection is the authentic atom, the elastic point. That is what Klee extracts as the genetic element of the active, spontaneous line. It testifies to his affinity for the Baroque and for Leibniz, and opposes him to Kandinsky, a Cartesian, for whom angles are firm, for whom the point is firm, set in motion by an exterior force. For Klee, however, the point as a "nonconceptual concept of noncontradiction" moves along an inflection. It is the point of inflection itself, where the tangent crosses the curve. That is the point-fold. Klee begins with a succession of three figures.[1] The first draws the inflection. The second shows that no exact and unmixed figure can exist. As Leibniz stated, there can never be "a straight line without curves intermingled," nor any "curve of a certain finite nature unmixed with some other, and in small parts as well as large," such that one "will never be able to fix upon a certain precise surface in a body as one might if there were atoms."[2] The third marks the convex side with shadow, and thus disengages concavity and the axis of its curve, that now and again changes sides from the point of inflection.

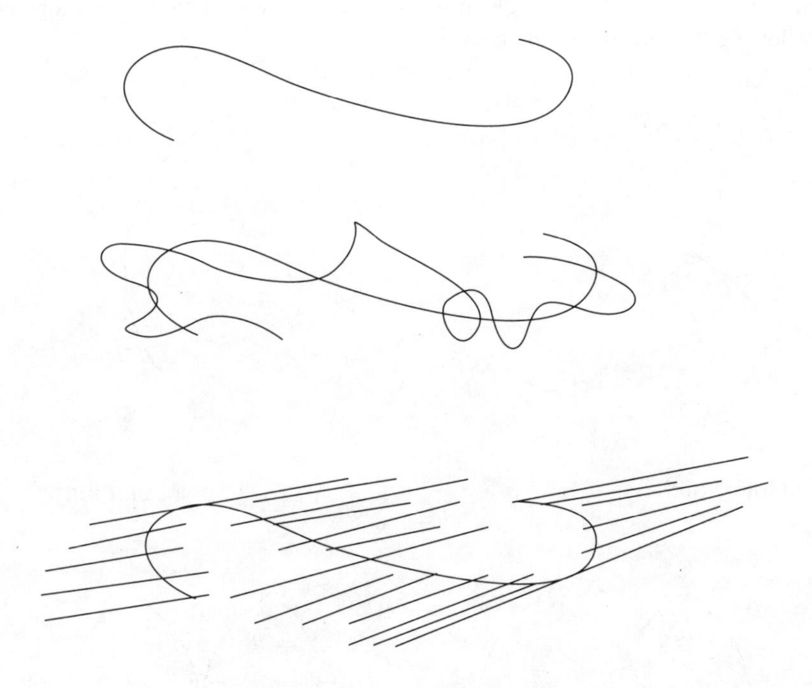

Bernard Cache defines inflection — or the point of inflection — as an intrinsic singularity. Contrary to "extrema" (extrinsic singularities, maximum and minimum), it does not refer to coordinates: it is neither high nor low, neither right nor left, neither regression nor progression. It corresponds to what Leibniz calls an "ambiguous sign." It is weightless; even the vectors of concavity still have nothing to do with a vector of gravity since the axes of the curve that they are determining oscillate around it. Thus inflection is the pure Event of the line or of the point, the Virtual, ideality par excellence. It will take place following the axes of the coordinates, but for now it is not yet in the world: it is the World itself, or rather its beginning, as Klee used to say, "a site of cosmogenesis," "a nondimensional point" "between dimensions." An event that would await an event? That is how the inflection already moves through virtual transformations, that is (for Cache), three transformations.[3]

The first are vectorial, or operate by symmetry, with an orthogonal or tangent plane of reflection. They work according to optical laws, transforming inflection at a turning point, in an ogive, or pointed arch. The ogive expresses the form of a moving body that espouses the configuration of lines of flowing liquid, and the return, the profile of the depth of a valley when waters are brought together following the line of a single course:

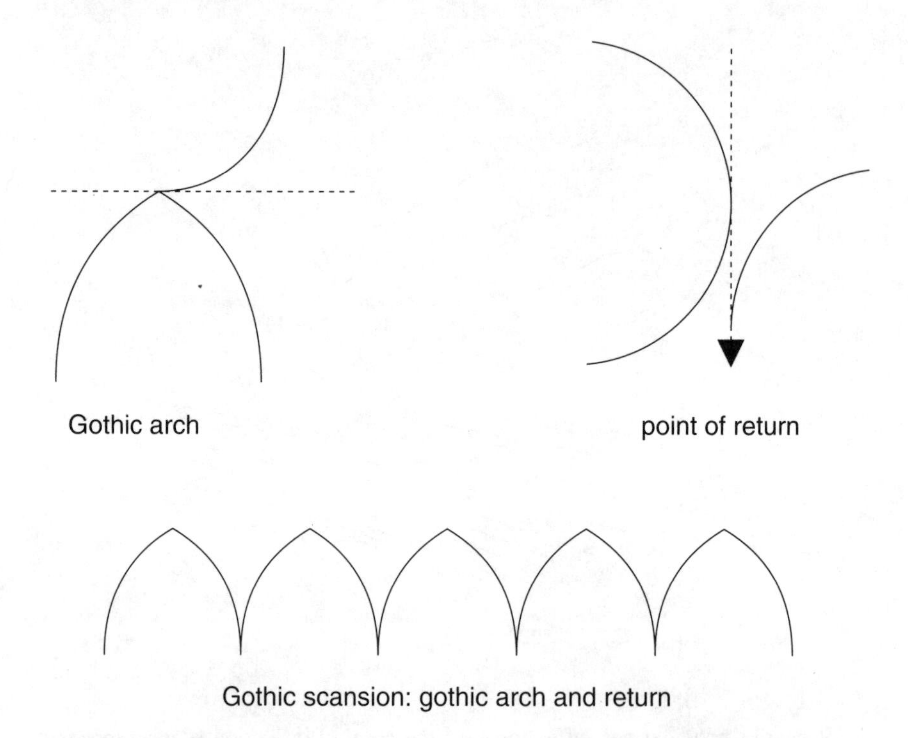

Gothic scansion: gothic arch and return

The second set of transformations is projective: such transformations convey the projection, on external space, of internal spaces defined by "hidden parameters" and variables or singularities of potential. René Thom's transformations refer in this sense to a morphology of living matter, providing seven elementary events: the *fold*; the crease; the dovetail; the butterfly; the hyperbolic, elliptical, and parabolic umbilicus.[4]

Finally, the inflection in itself cannot be separated from an infinite variation or an infinitely variable curve. Such is Koch's curve, obtained by means of rounding angles, according to Baroque requirements, by making them proliferate according to a law of homothesis.[5] The curve passes through an infinite number of angular points and never admits a tangent at any of these points. It envelops an infinitely cavernous or porous world, constituting more than a line and less than a surface (Mandelbrot's fractal dimension as a fractional or irrational number, a nondimension, an interdimension).[6] Nonethelesss homothesis causes variation to coincide with a change of scale, as in the case of the length of a geographical gradient. Everything changes when fluctuation is made to intervene in the place of internal homothesis. It is no longer possible to determine an angular point between two others, no matter how close one is to the other; but there remains the latitude to always add a detour by making each interval the site of a new folding. That is how we go from fold to fold and not from point to point, and how every contour is blurred to give definition to the formal powers of the raw material, which rise to the surface and are put forward as so many detours and supplementary folds. Transformation of inflection can no longer allow for either symmetry or the favored plane of projection. It becomes vortical and is produced later; deferred, rather than prolonged or proliferating: the line effectively folds into a spiral in order to defer inflection in a movement suspended between sky and earth, which either moves away from or indefinitely approaches the center of a curve and at each instant "rises skyward or risks falling upon us."[7] But the vertical spiral neither retains nor defers inflection without also promoting it and making it irresistible, in a transversal sense: a turbulence that is never produced on its own, whose spiral follows a fractal mode by which new turbulences are inserted between the initial ones.[8] Growing from other turbulences, in the erasure of contour, turbulence ends only in watery froth or in a flowing mane. Inflection itself becomes vortical, and at the same time its variation opens onto fluctuation, it becomes fluctuation.

The definition of Baroque mathematics is born with Leibniz. The object of the discipline is a "new affection" of variable sizes, which is variation itself. To be sure, in a fractional number or even in an algebraic formula, variability is not considered as such, since each of the terms has or must have a particular value. The same no longer holds either for the irrational number and corresponding serial calculus, or for the differential quotient and differential calculus, in which variation becomes presently infinite. The irrational number is the common limit of two convergent series, of which one has no maximum and the other no minimum. The differential quotient is the common limit of the relation between two quantities that are vanishing. But we can remark that in both cases the presence of a curved element acts as a cause. The irrational number implies the descent of a circular arc on the straight line of rational points, and exposes the latter as a false infinity, a simple undefinite that includes an infinity of lacunae; that is why the continuous is a labyrinth that cannot be represented by a straight line. The straight line always has to be intermingled with curved lines.

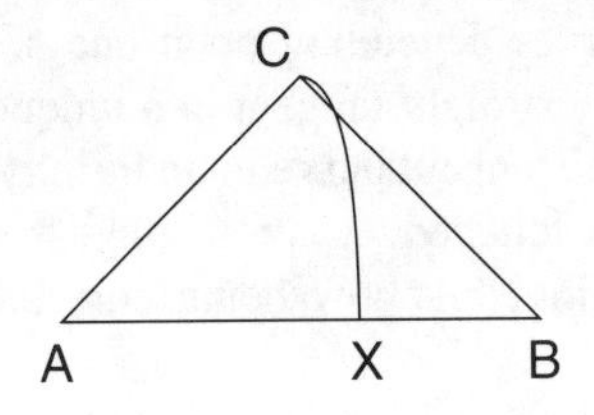

Between the two points A and B — no matter in what proximity they may be — there always remains the possibility for carrying out the right isosceles triangle, whose hypotenuse goes from A to B, and whose summit, C, determines a circle that crosses the straight line between A and B. The arc of the circle resembles a branch of inflection, an element of the labyrinth, that from an irrational number, at the meeting of the curved and straight lines, produces a point-fold. It is iden-

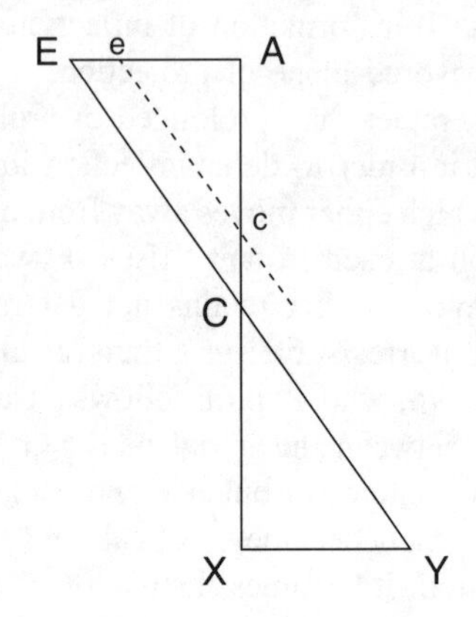

tical in the case of the differential quotient, with the point-fold A that retains the relation

$$\frac{c}{e}$$

when these two magnitudes vanish (that, too, is the relation between a radius and a tangent that fits the angle in C).[9] In short, there will always be an inflection that makes a fold from variation, and that brings the fold or the variation to infinity. The fold is Power, as we see in the irrational number that appears by way of an extraction from a root, and in the differential quotient that appears by way of the relation of a magnitude and a power, as a condition of variation. Force itself is an act, an act of the fold.

When mathematics assumes variation as its objective, the notion of function tends to be extracted, but the notion of objective also changes and becomes functional. In some especially important mathematical writings, Leibniz posits the idea of families of curves depending upon one or several parameters: "Instead of seeking the unique straight tangent in a unique point for a given curve, we can go about seeking the tangent curve in an infinity of points with an infinity of curves; the curve is not touched, it is touching, the tangent no longer either straight, unique, or touching, but now being curvilinear, an infinite, touched family" (the problem of the inverse of tangents).[10] There exists thus a series of curves that not only imply constant parameters for each and every curve, but the reduction of variables to a "single and unique variability" of the touching or tangent curve: the fold. The goal is no longer defined by an essential form, but reaches a pure functionality, as if declining a family of curves, framed by parameters, inseparable from a series of possible declensions or from a surface of variable curvature that it is itself describing.

This new object we can call *objectile*. As Bernard Cache has demonstrated, this is a very modern conception of the technological object: it refers neither to the beginnings of the industrial era nor to the idea of the standard that still upheld a semblance of essence and imposed a law of constancy ("the object produced by and for the masses"), but to our current state of things, where fluctuation of the norm replaces the permanence of a law; where the object assumes a place in a continuum by variation; where industrial automation or serial machineries replace stamped forms. The new status of the object no longer refers its condition to a spatial mold—in other words, to a relation of form-matter—but to a temporal modulation that implies as much the beginnings of a continuous variation of matter as a continuous development of form. In modulation "a pause never intervenes for withdrawal from the mold because the circulation of the source of energy amounts to a permanent withdrawal; a modulator is a continuous temporal mold . . . Molding amounts to modulating in a definitive way; modulating is molding in a continuous and perpetually variable fashion."[11] Can we not affirm that modulation is what Leibniz is defining when he states that the law of series posits curves as "the trace of the same line" in a continuous movement, continually touched by the curve of their convergence? His is not only a temporal but also a qualitative conception of the object, to the extent that sounds and colors are flexible and taken in modulation. The object here is manneristic, not essentializing: it becomes an event.

If the status of the object is profoundly changed, so also is that of the subject. We move from inflection or from variable curvature to vectors of curvature that go in the direction of concavity. Moving from a branching of inflection, we distinguish a point that is no longer what runs along inflection, nor is it the point of inflection itself; it is the one in which the lines perpendicular to tangents meet in a state of variation. It is not exactly a point but a place, a position, a site, a "linear focus," a line emanating from lines. To the degree it represents variation or inflection, it can be called *point of view*. Such is the basis of perspectivism, which does not mean a dependence in respect to a pregiven or defined subject; to the contrary, a subject will be what comes to the point of view, or rather what remains in the point of view. That is why the transformation of the object refers

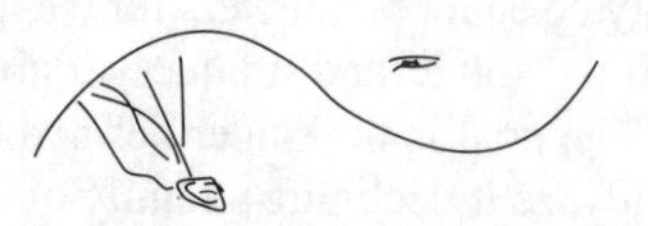

to a correlative transformation of the subject: the subject is not a sub-ject but, as Whitehead says, a "superject." Just as the object becomes objectile, the subject becomes a superject. A needed relation exists between variation and point of view: not simply because of the variety of points of view (though, as we shall observe, such a variety does exist), but in the first place because every point of view is a point of view on variation. The point of view is not what varies with the subject, at least in the first instance; it is, to the contrary, the condition in which an eventual subject apprehends a variation (metamorphosis), or: something = x (anamorphosis).[12] For Leibniz, for Nietzsche, for William and Henry James, and for Whitehead as well, perspectivism amounts to a relativism, but not the relativism we take for granted. It is not a variation of truth according to the subject, but the condition in which the truth of a variation appears to the subject. This is the very idea of Baroque perspective.

It might, however, be claimed that point of view explodes with the proximity of concavity: does there not exist a contradiction between continuity of infinite variation and the discontinuity of viewpoint? Is this not the same contradiction between the law of continuity and the principle of indiscernibles that many authors (following Kant) denounce in Leibniz? The question is moot if, from the outset, we try to not combine continuity and contiguity.[13] Although they are not contiguous, singularities, or unique points, belong fully to continuousness. Points of inflection make up a first kind of singularity in space, and constitute envelopes in accord with indivisible relations of distance. But neither one nor the other contradicts the continuous. There are as many points of view—whose distance in each case is indivisible—as inflections in inflection, whose length increases. Continuity is made up no less of distances between points of view than of the length of an infinity of corresponding curves. Perspectivism is clearly a pluralism, but it thus implies by its name distance and not discontinuity (certainly no void is given between two points of view). Leibniz can define extension (*extensio*) as "continuous repetition" of the *situs* or position—that is, of point of view: not that extension is therefore the attribute of point of view, but that the attribute of space (*spatium*), an order of distances between points of view, is what makes this repetition possible.[14]

Point of view on a variation now replaces the center of a figure or a configuration. The most famous example is that of conic sections, where the point of the cone is the point of view to which the circle, the ellipse, the parabola, and the hyperbola are related as so many variants that follow the incline of the section that is planned ("scenographies"). All these figures become so many ways by which a "flat projection" is mapped out. And this projection is not exactly the circle, which it would be only under the privilege of an old conception of perspective. Rather, it is the objectile that now declines or describes relations of curves: those of the second degree, in which the circle plays a role. This objectile or projection resembles an unfolding. But unfolding is no more the contrary of foldings than an invariant would be the contrary of variation. It is an invariant of transformation. Leibniz will designate it by an "ambiguous sign."[15] It is effectively enveloped in variation, just as variation is enveloped in point of view. It does not exist outside of variation, just as variation does not exist outside of point of view. That is why, at the basis of this new theory of conic sections, Desargues called the relation or the law enveloped by a variation "involution" (for example, a triangle that is supposed to turn around an axis, the dispositions of the points defined on the axis by the projection of three summits and by the prolongation of the three sides).[16]

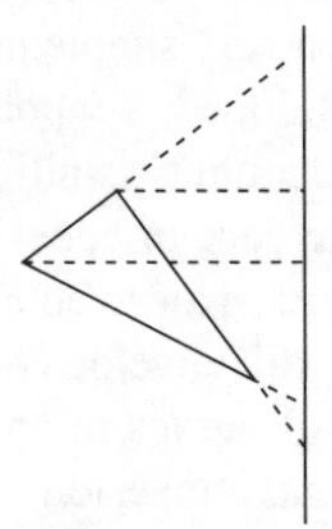

Michel Serres has analyzed superlatively both the consequences and the presuppositions of the new theory of conic sections: in a world of infinity, or of variable curvature that has lost notion of a center, he stresses the importance of setting point of view in the place of the missing center; of the new optical model of perception, and of geometry in perception, that casts aside tactile notions, contact and figure, in favor of an "architecture of vision"; of the status of the object, which now exists only through its metamorphoses or in the declension of its profiles; of perspectivism as a truth of relativity (and not a relativity of what is true). In each area point of view is a variation or a *power of arranging cases,* a condition for the manifestation of reality: thus the alternating series of conics, beginning with the summit of the cone (a finite point, an infinite straight line, a finite circle, an infinite parabola, a finite ellipse, an infinite hyperbola), or rather the series of powers to the second degree from the apex of the arithmetical triangle, and for every area the need to assign *the* point of view without which truth could not be proven, that is, to arrange series of variations or determine each case.[17] In all these areas Leibniz constructs the "table" of cases that refers to point of view as jurisprudence or the art of judgment. It comprises the need to find the correct point of view — or rather, the best — without which disorder or even chaos would reign. When we mentioned Henry James it was with respect to Leibniz's idea about point of view as the secret of things, as focus, cryptography, or even as the determination of the indeterminate by means of ambiguous signs: *what* I am telling to you, *what* you are also thinking about, do you agree to tell *him* about *it,* provided that we know what to expect of *it,* about *her,* and that we also agree about who *he* is and who *she* is? As in a Baroque anamorphosis, only point of view provides us with answers and cases.

We have gone from variable curvature to the origin of curvature (from the concave side), from variation to point of view, from the fold to envelopment, in a word, from inflection to inclusion. The transition cannot be discerned, somewhat like a right angle that is not measured by a great arc but by a tiny arc situated close to the summit: it is at the summit "that the angle or the inclination of the two lines is found."[18] We would nonetheless hesitate to say that visibility is located in point of view. We would need a more natural intuition to allow for this passage to the limit. Thus it is a very simple intuition: Why would something be folded, if it were not to be enveloped, wrapped, or put into something else? It appears that here the envelope acquires its ultimate or perhaps final meaning: it is no longer an envelope of coherence or cohesion, like an egg, in the "reciprocal envelopment" of organic parts. Nor even a mathematical envelope of adherence or adhesion, where a fold still envelops other folds, as in the enveloping envelope that touches an infinity of curves in an infinity of points. It is an envelope of inherence or of unilateral "inhesion": inclusion or inherence is *the final cause of the fold,* such that we move indiscernibly from the latter to the former. Between the two, a gap is opened which makes the envelope the reason for the fold: what is folded is the included, the inherent. It can be stated that what is folded is only virtual and currently exists only in an envelope, in something that envelops it.

From now on it is not exactly point of view that includes; or at least, it does so only as an agent, but not of a final cause or a finished act (entelechia). Inclusion or inherence has *a condition of closure or envelopment,* which Leibniz puts forward in his famous formula, "no windows," and which point of view does not suffice to explain. When inclusion is accomplished, it is done so continuously, or includes the sense of a finished act that is neither the site, the place, nor the point of view, but what remains in point of view, what occupies point of view, and without which point of view would not be. It is necessarily a soul, a subject. A soul always includes what it apprehends from *its* point of view, in other words, inflection. *Inflection is an ideal condition or a virtuality that currently exists only in the soul that envelops it.* Thus the soul is what has folds and is full of folds.

Folds are in the soul and authentically exist only in the soul. That is already true for "innate ideas": they are pure virtualities, pure powers whose act consists in habitus or arrangements (folds) in the soul, and whose completed act consists of an inner action of the soul (an internal deployment).[19] But this is no less true for the world: the whole world is only a virtuality that currently exists only in the folds of the soul which convey it, the soul implementing inner pleats through which it endows itself with a representation of the enclosed world. We are moving from inflection to inclusion in a subject, as if from the virtual to the real, inflection defining the fold, but inclusion defining the soul or the subject, that is, what envelops the fold, its final cause and its completed act.

Whence the distinction of three kinds of points as three kinds of singularities.[20] The *physical point* is what runs along inflection or is the point of inflection itself: it is neither an atom nor a Cartesian point, but an elastic or plastic point-fold. Thus it is not exact. On the one hand, it is important to note that it devalorizes the exact point while, on the other, it leads the *mathematical point* to assume a new status that is rigorous without being exact. On one side, the exact point is effectively not a part of extension, but a conventional extremity of the line. On the other side, the mathematical point in turn loses exactitude in order to become a position, a site, a focus, a place, a point of conjunction of vectors of curvature or, in short, point of view. The latter therefore takes on a genetic value: pure extension will be the continuation or diffusion of the point, but according to the relations of distance that define space (between two given points) as the "place of all places." However, if the mathematical point thus stops being the extremity of the line in order to become the point of focus, it is nonetheless a simple "modality." It is in the body, in the thing extended.[21] But in this way, as we have seen, it is only the projection of a third point in the body. That is the *metaphysical point,* the soul or the subject. It is what occupies the point of view, it is what is projected in point of view. Thus the soul is not in a body in a point, but is itself a higher point and of another nature, which corresponds with the point of view. *The point of inflection, the point of position, and the point of inclusion will thus be distinguished.*

Everyone knows the name that Leibniz ascribes to the soul or to the subject as a metaphysical point: the monad. He borrows this name from the Neoplatonists who used it to designate a state of One, a unity that envelops a multiplicity, this multiplicity developing the One in the manner of a "series."[22] The One specifically has a power of envelopment and development, while the multiple is inseparable from the folds that it makes when it is enveloped, and of unfoldings when it is developed. But its envelopments and developments, its implications and explications, are nonetheless particular movements that must be understood in a universal Unity that "complicates" them all, and that complicates all the Ones. Giordano Bruno will bring the system of monads to the level of this universal complication: the Soul of the world that complicates everything. Hence Neo-Platonic emanations give way to a large zone of immanence, even if the rights of a transcendent God or an even higher Unity are formally respected.

Explication-implication-complication form the triad of the fold, following the variations of the relation of the One-Multiple.[23] But if we ask why the name "monad" has been associated with Leibniz, it is because of the two ways that Leibniz was going to stabilize the concept. On the one hand, the mathematics of inflection allowed him to posit the enveloping series of multiples as a convergent infinite series. On the other hand, the metaphysics of inclusion allowed him to posit enveloping unity as an irreducible individual unity. In effect, as long as series remained finite or undefined, individuals risked being relative, called upon to melt into a universal spirit or a soul of the world that could complicate all series. But if the world is an infinite series, it then constitutes the logical comprehension of a notion or of a concept that can now only be individual. It is therefore enveloped by an infinity of individuated souls of which each retains its irreducible point of view. It is the accord of singular points of view, or harmony, that will replace universal complication and ward off the dangers of pantheism or immanence: whence Leibniz's insistence upon denouncing the hypothesis, or rather the hypostasis, of a Universal Spirit that would turn complication into an abstract operation in which individuals would be swallowed up.[24]

All this remains obscure. For if, by pushing to its limit a metaphor sketched by Plotinus, Leibniz makes of the monad a sort of point of view on the city, must we understand that a certain form corresponds to each point of view?[25] For example, a street of one form or another? In conic sections, there is no separate point of view to which the ellipse would return, and another for the parabola, and another for the circle. The point of view, the summit of the cone, is the condition under which we apprehend the group of varied forms or the series of curves to the second degree. It does not suffice to state that the point of view apprehends a perspective, a profile that would each time offer the entirety of a city in its own fashion. For it also brings forth the connection of all the related profiles, the series of all curvatures or inflections. What can be apprehended from one point of view is therefore neither a determined street nor a relation that might be determined with other streets, which are constants, but the variety of all possible connections between the course of a given street and that of another. The city seems to be a labyrinth that can be ordered. The world is an infinite series of curvatures or inflections, and the entire world is enclosed in the soul from one point of view.

The world is the infinite curve that touches at an infinity of points an infinity of curves, the curve with a unique variable, the convergent series of all series. But why then is there not a single and universal point of view? Why does Leibniz so strongly deny "the doctrine of a universal spirit"? Why are there several points of view and several irreducible souls, an infinity? We can consider the series of the twelve sounds: the series can undergo in turn many variations that are both rhythmic and melodic, but that also follow the contrary, or retrograde, movement. With greater reason an infinite series, even if the variable is unique, cannot be separated from an infinity of variations that make it up: we necessarily take it in accord with all possible orders, and we favor this or that partial sequence at this or that time. That is why only one form — or one street — recovers its rights, but only in respect to the entire series.

As an individual unit each monad includes the whole series; hence it conveys the entire world, but does not express it *without expressing more clearly a small region of the world, a "subdivision," a borough of the city, a finite sequence.* Two souls do not have the same order, but neither do they have the same sequence or the same clear or enlightened region. It might even be stated that insofar as it is filled with folds that stretch to infinity, the soul can always unfold a limited number of them inside itself, those that make up its subdivision or its borough.[26] A definition of individuation remains to be clarified: if only individuals exist, it is not because they include the series in a certain order and according to a given region; it is even the inverse that holds.

Thus for the moment we only have a nominal definition of the individual. The definition suffices all the same to show that there necessarily exists an infinity of souls and an infinity of points of view, although each included soul and each point of view may grasp the infinitely infinite seriality. Each grasps or includes it in a different order and from the standpoint of a different borough. If we return to the elementary schema of the two foci of inflection, we see that, in truth, each of them is a point of view on inflection in general, but that it is in an inverse order (a retrograde movement) and in accord with an opposed subdivision (one of the two branches).

But why it is necessary to *depart* from the world or the serial order? If not, the theme of the mirror and of point of view would lose all meaning. We move from inflections of the world to inclusion in its subjects: how can this be possible since the world only exists in subjects that include it? In this respect the first letters to Arnauld specify the conciliation of the two essential propositions. On the one hand, the world in which Adam committed sin exists only in Adam the sinner (and in all other subjects who make up this world). On the other hand, God creates not only Adam the sinner but also the world in which Adam has committed sin. In other words, if the world is in the subject, the subject is no less *for the world*. God produces the world "before" creating souls since he creates them for this world that he invests in them. In this very way the law of infinite seriality, the "law of curvatures," no longer resides in the soul, although seriality may be the soul, and although curvatures may be in it.

It is in this sense too that the soul is a "production," a "result." The soul results from the world that God has chosen. Because the world is in the monad, each monad includes every series of the states of the world; but, because the monad is for the world, no one clearly contains the "reason" of the series of which they are all a result, and which remains outside of them, just like the principle of their accord.[27] We thus go from the world to the subject, at the cost of a torsion that causes the monad to exist currently only in subjects, but that also makes subjects all relate to this world as if to the virtuality that they actualize. When Heidegger tries to surpass intentionality as an overly empirical determination of the subject's relation to the world, he envisions how Leibniz's formula of the monad without windows is a way to get past it, since the *Dasein,* he says, is already open at all times and does not need windows by which an opening would occur to it. But in that way he mistakes the condition of closure or concealment enunciated by Leibniz; that is, the determination of a being-for the world instead of a being-in the world.[28] Closure is the condition of being for the world. The condition of closure holds for the infinite opening of the finite: it "finitely represents infinity." It gives the world the possibility of

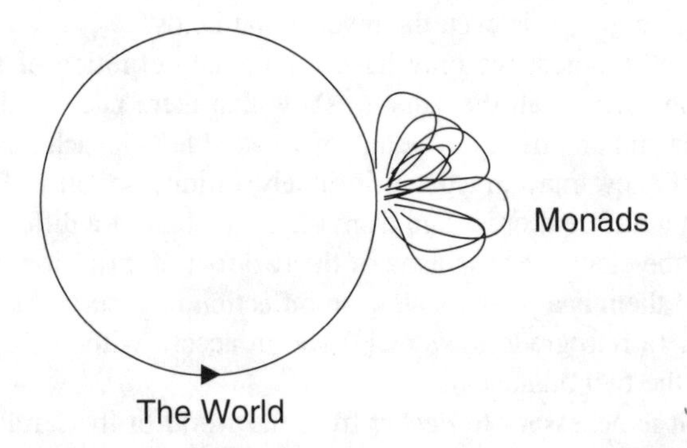

beginning over and again in each monad. The world must be placed in the subject in order that the subject can be for the world. This is the torsion that constitutes the fold of the world and of the soul. And it is what gives to expression its fundamental character: the soul is the expression of the world (actuality), but because the world is what the soul expresses (virtuality). Thus God creates expressive souls only because he creates the world that they express by including it: from inflection to inclusion. Finally, in order that the virtual can be incarnated or effectuated, is something needed other than this actualization in the soul? Is a realization in matter also required, because the folds of this matter might happen to reduplicate the folds in the soul? We cannot yet be sure, although the preceding chapter invites us to believe it.

Chapter 3
What Is Baroque?

Monads "have no windows, by which anything could come in or go out." They have neither "openings nor doorways."[1] We run the risk of understanding the problem vaguely if we fail to determine the situation. A painting always has a model on its outside; it always is a window. If a modern reader thinks of a film projected in darkness, the film has nonetheless been projected. Then what about invoking numerical images issuing from a calculus without a model? Or, more simply, the line with infinite inflection that holds for a surface, like the lines of Pollock's or Rauschenberg's painting? More exactly, in Rauschenberg's work we could say that the surface stops being a window on the world and now becomes an opaque grid of information on which the ciphered line is written.[2] The painting-window is replaced by tabulation, the grid on which lines, numbers, and changing characters are inscribed (the objectile).

Leibniz is endlessly drawing up linear and numerical tables. With them he decorates the inner walls of the monad. Folds replace holes. The dyad of the city-information table is opposed to the system of the window-countryside.[3] Leibniz's monad would be just such a grid—or better, a room or an apartment—completely covered with lines of variable inflection. This would be the camera obscura of the *New Essays*, furnished with a stretched canvas diversified by moving, living folds. Essential to the monad is its *dark background*: everything is drawn out of it, and nothing goes out or comes in from the outside.

In this sense, it would be pointless to imagine overly modern situations unless they can help us understand what the Baroque had really entailed. For ages there have been places where what is seen is inside: a cell, a sacristy, a crypt, a church, a theater, a study, or a print room. The Baroque invests in all of these places in order to extract from them power and glory. First of all, the camera obscura has only one small aperture high up through which light passes, then through the relay of two mirrors it projects on a sheet the objects to be drawn that cannot be seen, the second mirror being tilted according to the position of the sheet.[4] And then transformational decors, painted skies, all kinds of trompe l'oeil that adorn the walls: the monad has furniture and objects only in trompe l'oeil. Finally, the architectural ideal is a room in black marble, in which light enters only through orifices so well bent that nothing on the outside can be seen through them, yet they illuminate or color the decor of a pure inside. (Is it not the Baroque manner, such as this, that inspires Le Corbusier in the Abbey of La Tourette?) The Leibnizian monad and its system of light-mirror-point of view-inner decor cannot be understood if they are not compared to Baroque architecture. The architecture erects chapels and rooms where a crushing light comes from openings invisible to their very inhabitants. One of its first acts is in the Studiolo of Florence, with its secret room stripped of windows. The monad is a cell. It resembles a sacristy more than an atom: a room with neither doors nor windows, where all activity takes place on the inside.

The monad is the autonomy of the inside, an inside without an outside. It has as its correlative the independence of the façade, an outside without an inside. Now the façade can have doors and windows — it is riddled with holes — although there may be no void, a hole being only the site of a more rarefied matter. The doors and windows of that matter open or even close only from the outside and onto the outside. To be sure, the organic matter already sketches an interiorization, but a relative one, that is always ongoing and forever unfinished. It is because a fold passes through living material in order to allot to the absolute interiority of the monad the metaphysical principle of life, and to make the infinite exteriority of matter the physical law of phenomena. We have two infinite sets, whereby the one never rejoins the other: "Since infinite division of exteriority is extended endlessly and remains open, we are required to exit from the outside in order to posit an inner punctual unity. . . . The physical, natural, phenomenal, contingent world is plunged entirely in the infinite repetition of open linkages: in this way it is not metaphysical. The world of metaphysics is beyond, and closes repetition . . . the monad is this fixed point that infinite partition never attains, and that closes infinitely divided space."[5]

Baroque architecture can be defined by this severing of the façade from the inside, of the interior from the exterior, and the autonomy of the interior from the independence of the exterior, but in such conditions that each of the two terms thrusts the other forward. Wölfflin states as much in his own way ("It is precisely the contrast between the exacerbated language of the façade and the serene peace of the inside that constitutes one of the most powerful effects that

Baroque art exerts upon us"), although he may be misled in thinking that the excess of inner decoration ends up by jostling the contrast, or that the absolute inside in itself is peaceful. Likewise, Jean Rousset defines the Baroque through the severing of the façade from the inside, although he also believes that decoration may risk making the inside "explode." Yet the inside remains perfectly integral from the point of view, or in the mirror, that oversees its decoration, no matter how complicated it might be. A new kind of link, of which pre-Baroque architecture had no inkling, must be made between the inside and outside, or the spontaneity of the inside and the determination of the outside. "What necessary and direct relation can be found between the inside of Saint Agnes and its façade? . . . Far from being adjusted to the structure, the Baroque façade only tends to thrust itself forward," while the inside falls back on itself, remains closed, and tends to be offered to the gaze that discovers it entirely from one point of view, "a little coffin containing the absolute."[6]

What makes the new harmony possible is, first, the distinction between two levels or floors, which resolves tension or allots the division. The lower level is assigned to the façade, which is elongated by being punctured and bent back according to the folds determined by a heavy matter, forming an infinite room for reception or receptivity. The upper level is closed, as a pure inside without an outside, a weightless, closed interiority, its walls hung with spontaneous folds that are now only those of a soul or a mind. This is because, as Wölfflin has shown, the Baroque world is organized along two vectors, a deepening toward the bottom, and a thrust toward the upper regions. Leibniz will make coexist, first, the tendency of a system of gravity to find its lowest possible equilibrium where the sum of masses can descend no further and, second, the tendency to elevate, the highest aspiration of a system in weightlessness, where souls are destined to become reasonable. The coexistence resembles Tintoretto's paintings. That one is metaphysical, dealing with souls, or that the other is physical, entailing bodies, does not impede the two vectors from comprising a similar world, a similar house. And not only are they distributed as a function of an ideal line which is actualized on one level and realized on another; a higher analogy endlessly relates the one to each other.

Domestic architecture of this kind is not a constant, either of art or of thinking. What is Baroque is this distinction and division into two levels or floors. The distinction of two worlds is common to Platonic tradition. The world was thought to have an infinite number of floors, with a stairway that descends and ascends, with each step being lost in the upper order of the One and disintegrated in the ocean of the multiple. The universe as a stairwell marks the Neoplatonic tradition. But the Baroque contribution par excellence is a world with only two floors, separated by a fold that echoes itself, arching from the two sides according to a different order. It expresses, as we shall see, the transformation of the cosmos into a "mundus."

Among the apparently Baroque painters, Tintoretto and El Greco shine, and are incomparable. And yet they have in common this same Baroque trait. *The Burial of Count Orgaz* is, for instance, divided in two by a horizontal line. On the bottom bodies are pressed leaning against each other, while above a soul rises, along a thin fold, attended by saintly monads, each with its own spontaneity. In Tintoretto the lower level shows bodies tormented by their own weight, their souls stumbling, bending and falling into the meanders of matter; the upper half acts like a powerful magnet that attracts them, makes them ride astride the yellow folds of light, folds of fire bringing their bodies alive, dizzying them, but with a "dizziness from on high": thus are the two halves of the *Last Judgment*.[7]

The severing of the inside from the outside in this way refers to the distinction between the two levels, but the latter refers to the Fold that is actualized in the intimate folds that the soul encloses on the upper level, and effected along the creases that matter brings to life always on the outside, on the lower level. Hence the ideal fold is the *Zweifalt*, a fold that differentiates and is differentiated. When Heidegger calls upon the *Zweifalt* to be the differentiator of difference, he means above all that differentiation does not refer to a pregiven undifferentiated, but to a Difference that endlessly unfolds and folds over from each of its two sides, and that unfolds the one only while refolding the other, in a coextensive unveiling and veiling of Being, of presence and of withdrawal of being.[8] The "duplicity" of the fold has to be reproduced from the two sides that it distinguishes, but it relates one to the other by distinguishing them: a severing by which each term casts the other forward, a tension by which each fold is pulled into the other.

The fold is probably Mallarmé's most important notion, and not only the notion but, rather, the operation, the operative act that makes him a great Baroque poet. *Hérodiade* is already the poem of the fold. The fold of the world is the fan or "l'unanime pli" (unanimous fold). At times the open fan makes all particles of matter, ashes, and fog rise and fall. We glimpse the visible through the mist as if through the mesh of a veil, following the creases that allow us to see stone in the opening of their inflections, "fold after fold," revealing the city. The fan reveals absence or withdrawal, a conglomeration of dust, hollow collectivities, armies and hallucinating assemblies. Ultimately the fold pertains to the sensitive side of the fan, to sensitivity itself, stirring up the dust through which it is visible, and exposing its own inanity. And at others, from the other side of the fan that is now closed ("le sceptre des rivages roses . . . ce blanc vol fermé que tu poses") [the scepter of the rosy shores . . . this white closed flight you pose], the fold no longer moves toward pulverization, it exceeds itself or finds its finality in an inclusion, "tassement en épaisseur, offrant le minuscule tombeau, certes, de l'âme" [thick layerings, offering the tiny tomb, surely, of the soul].

The fold is inseparable from wind. Ventilated by the fan, the fold is no longer made of matter through which we see, but of the soul in which we read "plis jaunes de la pensée" [yellow folds of thought], the Book or the monad with multiple leaves. Now it contains every fold, since the combinations of its pages are infinite; but it includes them in its closure, and all its actions are internal. However, these are not two worlds: the fold of the newpaper, dust or mist, inanity, is a fold of circumstance that must have its new mode of correspondence with the book, the fold of the Event, the unity that creates being, a multiplicity that makes for inclusion, a collectivity having become consistent.

For Leibniz, these were not the folds of the fan, but veins in marble. And on one side there are all these creases of matter following which we behold living matter in the microscope, collectivities through the folds of dust that they are stirring up, armies and flocks, greenery seen through blue and yellow dust, inanities or fictions, swarming holes that endlessly feed our disquiet, our boredom, or our giddiness. And then, on the other side, there are these folds in the soul, where inflection becomes inclusion (just as Mallarmé writes that folding becomes a layering): we're no longer seeing, we're reading. Leibniz begins to use the word "to read" at once as the inner act in the privileged region of the monad, and as the act of God in all of the monad itself.[9]

It is well known that the total book is as much Leibniz's dream as it is Mallarmé's, even though they never stop working in fragments. Our error is in believing that they did not succeed in their wishes: they made this unique Book perfectly, the book of monads, in letters and little circumstantial pieces that could sustain as many dispersions as combinations. The monad is the book or the reading room. The visible and the legible, the outside and the inside, the façade and the chamber are, however, not two worlds, since the visible can be read (Mallarmé's journal), and the legible has its theater (both Leibniz's and Mallarmé's theaters of reading). Combinations of the visible and the legible make up "emblems" or allegories dear to the Baroque sensibility. We are always referred to a new kind of correspondence or mutual expression, an *entr'expression,* fold after fold.

The Baroque is inseparable from a new regime of light and color. To begin, we can consider light and shadows as 1 and 0, as the two levels of the world separated by a thin line of waters: the Happy and the Damned.[10] An opposition is no longer in question. If we move into the upper level, in a room with neither door nor window, we observe that it is already very dark, in fact almost decorated in black, "fuscum subnigrum." This is a Baroque contribution: in place of the white chalk or plaster that primes the canvas, Tintoretto and Caravaggio use a dark, red-brown background on which they place the thickest shadows, and paint directly by shading toward the shadows.[11] The painting is transformed. Things jump out of the background, colors spring from the common base that attests to their obscure nature, figures are defined by their covering more than their contour. Yet this is not in opposition to light; to the contrary, it is by virtue of the new regime of light. Leibniz makes the point in the *Profession de foi du philosophe*: "It slides as if through a slit in the middle of shadows." Should we be given to understand that it comes from a vent, from a thin opening, angled or folded, by intermediary mirrors, the white consisting "in a great number of small reflecting mirrors"?

More exactly, since monads have no openings, a light that has been "sealed" is lit in each one when it is raised to the level of reason. A whiteness is produced through all the tiny inner mirrors. It makes white, but shadow too: it makes the white that is confounded with the illuminated area of the monad, that soon becomes obscure or shades toward the dark background, the *fuscum,* whence things emanate "by means of shadows and fairly strong and well-handled colors." As with Desargues, we only have to invert perspective or to place "the luminous in place of the eye, the opaque in place of the object, and shadow in place of the projection."[12] Wölfflin has summarized the lessons of this progressivity of light that grows and ebbs, and that is transmitted by degrees. It is the relativity of clarity (as much as of movement), the inseparability of clarity from obscurity, the effacement of contour—in short, the opposition to Descartes, who remained a man of the Renaissance, from the double point of view of a physics of light and a logic of the idea.

Clarity endlessly plunges into obscurity. Chiaroscuro fills the monad following a series that can move in either of two directions: at one end is a dark background and at the other is light, sealed; when it is lit, the monad produces white light in an area set aside, but the white is progressively shaded, giving way to obscurity, to a thicker and thicker shadow, as it spreads toward the dark background in the whole monad. Outside of the series we have God on one side, who said let there be light, and with it the white-mirror, but on the other side the shadows or absolute blackness, made up of an infinity of holes that can no longer reflect the received rays. An infinitely spongy and cavernous matter ultimately contains all of these holes.[13] Does the line of light—or fold of the two levels—pass between the shadows and the dark background being withdrawn from it? Ultimately, yes, insofar as the lower level is now no more than a cave hollowed out by caves, and matter, forced back under the waters, is almost reduced to nothing. But concrete matter is above, its holes already filled with an increasingly vaporous matter, such that the fold of the two levels appears to be the common limit of two kinds of full folds.

Germany's entry on the philosophical scene implies the entire German soul that, according to Nietzsche, comes forward less as something "deep" than full of folds and pleats.[14] How can a portrait be made of Leibniz's person without marking the extreme tension of an open façade and a hermetic inner volume, each being independent of the other and both regulated by a strange preestablished connection? It is an almost schizophrenic tension. Leibniz comes forward in Baroque strokes. "As a German type Leibniz is more interesting than Kant: simple-minded, full of noble words, ruseful, supple, malleable, a mediator (between Christianism and mechanistic philosophy), and in his own heart having enormous audacity, sheltered under a mask and courteously intrusive, modest in appearance. . . . Leibniz is dangerous, a good German who needs façades and philosophies of façades, but bold and basically mysterious in the extreme."[15] The courtly wig is a façade, an entry, like the vow to hurt no one's established feelings, and the art of presenting his system from one point of view or another, in such and such a mirror, following the apparent intelligence of a correspondent or of an opponent knocking on his door, while the System itself is up above, turning about itself, ceding absolutely nothing to the compromises, down below, whose secret he keeps, taking, on the contrary, "the best of all sides" in order to deepen or to make another fold in the room with closed doors and with sealed windows, the room in which Leibniz is confined when he states, "Everything is always the same, with degrees of perfection excepted."

The best inventors of the Baroque, the best commentators have had their doubts about the consistency of the notion, and have been bewildered by the arbitrary extension that, despite themselves, the notion risked taking. The Baroque was seen as being restricted to one genre (architecture), or to an increasingly restrictive determination of periods and places, or yet again to a radical disavowal: the Baroque never existed. It is nonetheless strange to deny the existence of the Baroque in the way we speak of unicorns or herds of pink elephants. For in this case the concept is given, while in the case of the Baroque the question entails knowing if a concept can be invented that is capable (or not) of attributing existence to it. Irregular pearls exist, but the Baroque has no reason for existing without a concept that forms this very reason. It is easy to call the Baroque inexistent; it suffices not to propose its concept. We thus have to go back and wonder if Leibniz is the Baroque philosopher par excellence or if his work forms a concept capable of making the Baroque exist in itself. In this respect, those who have compared Leibniz to the Baroque have often done so in the name of too broad a concept, such as Knecht with his "coincidence of opposites." Christine Buci-Glucksmann proposes a much more interesting criterion, a dialectics of seeing and gazing, but this criterion might in turn be too restrictive, allowing only the definition of an optical fold.[16] For our purposes the criterion or operative concept of the Baroque is the Fold, everything that it includes, and in all its extensiveness.

Fold after fold: if the Baroque can be stretched beyond its precise historical limits, it appears to us that it is always by virtue of this criterion, which inspires us to recall Michaux when he writes of *La vie dans les plis* (Life in the folds), or Boulez when he looks to Mallarmé and composes "Fold after Fold," or Hantaï when he constructs a method from folding. And if, in the other direction, we return to the past, why would we not find the Baroque already, for instance, in Uccello? Because he is not satisfied with painting blue and pink horses, and lances arched as if they were strokes of light directed on all points of the sky, he endlessly draws "*mazocchi,* that are wooden circles covered with cloth that is placed on the head, so that the folds of the remaining fabric turn about the whole face." He comes up against his contemporaries' incomprehension because "the power of *sovereignly developing* all things and the strange series of hoods with folds seem to him more revealing than the magnificent marble figures of the great Donatello."[17] Thus a Baroque line would move exactly according to the fold, and that would bring together architects, painters, musicians, poets, and philosophers. To be sure, it might be argued that the concept of the fold also remains too broad: If we restrict ourselves to the plastic arts, what period and what style would fail to recognize the fold as a trait of painting or of sculpture? It is not only in clothing, but includes the body, rocks, waters, earth, and line. Baltrušaitis generally defines the fold by severing but a severing that casts forth each of the divided terms next to the other. In this way he defines the Romanesque fold by the severing-casting forth of figuration and of geometry.[18]

Cannot the Oriental fold also be defined by what is void and what is full? And all the others will have to be defined, one after the other, through comparative analysis. Uccello's folds are not really Baroque because they are held in solid, polygonal, inflexible—even if ambiguous—geometrical structures. Should we wish to maintain the working relation of the Baroque and the fold, we shall therefore have to show that the fold remains limited in the other cases, and that in the Baroque it knows an unlimited freedom whose conditions can be determined. Folds seem to be rid of their supports—cloth, granite, or cloud—in order to enter into an infinite convergence, as in El Greco's *Christ in the Mountolive Garden* (that of the National Gallery). Or then, notably in *The Baptism of Christ,* the counter-fold of the calf and knee, the knee as an inversion of the calf, confers on the leg an infinite undulation, while the seam of the cloud in the middle transforms it into a double fan. . . .

These are the same traits, taken in their rigor, that have to account for the extreme specificity of the Baroque, and the possibility of stretching it outside of its historical limits, without any arbitrary extension: the contribution of the Baroque to art in general, and the contribution of Leibnizianism to philosophy.

1. *The fold*: the Baroque invents the infinite work or process. The problem is not how to finish a fold, but how to continue it, to have it go through the ceiling, how to bring it to infinity. It is not only because the fold affects all materials that it thus becomes expressive matter, with different scales, speeds, and different vectors (mountains and waters, papers, fabrics, living tissues, the brain), but especially because it determines and materializes Form. It produces

a form of expression, a *Gestaltung,* the genetic element or infinite line of inflection, the curve with a unique variable.

2. *The inside and the outside*: the infinite fold separates or moves between matter and soul, the façade and the closed room, the outside and the inside. Because it is a virtuality that never stops dividing itself, the line of inflection is actualized in the soul but realized in matter, each one on its own side. Such is the Baroque trait: an exterior always on the outside, an interior always on the inside. An infinite "receptivity," an infinite "spontaneity": the outer façade of reception and inner rooms of action. Up to now Baroque architecture is forever confronting two principles, a bearing principle and a covering principle (on the one hand, Gropius, and on the other, Loos).[19] Conciliation of the two will never be direct, but necessarily harmonic, inspiring a new harmony: it is the same expression, the line, that is expressed in the elevation of the inner song of the soul, through memory or by heart, and in the extrinsic fabrication of material partitions, from cause to cause. But, justly, what is expressed does not exist outside its expressions.

3. *The high and the low*: the perfect accord of severing, or the resolution of tension, is achieved through the division into two levels, the two floors being of one and the same world (the line of the universe). The façade-matter goes down below, while the soul-room goes up above. The infinite fold then moves between the two levels. But by being divided, it greatly expands on either side: the fold is divided into folds, which are tucked inside and which spill onto the outside, thus connected as are the high and the low. Pleats of matter in a condition of exteriority, folds in the soul in a condition of closure. Pleats of the partition and folds of the song. Baroque is abstract art par excellence: on the lower floor, flush with the ground, within reach, the art comprehends the textures of matter (the great modern Baroque painters, from Paul Klee to Fautrier, Dubuffet, Bettencourt . . .). But abstraction is not a negation of form: it posits form as folded, existing only as a "mental landscape" in the soul or in the mind, in upper altitudes; hence it also includes immaterial folds. Material matter makes up the bottom, but folded forms are styles or manners. We go from matter to manner; from earth and ground to habitats and salons, from the *Texturologie* to the *Logologie*. These are the two orders, Dubuffet's two levels, with the discovery of their harmony that must go as far as indiscernibility. Is it a texture, or a fold of the soul, of thought?[20] Matter that reveals its texture becomes raw material, just as form that reveals its folds becomes force. In the Baroque the coupling of material-force is what replaces matter and form (the primal forces being those of the soul).

4. *The unfold*: clearly this is not the contrary of the fold, nor its effacement, but the continuation or the extension of its act, the condition of its manifestation. When the fold ceases being represented in order to become a "method," a process, an act, the unfold becomes the result of the act that is expressed exactly in

this fashion. Hantaï begins by representing the fold—tubular and swarming—but soon folds the canvas or paper. Then, it resembles two axes, one of "Studies" and another of "Tables." Sometimes the surface is locally or irregularly folded. These are the outer sides of the open fold that are painted, such that stretching, splaying, and unfolding cause surfaces of color to alternate with zones of white that all modulate over one another. Sometimes it is the solid that projects its inner sides on a regularly folded plane surface in accord with the creases: here the fold has a fulcrum, it is knotted and closed at each intersection, and is unfolded to cause the inner white to circulate.[21]

Sometimes light vibrates color in the pleats and crannies of matter, sometimes light vibrates in the folds of an immaterial surface. However, what is it that makes the Baroque line only a possibility for Hantaï? He never stops facing another possibility, which is that of the Oriental line. Painted and nonpainted surfaces are not divided as are form and content, but as the full and the void in a reciprocal becoming. That is how Hantaï hollows out the eye of the fold and paints only the sides (the Oriental line); but sometimes he makes successive foldings in the same area that leave no place for voids (a full Baroque line). It may be that the Baroque will have to confront the Orient profoundly. This happened to be Leibniz's adventure with his binary arithmetic: in one and zero Leibniz acknowledges the full and the void in a Chinese fashion; but the Baroque Leibniz does not believe in the void. For him it always seems to be filled with a folded matter, because binary arithmetic superimposes folds that both the decimal system—and Nature itself—conceal in apparent voids. For Leibniz, and in the Baroque, folds are always full.[22]

5. *Textures*: Leibnizian physics includes two principal chapters, the one involving active or so-called derivative forces related to matter, and the other involving passive forces, or the resistance of material or texture.[23] Perhaps only at the limit does texture become most evident, before rupture or tearing, when stretching, no longer being opposed to the fold, now expresses it in its pure state, according to a Baroque figure that Bernard Cache has indicated (hysteresis more than stretching).[24] Not belonging to the same pictorial vision, here the fold still pushes back the opening or the hole. As a general rule the way a material is

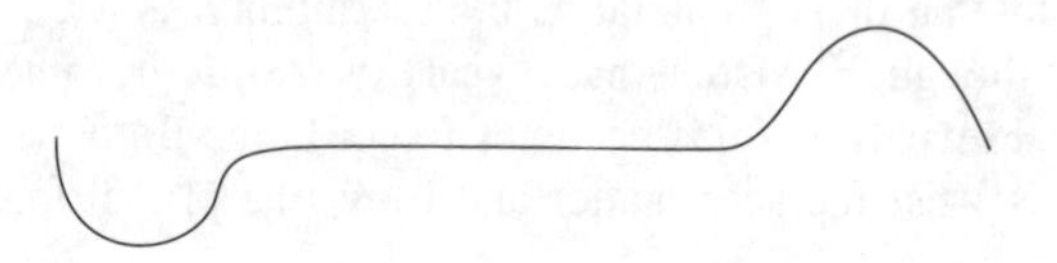

folded is what constitutes its texture. It is defined less by its heterogenous and really distinct parts than by the style by which they become inseparable by virtue of particular folds. Whence the concept of Mannerism in its working relation with the Baroque. That is what Leibniz stated when he invoked the "paper or the tunic." Everything is folded in its own manner, cord and rod, but also colors distributed according to the concavity and convexity of the luminous rays, sounds, all the more strident where "the trembling parts are shorter and more taut." Hence texture does not depend on the parts themselves, but on strata that determine its "cohesion."

The new status of the object, the objectile, is inseparable from the different layers that are dilating, like so many occasions for meanders and detours. In relation to the many folds that it is capable of becoming, matter becomes a matter of expression. In this respect, the fold of matter or texture has to be related to several factors, first of all, light, chiaroscuro, the way the fold catches illumination and itself varies according to the hour and light of day (Tromeur's and Nicole Grenot's contemporary research). But then, depth: how does the fold itself determine a "thin" and superimposable depth, the paper fold defining a minimum of depth on our scale of things, as we see in Baroque letter holders in trompe l'oeil, where the representation of a pleated card casts a sense of depth in front of the wall. And third, there is the soft and overlaid depth of fabric that has never ceased to inspire painting, brought to new power in our time by Helga Heinzen: her representation of striped and folded fabrics covers the entire painting, the body disappears in the falls and rises, the waves and sums, which follow a line now coming from Islam.

But still the theater of matter, to the extent a material can be grasped, hardened in its distortion or its hysteresis, is apt to express within itself the folds of another material, as in Renonciat's wooden sculpture, where Lebanese cedar turns into a plastic dropcloth, or the Paraña pine becomes "cotton and feathers." Finally, the way that all these textures of matter tend toward a higher point, a spiritual point that envelops form, that holds it enveloped, and that contains alone the secret of material folds below. Where would these come from? They are not explained by composite parts, since the "swarming," the perpetual displacement of contour, originates in the projection of something spiritual into matter. Are they a phantasmagoria of the order of thought, as Dubuffet would say? In another manner, the sculptor Jeanclos finds an analogous way when he goes from physical leaves of cabbage—infinitely folded, tied, bloodied—or infinitely stretched sheets, to metaphysical peas, spiritual crabs, heads of monads that concretize the meaning of the expression "the folds of sleep."[25] Whether active or passive, derivative forces of matter refer to primitive forces which are those of the soul. But always the two levels, their harmony, and their harmonization.

6. *The paradigm*: the search for a model of the fold goes directly through the choice of a material. Would it be the paper fold, as the Orient implies, or the fold of fabric, that seems to dominate the Occident? But the point is that the composite materials of the fold (texture) must not conceal the formal element or

form of expression. In this respect, the Greek fold is not satisfactory, even if it has the correct ambition to be worthy of the highest areas, in political force, and in the power of thinking: the Platonic paradigm of weaving as interlacing is contained in textures but does not extract the formal elements of the fold. It is because the Greek fold, as the *Politics* and the *Timaeus* have shown, presupposes a common measure of two terms that are mixed, and thus operates through encirclements that correspond to the repetition of proportion. That is why, for Plato, forms are folded. The formal element of the fold is not attained. This formal element appears only with infinity, in what is incommensurable and in excess, when the variable curve supersedes the circle.[26] Such is the case for the Baroque fold, with its corresponding status of a power of thinking and political force. The paradigm becomes "mannerist," and proceeds to a formal deduction of the fold.

In this way the psychiatrist Clérambault's taste for folds of Islamic origin, and his extraordinary photogaphs of veiled women—true paintings that resemble those of Helga Heinzen nowadays—amounts, despite what has been said, to much more than a simple personal perversion. So does Mallarmé's shawl, or the poet's wish to edit a fashion journal. If Clérambault manifests a delirium, it is because he discovers the tiny hallucinatory perceptions of ether addicts in the folds of clothing. It falls upon formal deduction to straddle many diverse materials and areas. It will have to distinguish: simple and composite Folds; Hems (knots and seams being corollaries of the fold); Drapes, with their proppings.[27] Only then will ensue material Textures and, finally, Agglomerations or Conglomerations (felt made by fulling and not by weaving). We will see to what extent this deduction is properly Baroque or Leibnizian.

Part II
Inclusions

Chapter 4
Sufficient Reason

"Everything has a reason . . ." This vulgar formulation already suffices to suggest the exclamatory character of the principle, the identity of the principle and of the cry, the cry of Reason par excellence. Everything is everything that happens, no matter what happens. Everything that happens has a reason![1] It is understood that a cause is not the reason being sought. A cause is of the order of what happens, either to change a state of things, or to produce or destroy the thing. But the principle claims that everything that happens to a thing—causations included—has a reason. If an event is called what happens to the thing, whether it undergoes the event or makes it happen, it can be said that sufficient reason is what includes the event as one of its predicates: the concept of the thing, or the notion.

"Predicates or events," says Leibniz.[2] Whence the path that we have just followed in the chapters above, from inflection to inclusion. Inflection is the event that happens to the line or to the point. Inclusion is the predication that places inflection in the concept of the line or the point, that is, in this *other point* that will be called metaphysical. We go from inflection to inclusion just as we move from the event of the thing to the predicate of the notion, or from "seeing" to "reading." What we see on the thing we read in its concept or notion. The concept resembles a signature or an enclosure. Sufficient reason is inclusion; in other words, the identity of the event and the predicate. Sufficient reason proclaims, "Everything has a concept!" Its metaphysical formulation goes as follows: "All predication is grounded in the nature of things"; as a logical formulation: "Every predicate is in the subject," the subject or nature of things being the notion, the concept of the thing.

The Baroque is widely known to be typified by the "concetto," but only insofar as the Baroque *concetto* can be opposed to the classical *concept*. It is also widely held that Leibniz brings a new conception to the concept, with which he transforms philosophy. But we have to wonder about the composition of this new, Leibnizian conception. That it is opposed to the "classical" conception of the concept—in the way that Descartes had invented it—is best shown in Leibniz's correspondence with De Volder, a Cartesian. First of all, the concept is not a simple logical being, but a metaphysical being; it is not a generality or a universality, but an individual; it is not defined by an attribute, but by predicates-as-events.

But does this hold for every inclusion? In response to the question we encounter the distinction of two great types of inclusion or analysis, analysis being the operation that discovers a predicate in a notion taken as a subject, or a subject for an event taken as a predicate. Leibniz seems to be saying that in the case of necessary propositions or truths of essence ("2 plus 2 equal 4"), the predicate is *expressly* included in the notion, while, for contingent existences ("Adam sins," "Caesar crosses the Rubicon"), inclusion is only *implicit or virtual.*[3] Must we be led to understand, as Leibniz sometimes suggests, that analysis is finite in one case and indefinite in the other? Yet beyond the fact that in each case we cannot be sure of what the concept or subject is made, we run the risk of a double misreading if we associate "expressed intention" with the finite, and the "implicit or virtual" with the indefinite. It would be astonishing to find that the analysis of essences is finite, since the latter are inseparable from the infinity of God himself.

In turn, the analysis of existences cannot be separated from the infinity of the world, which is no less existent than all other infinity: were the indefinite existing in the world, God would not be submitted to it, and would thus see the end of analysis, which is not the case.[4] In short, we can no more identify the virtual that Leibniz invokes with an inexistent indefinite than we can identify express intention with finitude. Difficulties accrue if we consider crucial texts in which Leibniz presents the implicit or the virtual, not as what has pertained to inclusions of existence, but now as a type of inclusion of essence: these are necessary propositions that are divided in case of an intentional inclusion ("2 plus 2 equal 4"), and in the case of stated inclusion ("every duodenary is a sonary").[5] We might even say that propositions of essence attend to all analysis—intended or implicit—while propositions of existence ultimately escape it.

The first task would entail defining essences. Yet we cannot do so without knowing what a definition is, because we begin from already definable essences without any inkling about what they presuppose. A definition posits the identity of one term (the defined) with at least two other terms (definers or reasons). The definition can possibly be substituted for the defined, this substitution being the *reciprocal inclusion*: for example, I define 3 by 2 and 1. Several remarks must follow. First, at stake are real or genetic definitions that reveal the possibility of the defined: we do not define 3 by 1, 1, plus 1, nor by 8 minus 5, but by the first numbers that the defined includes and that include it. Second, definitions of this kind never operate by genre and difference. They solicit neither the comprehension, the extension of a concept, abstraction, nor generality that would, moreover, go back to nominal definitions. Third, the demonstration can be defined as a chain of definitions, that is, as a concatenation of reciprocal inclusions: thus we demonstrate that "2 plus 2 equal 4."[6] Finally, we predict that antecedence, what Aristotle previously had called the before and the after—although no temporal order is in question here—is a complicated notion: the definers or reasons must precede the defined since they determine its possibility, but only by following the "power," and not the "act" that, on the contrary, would suppose the antecedence of the defined. Whence, justly, reciprocal inclusion and the absence of all temporal relations.

From then on it goes without saying that, from one definition to another, if we go back along the nontemporal chain, we arrive at undefinables; in other words, definers that are last reasons, and that can no longer be defined. Why not proceed indefinitely? This question loses all meaning as soon as we are placed in the midst of real definitions, for the indefinite would furnish or have furnished only nominal definitions. Had we known from the beginning what a real definition was, we would have had to begin with undefinables. But we get there through this intermediary, and we discover them as absolutely first in the order of the before and after: they are called "simple primitive notions." From definition to definition (demonstration), everything can only begin with undefinable terms that enter into the initial definitions. These undefinables are obviously not reciprocal inclusions, like definitions, but they are *auto-inclusions*: they are Identicals in the pure state, each of which includes itself and includes only itself, each only capable of being identical to itself. Leibniz draws identity into infinity: the Identical is an auto-position of the infinite, without which identity would remain hypothetical (if A is, then A is A . . .).

This mark of identity can allow us to demonstrate that Leibniz makes a very special, indeed Baroque, conception from these principles. In this respect Ortega y Gasset makes a set of subtle remarks: on the one hand, Leibniz loves principles, and he is probably the only philosopher who invents them endlessly. He invents them with pleasure and enthusiasm, and he brandishes them like swords. But on the other hand, he plays with principles, multiplies formulas, varies their relations, and incessantly wants to "prove" them as if, loving them too much, his respect for them were lacking.[7] Leibniz's principles are not universal empty forms; nor are they hypostases or emanations that might turn them into beings. But they are the determination of classes of beings.

If the principles appear to us as cries, it is because each one signals the presence of a class of beings that are themselves crying and draw attention to themselves by these cries. In this way we could not be led to believe that the principle of identity causes us to be aware of nothing, even if it does not make us penetrate into this awareness. The principle of identity or, rather, the principle of contradiction, as Leibniz says, makes us become aware of a class of beings, that of the Identicals, which are complete beings. The principle of identity — or rather, of contradiction — is only the cry of the Identicals. It cannot be an abstraction. It is a signal. Identicals are undefinables in themselves and exist perhaps beyond our ken; they have, no less, a criterion that the principle makes us aware of or able to hear.

Every form that can be thought of as infinite by itself would be identical to itself, capable of being raised directly to infinity, by itself, and not by means of a cause: "nature susceptible to the last degree." Such is the criterion. For example, can we imagine a speed, a number, or a color as infinite? In contrast, thought appears to be a form that can be raised to infinity, or even extension, *under the condition that these forms are not wholes, and that they do not have parts*: these are "absolutes," "fundamental qualities," "distinctly knowable qualities," A, B, C . . . [8] Each one, being included in itself and including only itself, not being a whole and having no parts, has strictly no relation with an other. These are pure "disparities," diverse absolutes that cannot be contradicted since no element exists that one can affirm or the other can deny. They are, as Blanchot would say, in a "nonrelation." And this is just what the principle of contradiction states: it states that since two distinct Identicals cannot be contradicted by each other, they surely form a category.

They might be called "attributes" of God. There we find in fact the only thesis that ties Spinoza to Leibniz, their common manner of requiring in the ontological proof of the existence of God a detour that Descartes had confidence enough to cut short: before concluding that an infinitely perfect being necessarily exists, it had to be shown that it is possible (a real definition), and that it does not imply contradiction. Now it is precisely because all absolute forms are incapable of being contradicted that they can belong to a same Being and, in being able to, they effectively belong to it. Since they are forms, their real distinction is formal and carries no ontological difference among beings to which each might be attributed: they are all attributed to a single and same Being that is both ontologically one and formally diverse.[9] There the real distinction already does not involve separability. As Kant will state, the ontological proof goes from totality of all possibilities to the individuality of a necessary being:

$$\frac{\infty}{1}$$

Identicals are a class of beings but *a class with one sole member.* Here we find the law of antecedence, since absolute forms precede God as do the first elements of his possibility, although God precedes them "in re" and "in actu."

How do we go from Identicals to Definables? Identicals are absolutely simple primitive notions, A, B, . . ., that metaphysically "compose" a unique Being, AB . . . But the metaphysical composition and the logical derivation cannot be confused. Definables are derived notions: they can be simple if they are first in their order, but they always presuppose at least two primitives that define them in a relation, under a "vinculum," or through the intermediary of a particle that itself can be simple or complex (for example, A *in* B). That is the Combinatory that goes thus from Identicals to Definables, from primary to derived beings, through a distinction of levels: level I includes the primary or the indefinable Identicals; level II is composed of the simple derived beings, defined by two primary beings in a simple relation; level III is composed of composite derived beings defined by three primaries, or by a simple primary and a simple derived being in a relation that is itself composite . . .[10]

We can take an example that works by analogy: even if we cannot begin from absolute primaries in order to deduce our thought, we can always convene relative primaries in an area (they presuppose the area instead of engendering it); thus the first numbers are prime in arithmetic because, being divisible only by itself or by unity, each is a phenomenon of auto-inclusion. Or else the undefinable axioms in geometry (for instance "point," "space," "intermediary" . . .) form a level I, from which derives a level II through the combination each time of two primaries, then a level III (line being the *intermediary space* between *two points*).[11] In the absolute God probably assures the passage from Identicals to Definables: he is composed of all absolute primary forms, but he is also the first and last definable, from which all others will derive. But we are thus not resolving the difficulty that weighs upon the whole combinatory. Couturat demonstrates it perfectly: How can an account be made of the relations marked by articles, prepositions, verbs, and cases that surge forth from level II on? We began from absolute forms taken in their nonrelation. And all of a sudden relations or "particles" spring up, not only for our understanding, but in the understanding of God himself. How could the relation jump out of the nonrelation?

Clearly many areas are found in the understanding of God. We can state that the relations surge up in a region that no longer involves God himself, but the possibility of creation. That is at least an indication, even if the question does not entail knowing whence the relations spring forth, but how they do. Baroque thinking has in fact ascribed a particular importance to the distinction of several orders of infinity. And in the first place, if absolute forms constitute God as an infinity by itself, which excludes wholes and parts, the idea of creation goes back to a second infinity, through cause. *It is this infinity by way of cause that constitutes wholes and parts,* without there being either a largest or a smallest part. It is no longer a whole, but a series that has neither a final term nor a limit. It is not quite ruled by the principle of identity, but by a principle of similitude or of homothesis that signals a new class of beings. Here is everything that might be called *extensions* or *extensities*: not only extension strictly speaking, but also time, number, infinitely divisible matter, everything that is "partes extra partes," and, as such, submitted to the principle of similitude. Thus each term of the series, which forms a whole for the precedents and a part for everything that ensues, is defined by two or several simple terms which assume an assignable relation in this new function, and which no longer play the role of *parts,* but of *requisites,* of reasons or constituent elements.

Thus, in a numerical set, each as whole and part is defined by the first numbers that enter into the relation in this respect: 4, which is twice 2 and half of 8, is defined by 3 and 1. Or else, in the arithmetical triangle, each line as a series of numbers is twice its precedent, but is defined by a power of two that places the requisite in a relation of multiplication with itself (and the requisites in relation to one another). We need only understand that the whole and the parts (and similitude) are not already related, but the original formula of a derived infinity, a sort of intelligible matter for every possible relation: thus the primary terms, without relations in themselves, *acquire relations* by becoming the requisites or the definers of the derived, in other words, the shapers of this material. As long as the primaries were without relation, as simple auto-inclusions, they were attributes of God, predicates of an absolutely infinite Being.

But as soon as we consider an infinity of a second order that derives from this Being, predicates abandon being attributes in order to become relations. They enter into relations that define wholes and parts to infinity, and are themselves in reciprocal inclusion with the defined, in accord with the double antecedence. Here we have entered into "sufficient reason," simply because the definers in their relation are in each instance the reason of the defined. Were a relation to be defined, we would say that it is the unity of the nonrelation with matters of wholes-and-parts. If it has often been held that relations presented Leibniz with an irreducible difficulty, it is because predicates and attributes were lumped together, in a confusion that is legitimate only at the level of absolutely simple notions specifically excluding all relation, but is not so at the level of the derived forms, or Predicate = relation, in the reciprocal inclusion of the predicate-relation with the defined subject (4 is 3R1). And even when the subject will be the monad without parts, predicates will continue to be "affections and relations," at least in the lexicon of the *Monadology.*

But previously there exists a third order of infinity. The question involves series that do not always possess a last term, but that *are convergent and tend toward a limit.*[12] Extension no longer pertains, but intensions or intensities do. No longer relations, but rather laws. No longer Combinatory, but Characteristic. No longer matter, but something "real" in matter that fills extension (to be sure, a "possible" reality). It is the real in matter, the thing, that has inner characters whose determination enters each time into a series of magnitudes converging toward a limit, the relation between these limits being that of a new type,

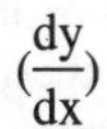

$$\left(\frac{dy}{dx}\right)$$

and making up a law. Hermann Weyl will state that a law of Nature is necessarily a differential equation. The notion of requisite, one of Leibniz's most original notions, no longer designates definers but takes on its most rigorous, autonomous meaning by designating conditions, limits, and differential relations among these limits.

Parts or wholes do not exist any more; they are replaced by degrees for each character. The inner characters of a sound include an actual intensity, a pitch, a duration, a timbre; a color has a tint, a saturation, a value; gold, in an example that Leibniz often uses, has a color, a weight, a malleability, a resistance to melting and to dissolution in nitric acid. The real in matter is not only extension; it possesses an "impenetrability, inertia, impetuosity and attachment." It is what is called the *texture* of a body, it is specifically the sum of its inner qualities, the latitude of their variation and the relation of their limits: hence the texture of gold.[13] Insofar as the Requisites are thus distinguished from the Definables (although they can furnish definitions), we discover that we are facing a third type of inclusion, in this instance a nonreciprocal and *unilateral* one: here sufficient reason becomes a principle. Everything real is a subject whose predicate is a character put into a series, the sum of predicates being the relation among the limits of these series (we shall avoid confusing limit and subject).

We have to mark at once the irreducibility of this new area from the point of view of an object of knowledge; but we also have to account for its transitory role, in another sense, from the point of view of knowledge itself. On the one hand, requisites are in fact neither presupposed, intuitive essences of the first infinity, nor theorematic essences of the second infinity in definitions and demonstrations. They are problematic essences that correspond to the third infinity. Leibniz's mathematics are forever forging an irreducible instance from problems; it is added to the concatenations of definitions, but without it, perhaps, definitions would not concatenate: if there are exchanges of mathematical letters, it is because we are thrown into problems before being sent off to theorems.[14] In this sense, axioms deal with problems, and surely escape demonstration. If the Characteristic is distinguished from the Combinatory, it is because it is a veritable calculus of problems or of limits. Requisites and axioms are conditions; not always conditions of experience in the Kantian fashion that still turns them into universals, but the conditions of a problem to which the thing responds in one case or another, the cases referring to values of the variable in the series.

What appears is that we are linked—almost fixed—to requisites: even the definers that we attain, in arithmetic or in geometry for example, have value only through analogy, and are in fact the inner characters of a presupposed domain (thus the first numbers whose converging series are sought). The theorem, the demonstration as a concatenation of definitions, can appeal to syllogistic form; but we go by "enthymemes," which hold only for syllogisms, and which work by means of "inner suppressions," ellipses, and problematic shortcuts.[15] In short, if the Combinatory realizes something of its dream, it can do so only through the Characteristic. Yet at this point we move over to the other aspect of the question, which now involves knowledge itself and not its nearest object.

The inner characters of the thing can in fact be understood from the outside and through successive experiments. As happens with animals, their relation remains in the state of simple empirical consecutiveness. However, according to every given case, we can also attain the texture, that is, the true connection of these characters, as in the intrinsic relations between the limits of their respective series (reason): there, we have a rational knowledge, and that is what explains how the inner characters already hold for definitions, the calculus of limits, for demonstrations, and how enthymemes work for complete syllogisms.[16] Whence Leibniz's worry over reintegrating axioms in the order of necessary truths and demonstrations (if they escape demonstrations inasmuch as they are requisites, it must all the more be shown that they involve the form of the whole and of parts). Thus characters have to lead us at times downward, toward knowledge of animals, and at others upward, toward rational, definitive, and demonstrative knowledge.

We therefore have three types of inclusion: auto-inclusions, reciprocal inclusions, and unilateral inclusions that can be localized at their limits. Their corresponding term, the *absolute-simples,* Identicals or infinite forms lacking any relation to each other; the *relative-simples,* the Definables, that enter into infinite series of wholes and parts, while their definers enter into relations; the *limitative-simples,* Requisites or converging series that tend toward limits, with their relations among limits. It is the Alphabet, the Combinatory, and the Characteristic.

If we go back to the model of the Baroque fabric, it could be stated that knowledge is known only where it is folded. Leibniz remarks that concatenations of syllogisms or definitions are a "fabric." But "there exists an infinity of other, more composite fabrics," folded like their enthymemes, that are always available for our use.[17] Even the purest syllogistic fabric has been folded according to different speeds of thinking. Ideas are so folded in the soul that we can't always unfold or develop them, just as things themselves are inextricably wrapped up in nature. Malebranche's error is to have believed that in God we see completely unfolded Ideas. But even for God notions have folds that adorn infinite understanding. Absolute Forms, Identicals, are simple and separated folds; Definables are already composite folds; Requisites with their limits resemble even more complex hems (and take up textures). Monads, that necessarily imply a point of view or a grounding, cannot fail to bear resemblance to draped forms.

Now we come to the fourth category of notions: individual notions or monads, that are no longer possible things, but now possible existants (substances). The complete schema is therefore: identities, extensities, intensities, individualities; *forms, magnitudes, things, substances.* Are the latter still simple or individual-simple notions, and in what sense? In every event it is clear that predicates of a given notion taken as a subject form yet another infinite convergent series that tends toward a limit. That is why the individual naturally has a presently infinite comprehension; it "envelops the infinite."[18] The individual notion, the monad, is exactly the inverse of God to the degree that reciprocals are numbers that exchange their numerator and their denominator: 2, or $\frac{2}{1}$, has as a reciprocal $\frac{1}{2}$. And God, whose formula is $\frac{\infty}{1}$, has as its reciprocal the monad, $\frac{1}{\infty}$. Now the question entails knowing if the infinite convergent series in the monad, in the individual, is of the same type as that of the intentions [intensions], or if indeed another case is involved, of another, fourth type of inclusion. Clearly we can and must present individual substances as having requisites and inner characters.

In fact that is how Leibniz salvages Aristotle, by making requisites of substance from both form and matter and powers both active and passive. Great differences are no less marked between the thing and substance, or the thing and the existant. The first difference is that the thing has several internal characters, x, y, . . . and therefore figures in several series, each of which tends toward its limit, the reason or connection of the series in the thing being a differential relation of the order

$$\frac{dy}{dx}.$$

It might be said that our perception of things is a "pleonasm" or that, in the instance of things, "we have more than one notion of a same subject," for example, weight and malleability for gold.[19] Now the same does not hold for individuals: we have seen that the world was a unique, infinitely infinite, converging series, and that each monad expressed it in its entirety, even though it clearly expressed only one portion of the series. But, rightly, the clear region of a monad *is extended* in the clear portion of another, and in a same monad the clear portion is prolonged infinitely into the obscure zones, since each monad expresses the entire world. A searing pain in me is only the prolongation of a series that led me into it, even if I did not notice it, and now it is continued in the series of my pain. *There is a prolongation or continuation of convergent series, one into the other.*

That is the very condition of "compossibility," in a manner of reconstituting over and again one and the same, infinitely infinite, converging series, the World, made of all series, its curvature having a unique variable. The differential relation thus acquires a new meaning, since it expresses the analytical extension of one series into another, and no more the unity of converging series that would not diverge in the least from each other. Now then, infinity also changes meaning. It acquires a fourth and still current dimension: it is no longer defined either by itself or by the "limit" of a series, but by a law of order or continuity that classifies limits or transforms series into a "totality" (the presently infinite totality of the world, or the transfinite). Just as each monad conveys the entire world, so then a single notion can no longer pertain for one subject, and subject-monads will now be distinguished only by their inner manner of expressing the world: the principle of sufficient reason will become a principle of indiscernibles. Since there never exist two identical subjects, there can be no apparently identical individuals.

There is a second difference that does not seem to be to the monad's liking. The thing in its texture surely contained the serial law that determined the play of its characters and the differential relation between limits. Whereas monads in their folds, including the same world in one order or another, contain the infinite series, they do not contain the law of this unique series. Differential relations, different orders refer to a totality of all orders that exists outside of the monad. In this way the world is in the monad, but the monad lives for the world: God himself conceives individual notions only as a function of the world that they express, and chooses them only through a calculus of the world. With all series being extended into each other, law or reason appears to be pushed back into transfinite totality, into the whole of the infinitely infinite series, the world, and the limits or relations among limits, in God who conceives and chooses the world.

Whence the cosmological proof of God's existence, which goes from the series to the whole, and from the whole to God.[20] The whole series is clearly in the monad, but the reason of the series — from which the monad receives only its particular effect or individual capacity to complete a part of it — is not. The limit remains *extrinsic* and appears only in a harmony *preestablished* among the monads. But perhaps the monad draws its force from it instead of being impoverished by it: the exteriority of reason is only the consequence of the positive possibility of prolonging the series into each other; not only the finite series that correspond to the clear expression of each monad, but the infinite series that correspond to the order or to the point of view of each individual. It is because each monad includes the entire world that it cannot include the serial reason common to all monads. We thus face a fourth type of inclusion. Inclusion of the world in the monad is surely unilateral, but *cannot be localized.* It cannot be localized at the limit, since the limit is outside of the monad. There exist four inclusions just as there are four infinities: the infinite sum of primitive forms (= God); infinite series without limits; infinite series with intrinsic limits; infinite series with extrinsic limits that restore an infinite whole (= World).

From this point we can dissipate the ambiguities of the beginning. First of all, why does Leibniz appear to present the truths of essences being amenable to a finite analysis that leads them back to Identicals, while the truths of existence would refer solely to an infinite analysis and would be "irreducible to identical truths"? But the two hypotheses are false. Whether intuitive, theorematic, or problematic, essences are always understood in an infinity. Identicals themselves are intuitive essences, in this way taken as infinite forms. In contrast, it is true that in the area of essences *we can always stop,* and make use of a definition as if it were a final Identical, or of a Requisite as if it were a definition, of a Limit, as if it had been reached. In the area of existences, to the contrary, we cannot stop, because series are liable to be extended and must be so because inclusion cannot be localized.

In the second place, we are not any more exact when we state that the analysis of existences is virtual, while that of essences would only be actual. All analysis is infinite, and in analysis the present or actual exists only in infinity. That inclusion is virtual in propositions of existence signifies merely that nothing is included in an existent unless it may be the entire world, and unless the world currently exists only in the existents that include it: there still, "virtual" designates the character of current inclusion that cannot be localized. There is always a double antecedence: the world is virtually first, but the monad is actually first. Now we understand that the word "virtual" also fits certain propositions of essence. In respect to those concerning Requisites, the word designates the unilateral character of inclusion. If we return to the text of *De la liberté,* we see that the virtual inclusion is based on a non-reciprocal proposition: "Every bino-binary ternary is binary-ternary." Inclusion is virtual, Leibniz specifies, because it has to be extracted, and because the predicate is included in the subject only "under a certain power."[21]

Here it seems that the arithmetical example is clear and simple, but not adequate. The adequate example, as the rest of the text affirms, is the irrational number because it is a root that has to be extracted, or even the differential relation because it involves quantities that are not of the same power. This is how Leibniz regroups the two cases of nonreciprocal inclusion: irrational and existent numbers. The analysis of things is effectively a determination of predicates as requisites, which is accomplished through the extraction of the root or even by a depotentialization of magnitudes, in line with the idea of intrinsic limits. The analysis of existents is a determination of predicates as world, which is accomplished through the prolongation of series of powers, in line with the idea of extrinsic limits. Time and again we discover an incertitude that is objective: On the one hand, does the fold pass between essences and existents or, on the other, between essences of God and what follows? Or between the essences of things and existents?

Predicates are never attributes except in the case of infinite forms or first quiddities; and even there they are more like conditions of possibility for the notion of God, nonrelations that would condition any possible relation. Now in all other cases the predicate is only a relation or an event. Relations themselves are types of events, and problems in mathematics. In antiquity predicates were defined by events that happen to figures. Events in their turn are types of relations; they are relations to existence and to time.[22] Included in the notion as subject is forever an event marked by a verb, or a relation marked by a preposition: I am writing, I am going to Germany, I cross the Rubicon . . . (and, if things had the gift of speech, they would say, as might, for example, gold: "I will resist melting and nitric acid"). How strange it was to think that the unilateral inclusion carried with it the reduction of the proposition to a judgment of attribution.

Attribution, to the contrary, is what Arnault *opposes* to Leibniz in order to criticize inclusion and to salvage the Cartesian conception of substance (I am a thinking being, I am a thing that thinks . . .). The attribute expresses a quality and designates an essence; now Leibniz refuses to define the predicate by a quality, or by the existing subject, even "sub ratione possibilitatis," as an essence. The subject is defined by its unity, and the predicate as a verb expressing an action or a passion. Leibniz knows well the scheme of the attribution of the subject-copula-attribute: I am writing, I am traveling. . . . But this scheme of a "general grammar" that is so dear to Arnauld implies a conception of affirmation and a theory of distinction that hardly favors inclusion.[23] *Leibnizian inclusion is based upon a scheme of subject-verb-object that since antiquity resists the scheme of attribution.* Here we have a Baroque grammar in which the predicate is above all a relation and an event, and not an attribute. When Leibniz uses the attributive model, he does so from the point of view of a classical logic of genres and species, which follows only nominal requirements.[24] He does not use it in order to ground inclusion. Predication is not an attribution. The predicate is the "execution of travel," an act, a movement, a change, and not the state of travel.[25] The predicate *is the proposition itself.* And I can no more reduce "I travel" to "I am a traveling being" than I can reduce "I think" to "I am a thinking being." Thought is not a constant attribute, but a predicate passing endlessly from one thought to another.

That the predicate is a verb, and that the verb is irreducible to the copula and to the attribute, mark the very basis of the Leibnizian conception of the event. In the first place the event is deemed worthy of being raised to the state of a concept: the Stoics accomplished this by making the event neither an attribute nor a quality, but the incorporal predicate of a subject of the proposition (not "the tree is green," but "the tree greens . . ."). They conclude that the proposition stated a "manner of being" of the thing, an "aspect" that exceeded the Aristotelian alternative, essence-accident: for the verb "to be" they substitute "to follow," and they put manner in the place of essence.[26] Then Leibniz implemented the second great logic of the event: the world itself is an event and, as an incorporeal (= virtual) predicate, the world must be included in every subject as a *basis* from which each one extracts the manners that correspond to its point of view (aspects). The world is predication itself, manners being the particular predicates, and the subject, what goes from one predicate to another as if from one aspect of the world to another. The coupling *basis-manners* disenfranchises form or essence: Leibniz makes it the mark of his philosophy.[27] The Stoics and Leibniz invent a mannerism that is opposed to the essentialism first of Aristotle and then of Descartes. Mannerism as a composite of the Baroque is inherited from a Stoic mannerism that is now extended to the cosmos. A third great logic of the event will come with Whitehead.

It is very curious to hear Russell state that Leibniz encounters great difficulty in pondering relations. In a certain fashion all Leibniz does is ponder relations, and Russell is aware of the fact. The only difficulties originate in what cannot be easily extracted, beginning with sentences, in which propositions of inherence show that the predicate is an internal relation. Sometimes the predicate is not given in the sentence, while at others the subject is missing, and at others both of them are lacking. When I say, "Here are three men," the real subject is an *extension* 3, which is only qualified as human, and quantified by three parts; but the predicate is 2 and 1 (men), the internal relation. If I say, "Water boils at 100° C," the subject is clearly a *thing,* water, but the predicate is a vaporization curve that enters into relation with the fusion curve and the sublimation curve at a triple point. And if I say, "Peter is smaller than Paul," "Paul is bigger than Peter," clearly this time the subjects are *substances,* but the relation in each case is not between the two subjects: the true relation is the predication of a "representative of Paul" in the subject Peter, in the aspect of length, or of a "representative of Peter" in the subject Paul, this relation or this predicate always being internal. And size itself refers to the preceding cases, sometimes the extension-subject, sometimes the predicate of the thing (the body). In short, in Leibniz we have an entire history of the concept that goes through the wholes-and-parts, things and substances, by means of extensions, intensions, and individuals, and by which the concept itself, in conformity with each level, becomes a subject. A rupture is opened with the classical conception of the concept as a being of reason: the concept is no longer the essence or the logical possibility of its object, but the metaphysical reality of the corresponding subject. It can be stated that all relations are internal, precisely because the predicates are not attributes (as in the logical conception).

The proof would come from Leibniz's theory of substance. This theory appears to be made expressly for this proof. The two nominal characters on which everyone agrees in principle, from Aristotle to Descartes, are: on the one hand, substance, what is concrete, determined, individual, in the sense that Aristotle speaks of *this,* and Descartes, of *that* stone; on the other hand, substance is subject to inherence or inclusion, in the way that Aristotle defines accident as "what is present in substance," and Descartes states that substance is a "thing *in which* what we conceive exists formally or eminently."[28] But no sooner than we search for a real definition of substance, it appears that the two characters are removed for the sake of an essential, necessary, and universal essence or attribute in the concept. Thus, for Aristotle, the attribute is not in the subject as if by accident, but is affirmed by the subject, such that it can be treated as a second substance. And for Descartes the essential attribute is confused with substance, to the point that individuals now tend only to be modes of the attribute as it generally is. Far from proving individuality and inclusion, attribution and the definition of substance call them into question.

According to Descartes, the initial criterion of substance is the simple, simple notion: that from which elements can be distinguished only by abstraction or distinction of reason (thus extension and the body, thought and the mind). Substance is simple because it can be distinguished from its attribute only by abstraction. Now Leibniz denounces simplicity as a pseudo-logical criterion, for the reason that many simple notions — three at least — are lacking in substance. Only later does he speak of the monad as a simple notion, when he feels that all dangers are set aside, and when he will bring forward two kinds of substance in the problem, of which some are said to be simple only because the others are composite. Yet from one end of his work to the other he invokes a *unity of being* as a metaphysical criterion instead of a simplicity of concept. Arnauld notes that it is an unusual procedure since one cannot then define substance by an essential attribute that would oppose it to "modality, or manner of being," that is, to movement or change. To which Leibniz responds ironically that he has his own "ordinary philosophers" who account for degrees of unity, Aristotle contra Descartes.

Leibniz specifically claims for substance *a unity that can be interior to movement, or a unity of change that can be active,* that excludes simple extension at the level of substances.[29] As long as movement is defined as "the successive existence of a moving body in different places," we apprehend only an accomplished movement, and not the inner unity to which it refers when it is in the act of moving. Movement that moves refers at once (1) to a unity in the instant, in the way that the following state must issue "from itself from the present through a natural force," and to (2) an inner unity for the totality of its duration (the physical criterion of substance). And more profoundly, the qualitative change refers (3) to an active unity that incites a state to move in a flash, but also assures the totality of the movement (a psychological criterion, perception and appetite).[30] Substance therefore represents the double spontaneity of movement as event, and of change as predicate. If the true logical criterion of substance is inclusion, it is because predication is not an attribution, because substance is not the subject of an attribute, but the inner unity of an event, the active unity of a change.

Beyond the Simple, Descartes proposed another criterion, the Complete, that refers to the real distinction. But the latter, no less than the distinction of reason, entails only the concept: the complete is not what is entire (what includes the sum of what belongs to the thing), but what is really distinct, in other words, what can be "thought" by itself by denying what belongs to other things. It is in this way, according to Descartes, that the thinking thing and the extended thing are in themselves, or really distinct, and thus separables. But there still, Leibniz shows that Descartes does not push the concept far enough: two things can be thought as being really distinct without being separable, no matter how little they may have requisites in common. Descartes does not see that even simple beings and even individual substances have requisites, even if it were in the common world that they express, or in the inner characters toward which they converge (form-matter, act-force, active unity-limitation). We have already seen that the really distinct is neither necessarily separate nor separable, and the inseparable can be really distinct.[31] At the limit, and as the Stoics stated, nothing is either separable or separated, but everything conspires, including substance, by virtue of requisites. It is false to state that a substance possesses only one attribute since it has an infinity of modes, but false too that several substances do not have a common attribute since they have requisites that still constitute one of their criteria (an epistemological criterion).[32] Thus there are five criteria of substance: (1) metaphysical, unity of being; (2) logical, inclusion of the predicate in the subject; (3) physical, inner unity in movement; (4) psychological, active unity of change; (5) epistemological, the requisites of inseparability. None permits substance to be defined by an essential attribute, or predication to be confused with an attribution.

Essentialism makes a classic of Descartes, while Leibniz's thought appears to be a profound Mannerism. Classicism needs a solid and constant attribute for substance, but Mannerism is fluid, and the spontaneity of manners replaces the essentiality of the attribute. Can we say that a pain is spontaneous in the soul of a dog that is flogged while it eats its meal, or in that of Caesar the baby when stung by a wasp while sucking at his mother's breast? But the soul is not flogged or stung. Instead of sticking to abstractions, we have to restore the series. The movement of the rod does not begin with the blow: carrying his stick, a man has tiptoed up to the dog from behind, then he has raised the instrument in order then to strike it upon the dog's body.

Just as this complex movement has an inner unity, so also, in the soul of the dog, the complex change has an active unity: pain has not abruptly followed pleasure, but has been prepared by a thousand minute perceptions — the pitter-patter of feet, the hostile man's odor, the impression of the stick being raised up, in short, an entire, imperceptible "anxiousness" from which pain will issue "sua sponte," as if through a natural force integrating the preceding modifications.[33] If Leibniz attaches so much importance to the question of the souls of animals, it is because he knows how to diagnose the universal anxiety of the animals watching out for danger, that seeks to grasp the imperceptible signs of what can turn its pleasure into pain, that will cause its quarry to flee, or turn its repose into movement. The soul *assigns itself* a pain that delivers to its consciousness a series of minute perceptions that it had almost failed to remark because they were first buried in its depths. Leibniz is haunted by depth of the soul, the dark depth, the "fuscum subnigrum." Substances or souls "draw everything from their own depths." That is the second aspect of Mannerism, without which the first would remain empty. The first is the spontaneity of manners that is opposed to the essentiality of the attribute. The second is the omnipresence of the dark depths which is opposed to the clarity of form, and without which manners would have no place to surge forth from. The entire formula of the Mannerism of substances is: "All is born to them out of their own depths, through a perfect spontaneity."[34]

Class of beings	Predicate	Subject	Inclusion	Infinity	Principle
Identicals (absolutely simple)	Forms or attributes	God	Auto-inclusion	Infinity by itself	Principle of contradiction
Definables (relatively simple)	Relations among definers	Extensions or Sizes (wholes and parts)	Reciprocal Inclusion	Infinity by the cause	Principle of similitude
Conditionables (limitatively simple)	Requisites (their relations or laws)	Intentions or Things (what has degrees & tends toward limits)	Inclusion unilateral localizable	Infinite Series with internal limit	Principle of sufficient reason
Individuals (wholly simple)	Events or Modes (relations with existence)	Existents or Substances	Inclusion unilateral cannot be localized	Infinite series with outer limit	Principle of indiscernibles

What founds Ortega y Gasset's impression, that of a play of principles within principles? It is because most of these terms are slippery. Or rather, they have been pigeonholed into boxes and columns, in places where they formerly unfolded themselves: they reign by unfolding themselves in a zone. But they already or still exist folded in what precedes, or they are folded into what follows. Thus sufficient Reason: it appears for itself in things, where inner characters begin to connect in order to provide the reason for the thing. But then, the principle of indiscernibles is only the explication of Reason at the level of individuals, at the point of appearing to be a simple dependency of sufficent reason.

And formerly, sufficient reason resided in the definables, like the relation among definers, such that it previously played in the frame or in the zone of the principle of similitude. And further, the principle of contradiction itself already expresses the very reason of the identicals, and is not limited to forming an alternative with the principle of sufficient reason. To the contrary, it rules in the zone where noncontradiction *suffices* as reason. In this sense the principle of contradiction is a case of sufficient reason.[35] But is not sufficient reason in its turn a case of noncontradiction? The same goes for substances and things, for conditionables and definables. And yet still we have considered only a small number of principles. There is a whole play of passages and transformations of principles: sufficient reason is the reciprocal of noncontradiction, as Couturat has observed.[36] But the principle of indiscernibles is also the inverse of the principle of sufficient reason inasmuch as the following can be stated: "a concept through a thing," and then: "a thing, and only one thing, through a concept" (in which case thing = individual).

There we have a unique trait that is found only in Leibniz's philosophy: the extreme taste for principles, far from favoring division into compartments, presides over the passage of beings, of things, and of concepts under all kinds of mobile partitions. In the midst of this extraordinary philosophical activity, which consists of the creation of principles, we might state that it is the least of principles that there are two poles, one toward which all principles are folding themselves together, the other toward which they are all unfolding, in the opposite way, in distinguishing their zones. These two poles are: Everything is always the same thing, there is only one and the same Basis; and: Everything is distinguished by degree, everything differs by manner . . . These are the two principles of principles. No philosophy has ever pushed to such an extreme the affirmation of a one and same world, and of an infinite difference or variety in this world.

Chapter 5
Incompossibility, Individuality, Liberty

Adam sinned, but his opposite, Adam the nonsinner, is neither impossible nor inherently contradictory (as would be "2 plus 2 do not equal 4"). Such is the tenor of propositions of existence. But we have to know where the problem is: between the two contraries, Adam the sinner and Adam the nonsinner, is a relation of contradiction. In contrast, an entirely different kind of relation must be added if we are to explain that Adam the nonsinner is not contradictory in itself. This other relation is not between the two Adams, but between the Adam nonsinner and the world in which Adam sinned. Surely, insofar as the world in which Adam sinned is included in Adam, we would fall back into a contradiction. But he is also included in an infinity of other monads. In this way there must be a relation of original exclusion between Adam the nonsinner and the world in which Adam sinned. Adam the nonsinner would include another world.

Between the two worlds there exists a relation other than one of contradiction (although there may be a local contradiction between the subjects that compose them, when taken two by two). It is a vice-diction, not a contradiction. That God chooses among an infinity of possible worlds is a rather conventional idea (found, for instance, in Malebranche). Leibniz innovates when he invokes a profoundly original relation among all possible worlds. By stating that it is a great mystery buried in God's understanding, Leibniz gives the new relation the name of *incompossibility.*[1] We discover that we are in a dilemma of seeking the solution to a Leibnizian problem under the conditions that Leibniz has established: we cannot know what God's reasons are, nor how he applies them in each case, but we can demonstrate that he possesses some of them, and what their principle may be.

We have seen that the world was an infinity of converging series, capable of being extended into each other, around unique points. Thus every individual, every individual monad expresses the same world in its totality although it only clearly expresses a part of this world, a series or even a finite sequence. The result is that another world appears *when the obtained series diverge in the neighborhood of singularities*. Compossibles can be called (1) the totality of converging and extensive series that constitute the world, (2) the totality of monads that convey the same world (Adam the sinner, Caesar the emperor, Christ the savior . . .). Incompossibles can be called (1) the series that diverge, and that from then on belong to two possible worlds, and (2) monads of which each expresses a world different from the other (Caesar the emperor and Adam the nonsinner). The eventual divergence of series is what allows for the definition of incompossibility or the relation of vice-diction.

By thus positing an infinity of possible worlds, Leibniz in no way reintroduces a duality that would turn our relative world into the reflection of a more profound, absolute world: to the contrary, he turns our relative world into the only existing world, a world that rejects all other possible worlds because it is relatively "the best." God chooses between an infinity of possible worlds, incompossible with each other, and chooses the best, or the one that has the most possible reality. While the Good was the criterion of the two worlds, the Best is the criterion of the unique and relative world. The principle of the best renews the issue of principles because it is the first time sufficient reason is applied to the world.

There is an antecedence to monads, although a world does not exist outside of the monads that express it. But God does not first of all create Adam, although he is free to have him sin or to be aware that he is sinning. He creates the world in which Adam sins, and also includes it in every individual that conveys it (Sextus raping Lucretia, Caesar crossing the Rubicon . . .). We begin with the world as if with a series of inflections or events: it is a *pure emission of singularities*. Here, for example, are three singularities: to be the first man, to live in a garden of paradise, to have a wife created from one's own rib. And then a fourth: sinning. Singularity-events of this kind hold a relation with "ordinaries" or "regulars" (the difference here being minimal). A singularity is surrounded by a cloud of ordinaries or regulars. And we can state that whatever is remarkable or singular is so to the degree that an inflection that erects a singular point can be made to move anywhere. But we can also state that everything is ordinary because a singular point is only the coincidence of two ordinary points from different vectors (point B of a square is the coincidence of *a*, the last point of the line AB, and of *c*, the first of the line BC).[2] When we follow the two poles of Leibniz's philosophy, we discover that Everything is regular! Everything, too, is singular! On a given scale, it remains for us to distinguish the singulars from the ordinaries or regulars in their relation with one another.

We can now return to our four singularities. We suppose that, every time, one of them can be extended into the neighboring area of the others, along regular lines that have common values in both directions. But then a fifth singularity appears: resistance to temptation. It is not simply that it contradicts the fourth, "sinning," such that a choice has to be made between the two. It is that the lines of prolongation that go from this fifth to the three others are not convergent, in other words, they *do not pass through common values*. It is neither the same garden, nor the same primeval world, nor even the same gynegenesis. A bifurcation takes place that we at least take for granted, since reason escapes us. We are satisfied to know that one exists. It always suffices to be able to say: that is what makes Adam the nonsinner to be supposed incompossible with this world, since it implies a singularity that diverges from those of this world.

That a calculus and even a divine play may exist at the origin of the world is a topic pondered among the greatest philosophers. But everything depends on the nature of the game, on its eventual rules and of the too human model that we are able to reconstitute from it. With Leibniz, it seems to us that in the first place there is a calculus of infinite series ruled by convergences and divergences.

Leibniz furnishes its great Baroque staging at the end of the *Théodicée*. The text responds marvelously to the general criteria of Baroque narrative: stories enclosed one in the other, and the variation of the relation of narrator-and-narration.[3] It is in fact a philosophical dialogue, in which a divinatory consultation of Apollo by Sextus Tarquin is inserted, followed by a direct meeting of Sextus and Jupiter in the presence of Theodorus, that gives way to Theodorus's conversation with Jupiter who sends him back to Pallas, until Theodorus's sublime dream precedes this new meeting. It is an architectural dream: an immense pyramid that has a summit but no base, and that is built from an infinity of apartments, of which each one makes up a world. It has a summit because there is a world that is the best of all worlds, and it lacks a base because the others are lost in the fog, and finally there remains no final one that can be called the worst. In every apartment a Sextus bears a number on his forehead. He mimes a sequence of his life or even his whole life, "as if in a theatrical staging," right next to a thick book.

The number appears to refer to the page that tells the story of the life of this Sextus in greater detail, on a smaller scale, while the other pages probably tell of the other events of the world to which he belongs. Here is the Baroque combination of what we read and what we see. And, in the other apartments, we discover other Sextuses and other books. Leaving Jupiter's abode, one Sextus will go to Corinth and become a famous man, while another Sextus will go to

Thrace and become king, instead of returning to Rome and raping Lucretia, as he does in the first apartment. All these singularities diverge from each other, and each converges with the first (the exit from the temple), only with values that differ from the others. All these Sextuses are possible, but they are part of incompossible worlds.

A bifurcation, like the exit from the temple, is called a point in the neighborhood of series' divergence. Borges, one of Leibniz's disciples, invoked the Chinese philosopher-architect Ts'ui Pên, the inventor of the "garden with bifurcating paths," a baroque labyrinth whose infinite series converge or diverge, forming a webbing of time embracing all possibilities. "Fang, for example, keeps a secret; a stranger knocks at his door; Fang decides to kill him. Naturally, several outcomes are possible: Fang can kill the intruder; the intruder can kill Fang; both of them can escape from their peril; both can die, etc. In Ts'ui Pên's work, all outcomes are produced, each being the point of departure for other bifurcations."[4] Another of Leibniz's disciples, the great popular novelist Maurice Leblanc, told the story of Balthazar's life. He was a "professor of everyday philosophy," for whom everything was ordinary, everything was always regular. . . . But, an orphan, he launched himself in a quest to find his father, with three singularities: his own fingerprints, the letters MTP tattooed on his chest, and the revelation of a clairvoyant who had told him that his father was headless. Then Count Coucy-Vendôme, who died with his throat cut, made Balthazar his inheritor in a document that bears the fingerprints and describes the tattoo. But Balthazar is intercepted by the Mastropieds gang (MTP) whose former head, a victim of the guillotine, claimed him as his son. He is taken away by an Englishman who hands him over to a pasha, who is soon decapitated, whose missing son, Mustapha (MTP) bore the same fingerprints. He is saved by a poet whose device is Mane Thecel Phares, who claims him in turn, but who loses his head in a fit of madness and assassinates a tramp. The final explanation is that the tramp had formerly organized a boarding school for rich children, four plus his own child. But, after a flood, he could not tell which of the five children remained. Having become an alcoholic, having also lost his head, he had sent to the four fathers the impression of the survivor's fingerprints and the sign of the tattoo, in order to persuade each of them that the child was his son.[5] Whence the entanglement of bifurcating stories that are developed simultaneously in divergent series in incompossible worlds. Balthazar cannot be the son of all these fathers in the same world. It is a multiple fraud.

It is clear why Borges invokes the Chinese philosopher rather than Leibniz. He wanted, just as did Maurice Leblanc, to have God pass into existence all incompossible worlds at once instead of choosing one of them, the best. And probably it would be globally possible, since incompossibility is an original relation, distinct from impossibility or contradiction. There would nonetheless be local contradictions, like that of Adam the sinner and Adam the nonsinner. But what especially impedes God from making all possibles—even incompossibles—exist is that this would then be a mendacious God, a trickster God, a deceiving God, such as Maurice Leblanc's tramp. Leibniz, who strongly distrusts the Cartesian argument of the nonmalevolent God, gives him a new basis at the level of incompossibility: God plays tricks, but he also furnishes the rules of the game (contrary to Borges's and Leblanc's game without rules). The rule is that possible worlds cannot pass into existence if they are incompossible with what God chooses. According to Leibniz, only novels of the order of D'Urfée's *L'Astrée* give us the idea of these incompossibles.[6]

Here we can deduce a definition of the individual and of the individual notion. We had seen that every monad conveyed the world (an inclusion that cannot be localized), but clearly conveyed only one partial zone or *subdivision* by virtue of its point of view (a localized borough). And this enlightened region probably passed through the body of every individual. But since we did not know what constituted the region of or relation to the body, only a nominal definition of the individual was offered. Now we can say that an individual is established first of all around a certain number of local singularities, which are its "primary predicates": thus for Adam the four predicates previously considered.[7] That is the real definition of the individual: *concentration, accumulation, coincidence of a certain number of converging preindividual singularities* (it being said that singular points can coincide in a same point, as the different summits of separate triangles coincide at the common summit of a pyramid). It resembles the nucleus of a monad. At the kernel of every monad, according to Gueroult's hypothesis, there exists no "simple notion."

Contrary to Leibniz's method, we would have to be satisfied with two extremes in a chain of notions.[8] At the core of every monad there exist singularities that in every case are the requisites of the individual notion. That each individual clearly expresses only a part of the world derives from the real definition: it clearly expresses the region determined by its constituent singularities. That every individual expresses the entire world also derives from the real definition: the constitutive singularities of each one are effectively extended in all directions up to the singularities of others, under the condition that the corresponding series converge, such that each individual includes the sum of a compossible world, and excludes only the other worlds incompossible with that world (where the series would diverge).

Whence Leibniz's stress when he states that God does not create a "vague" or vagabond Adam who straddles several incompossible worlds, but creates, "sub ratione possibilitatis," as many divergent Adams as there are worlds, each Adam containing the entire world to which he belongs (and to which, also by including it, belong all other compossible monads of such a world). In short, every possible monad is defined by a certain number of preindividual singularities, and is thus compossible with all the monads whose singularities converge with its own, and incompossible with those whose singularities imply divergence or nonprolongation.

But why is Adam's proper name given to all these divergent individuals in incompossible worlds? It is because a singularity can always be isolated, excised, or cut from its prolongations. Then it no longer matters if the garden in which Adam sins is not the same one in which Adam cannot sin. The singularity becomes indefinite, it is no more than *a* garden, and the primary predicate is no longer grasped in one world or another, but only considered "sub ratione generalitatis," at the same time its subject becomes *an* Adam in general, *a* Sextus. . . . From this we shall not conclude that individuation begins from these general predicates. They can be studied more closely later. Individuation does not go from a genre to smaller and smaller species, in accord with a law of differentiation, but goes from singularity to singularity, under the law of convergence or of prolongation that ties the individual to one world or another.

Individual difference is not specific, and the individual is not a last or final species.[9] However, Leibniz happens to say that the individual is like a "species infima" [lower species]; but that is merely a nominal definition of the individual, and Leibniz appeals to it for a specific end, that of breaking with everyone who opposes the individual to the concept. For some, the Nominalists, individuals would be the only existants, concepts being only carefully ordered words; for others, the Universalists, the concept has the power of being infinitely determinable, the individual referring only to accidental or extraconceptual determinations. But for Leibniz, at the same time only the individual exists, *and* it is by virtue of the power of the concept: monad or soul. Thus this power of the concept (to become a subject) does not consist in determining a genre to infinity, but in condensing and in prolonging singularities. The latter are not generalities but events, or droplets of an event. They are not in the least preindividual, insofar as the world is virtually first in respect to individuals that express it (God has created, not Adam the sinner, but the world in which Adam has sinned . . .). *In this sense the individual is the actualization of preindividual singularities,* and implies no previous determination. The contrary must be noted by observing that determination itself supposes individuation.

It is true for the two cases that Leibniz distinguishes: mathematical species and physical species. In the first case, "the least difference that causes two things not to resemble one another totally is enough to make them differ in species." All individual difference between two mathematical beings is necessarily specific, since it can be stated mathematically only in the form of a relation between definers (thus, for the ellipse, the relation of axes). It is even in this sense that the metaphysical individual can be assimilated to a "species infima." The comparison only works mathematically. In mathematics, specific difference is individuating, but because individual difference is already specific: there are as many species as individuals, and the differing material of two figures, whether iron or plaster, does not constitute them as two potential mathematical individuals. In mathematics, individuation is what constitutes a determination; now the same does not hold for physical things or organic bodies.[10] There, as we have observed, different characters make up series according to which the species never stops varying or dividing, at the same time that the thing or the body never stops changing. Series impose no evolutionism, but they do mark the relation of determination with the alteration of bodies. This multidetermination, which is confused with the diverse characters of classification, *assumes that the individuality of the body or the thing comes from elsewhere*. And in effect, what is individual and what individuates the alterable body is only the soul that is inseparable from it.[11] And even for the thing all substantial forms are everywhere within. It thus appears that determination assumes an individuation coming from without, and first of all in relation to species and genres.

We look in vain for the least opposition between the principle of indiscernibles and the law of continuity. The latter is a law of determination that rules in three principal areas: the mathematical domain of wholes and parts, the physical domain of species or corporeal characters, the cosmological domain of singularities (inasmuch as a singularity is extended as far as the neighborhood of another in a determined order. The principle of indiscernibles is a principle of individuation, according to which no two similar individuals could be distinguished solely from the outside by number, space, or time: in the first place, the soul is what is individual because it circumscribes a certain number of singularities that are distinguished from those of an other, although they all may be extensible. In the second place, the soul or souls individuate physical bodies taken in the continuity of their species. In the third place, if properly mathematical species are themselves individuating, it is because two figures of the same species are mathematically one and the same individual, referring to a same "soul or entelechia," even if they are physically different.

The principle of indiscernibles establishes divisions; but the divisions are not lacunae or ruptures of continuity; on the contrary, they divide continuity in such a fashion that there can be no holes, that is, in the "best" way (thus the irrational number). In order to oppose indiscernibles and continuity, we must hold to an overly rapid formulation of the two principles: thus it is said that the difference between two individuals must be internal and irreducible (= 1), while it must vanish and tend toward 0 by virtue of continuity. But never in any of its three meanings does continuity make difference vanish: what vanishes is merely all value that can be assigned to the terms of a relation for the gain of its inner reason, which precisely constitutes difference.[12] Difference no longer exists between the polygon and the circle, but in the pure variability of the sides of the polygon; difference is no longer between movement and inertia, but in pure variability of speed. Difference ceases being extrinsic and palpable (in this sense it vanishes) in order to become intrinsic, intelligible or conceptual, in conformity with the principle of indiscernibles.

And should we desire the most general formulation of the law of continuity, we might perhaps locate it in the concept, which is unknown and which cannot be known, *where the sensible ends and the intelligible begins*: this is a new way of saying that two worlds do not exist.[13] In the accord of the two instances, there is even a reflux of continuity on the souls. For if every individual is distinguished from all others by its primary singularities, the latter fall short of extending themselves as far as the primary singularities of other individuals, according to a spatiotemporal order that makes the "subdivision" of an individual be continued into the nearest subdivision and then into the subdivision following that, all the way up to infinity. The comparative extension and intensity of these subdivisions—favored zones that belong to each monad—even allow species of monads or souls to be divided into vegetal, animal, human, or angelic traits, "an infinity of degrees in the monads" in continuity.[14]

The play of the world has several aspects: it emits singularities; it puts forward infinite series that go from one singularity to another; it invents rules of convergence and divergence according to which these series of possibles are organized in infinite totalities, each totality being compossible, but two totalities together being incompossible with each other; it allots the singularities of each world in one way or another in the nucleus of monads or individuals that express this world. Thus God does not merely choose the best of all worlds—that is, the richest compossible totality in possible reality—but he also chooses the best allotment of singularities in possible individuals (other allotments of singularities and other demarcations of individuals could be conceived for the same world). Hence we have rules of the world's composition in a compossible architectonic totality, but also rules of the world's actualization in the individuals of this totality at the upper level and, finally, as we shall observe, rules for the realization of the world at the lower level, in a materiality proper to this totality.

Leibniz suggests in this regard that three intervening criteria come into play. One involves the building's tastefulness; the second, the "number and elegance of the rooms" on the inside; and the third, the convenience, the "rightness" of the grounds, of the materials, and even of the outer façade of a single adjacent part.[15] It is a vast play of architecture or of paved grounds: How can a space be filled with the fewest possible voids, and with the greatest possible number of figures? With this reservation excepted, space-time is not a grid or a preexisting receptacle that would be filled (for the best) by the chosen world: on the contrary, a space-time, as an order of indivisible distances from one singularity to another or from one individual to another, and even an extension, as a continuous prolongation in respect to distances, belong to each world. It is space, time, and extension that are in the world on each occasion and not the inverse. The play interiorizes not only the players who serve as pieces, but the board on which the game is played, and the material of that board.

Nietzsche and Mallarmé have rewarded us with the revelation of a Thought-world that throws dice. But for them the world lacks principle, has lost its principles. That is why the roll of the dice is the power of affirming Chance, of thinking of chance in sum, which is above all not a principle, but the absence of all principle. Thus Mallarmé gives to absence or nothingness what issues from chance, what claims to escape it all the while limiting it by principle: "The world is the anonymous domain of absence, from which things appear or into which they will then disappear. . . . The apparition is the mask behind which no one exists, behind which nothing really exists other than nothing," Nothing rather than something.[16] To think without principles, in the absence of God and in the absence of man himself, has become the perilous task of a child-player who topples the old Master of play, and who makes incompossibles enter into the same world, shattered (the board is broken to bits . . .).

But what happened in this long history of "nihilism," before the world lost its principles? At a point close to us human Reason had to collapse, like the Kantian refuge, the last refuge of principles. It falls victim to "neurosis." But still, before, a psychotic episode was necessary. A crisis and collapse of all theological Reason had to take place. That is where the Baroque assumes its position: Is there some way of saving the theological ideal at a moment when it is being contested on all sides, and when the world cannot stop accumulating its "proofs" against it, ravages and miseries, at a time when the earth will soon shake and tremble . . . ? The Baroque solution is the following: we shall multiply principles — we can always slip a new one out from under our cuffs — and in this way we will change their use. We will not have to ask what available object corresponds to a given luminous principle, but what hidden principle responds to whatever object is given, that is to say, to this or that "perplexing case." Principles as such will be put to a reflective use. A case being given, we shall invent its principle. It is a transformation from Law to universal Jurisprudence.[17]

We witness the honeymoon of singularity and the concept. Such is the Leibnizian revolution, and Leibniz is very close to Prospero, the Mannerist hero par excellence, "the mysterious Prospero, magician and rationalist, who knows the secrets of life, a mountebank, a dispenser of good fortune, but who is himself lost in his splendid isolation."[18]

It surely does not suffice to say that for Leibniz the game falls under the principle of the Best, with God being given to choose the best of all possible worlds. For the best is only a consequence and, as a consequence, it is immediately derived from the defeat of the Good (to save from the Good whatever can be saved . . .). The true character of the Leibnizian game — and what opposes it to the roll of the dice — is first of all a proliferation of principles: play is executed through excess and not a lack of principles; the game is that of principles themselves, of inventing principles. It is thus a game of reflection, of chess or checkers, where skill (not chance) replaces old gifts of wisdom or prudence. In the third place, it is a game of filling holes, in which emptiness is imagined and where players refuse to give way to absence: it is an inverted solitaire, the player "filling a square on which he lands" instead of jumping onto an empty spot, and removing the checker he lands on until the board is empty. Finally, it is a nonbattle closer to guerrilla warfare than a war of extermination, more like go than chess or checkers. You don't catch your adversary in order to reduce him to absence, you encircle his presence to neutralize him, to make him incompossible, to impose divergence upon him.[19] The Baroque is just that, at a time just before the world loses its principles. It is the splendid moment when Some Thing is kept rather than nothing, and where response to the world's misery is made through an excess of principles, a hubris of principles, and a hubris inherent to principles.

Leibniz's optimism is really strange.[20] Yet again, miseries are not what was missing; the best of all possibilities only blossoms amid the ruins of Platonic Good. If this world exists, it is not because it is the best, but because it is rather the inverse; it is the best because it is, because it is the one that is. The philosopher is still not the Inquisitor he will soon become with empiricism, and he is even less the Judge he will become with Kant (the tribunal of Reason). He is a Lawyer, or God's attorney. He defends God's Cause, following the word that Leibniz invents, "theodicy."[21] Surely the justification of God in the face of evil has always been a philosophical commonplace. But the Baroque is a long moment of crisis, in which ordinary consolation no longer has much value. There results a collapse of the world; the lawyer has to rebuild it, exactly the same world, but on another stage and in respect to new principles capable of justifying it (whence jurisprudence). An aggravated justification has to correspond to the enormity of the crisis: the world must be the best, not only in its totality, but in its detail or in all of its instances.[22]

We clearly witness a schizophrenic reconstruction: God's attorney convenes characters who reconstitute the world *with their inner, so-called autoplastic modifications*. Such are the monads, or Leibniz's Selves, automata, each of which draws from its depths the entire world and handles its relations with the outside or with others as an uncoiling of the mechanism of its own spring, of its own prearranged spontaneity. Monads have to be conceived as dancing. But the dance is the Baroque dance, in which the dancers are automata: there we have an entire "pathos of distance," like the indivisible distance between two monads (space); the meeting between the two of them becomes a parade, or development, of their respective spontaneities insofar as their distance is upheld; actions and reactions give way to a concatenation of postures allotted now and again through distance (Mannerism).[23]

The principle of optimism, or of the Best, saves the freedom of God: it is the game of the world and God that guarantees this liberty. In other possible worlds an Adam does not sin, and a Sextus does not rape Lucretia. That Caesar does not cross the Rubicon is not impossible, but only incompossible with the chosen, best world. That Caesar crosses the river is therefore not absolutely necessary, but relatively certain, at least in respect to our world. However, human liberty is not itself safeguarded inasmuch as it has to be practiced in this existing world. In human eyes it does not suffice that Adam may not sin in another world, if he is certainly sinning in this world. Leibniz leaves the impression that he is condemning us even more strongly than Spinoza, for whom there at least existed a process of possible liberation, whereas for Leibniz everything is sealed off from the beginning and remains in a condition of closure.

Most of the writings in which Leibniz promises us human liberty bifurcate at the simple liberty of God. To be sure, incompossibility allows Leibniz to resolve the ancient problem of future contingent events (Will a naval battle take place tomorrow?), without falling into the Stoics' aporias.[24] But it in no way guarantees the character of so-called voluntary events, or the freedom of whoever wants to engage a naval battle, or of whoever does not want to. How could there be free will, a will whose "individual notion encloses once and for all those who will never come to it?" How to conjoin liberty with a schizophrenic automaton's inner, complete, and preestablished determination?

We are thrown back to the inclusion of the predicate in the subject. And doubtless, if the predicate were an attribute, it would be hard to see what might salvage the liberty of the subject. But the predicate is an event, and appears in the subject as a change of perception: the event is voluntary when a motive can be assigned, such as reason or change of perception. In at least two writings—one short and the other extensive—Leibniz inaugurates the first great phenomenology of motives.[25] There he denounces two illusions: one consists in *objectifying* motives, as if they were weights placed on the pans of a scale, and as if deliberation were seeking to know in what direction, all conditions being equal, the scale would tip. The other illusion consists in *dividing* motives, since an infinity of subjective motives are needed so that a choice of objectified motives can be made, as if one might be able "to desire to desire." But in truth the soul is what invents its own motives, and these are always subjective. We have to begin from all of the smallest inclinations that ply our soul in every direction, in the flash of an instant, under the stress of a thousand "little springs": disquiet. That is the model of the pendulum or balance wheel, the *Unruhe,* that replaces the scale. The action is voluntary when the soul—instead of undergoing the total effect into which these little appeals enter—gives itself a certain amplitude, such that it bends entirely in one direction or toward one side.

For example, I hesitate between staying home and working or going out to a nightclub: these are not two separable "objects," but two orientations, each of which carries a sum of possible or even hallucinatory perceptions (not only of drinking, but the noise and smoke of the bar; not only of working, but the hum of the word processor and the surrounding silence . . .). And if we return to motives in order to study them for a second time, they have not stayed the same. Like the weight on a scale, they have gone up or down. The scale has changed according to the amplitude of the pendulum. The voluntary act is free because the free act is what expresses the entire soul at a given moment of its duration. That act is what expresses the self. Does Adam sin freely? In other words, at that instant his soul has taken an amplitude that is found to be easily filled by the aroma and taste of the apple, and by Eve's solicitations. Another amplitude—one having retained God's defense—is possible. The whole question turns on "laziness."

Going from inflection to inclusion, we have seen how inflections were naturally included in souls. Inclination is the fold in the soul, inflection the way the fold is included. Whence Leibniz's formula: the soul is inclined without being necessitated.[26] The motive is not even an internal determination, but an inclination. It is not the effect of the past, but the expression of the present. It must be observed to what degree Leibniz's inclusion is always coded in the present: I write, I travel. . . . If inclusion is extended to infinity in the past and the future, it is because it concerns first of all the living present that in each instance presides over their division. Because it includes what I am doing right now—what I am in the act of doing—my individual notion also includes everything that has driven me to do what I am doing, and everything that will result from it, all the way to infinity.[27] This privilege accorded to the present clearly refers to the function of inherence in the monad: the function does not include a predicate without giving it verbal value—that is, the unity of a movement in the act of being made. Inherence is the condition of liberty and not of impediment.

When Leibniz appeals to the perfect or completed act (entelechia), he is not dealing with an act that inclusion would require us to consider as past, and that would return to an essence. The condition of closure, of being shut off, has an entirely different meaning: *the perfect, completed act is that which receives from the soul that includes it the unity proper to a movement that is being made.* In this respect Bergson is very close to Leibniz, but in Leibniz the formula is expressed time and again: the present portends the future and is burdened with the past.[28] It is not a determinism—even an internal one—but an interiority that constitutes liberty itself. It is because the living present is essentially variable in both extension and intensity. At every moment, it is confused with the favored area or subdivision of the monad, the zone that it expresses clearly. Hence this is what constitutes the amplitude of the soul at a given instant. Extended more or less, more or less intense, the living present neither motivates the same action nor confers the same movement with a unity of its own. Adam might have been capable enough not to sin, but only if, at this moment, his soul could have taken another amplitude that might constitute the unity of another movement. The act is free because it expresses the wholeness of the soul in the present.

Nothing demonstrates the point better than the dark and wondrous theory of damnation. Even in this case the damned, Judas or Beelzebub, does not pay retribution for a past action, but for the hate of God that constitutes the present amplitude of his soul and fills it in the present. He is not damned for a past action, but by a present action that he renews at every moment. This hate of God in which he finds a horrible pleasure is rebegun endlessly so that "crime will pile upon crime." Judas is not damned because he betrayed God, but because, having betrayed God, he hates God all the more, and he dies of that hate. For a soul that is the absolute minimum of amplitude: to include in its clear region only a single predicate, that of "hating God." The only glimmer that remains for him — a uniquely pallid glimmer — is a "rage of Reason."

Were it to regain a little of its amplitude, and were it to refrain from hating in the present, the soul would immediately cease being damned — but it would be another soul causing the unity of another movement. As Leibniz states, a damned soul is not eternally damned, he is merely "forever damnable," and damns himself at every moment.[29] Thus the damned are free — and free in the present — as are the happy souls. What damns them is their current narrow-mindedness, their lack of amplitude. These are vengeful or resentful people, like those whom Nietzsche later describes. It is not as if they were undergoing the effects of their past, but as if they could not be done with the current and present wound they cannot keep themselves from scratching over and over again. Perhaps this vision of damnation is so deeply rooted in the Baroque as a function of a much broader context. The Baroque has conceived of death in the present, as a movement that is in the act of being completed, and that is unexpected, but that is "accompanied."[30]

If Adam were capable of not sinning, the damned could free themselves: it would suffice to have the soul take another amplitude, another fold, or another inclination. It can be stated that the soul cannot do so, except in another world, one that is incomposssible with ours. Yet clearly, that it cannot do so signifies that the soul would be other by doing so: what it does, it does entirely, that being what comprises its liberty. The soul is not determined to do it. It can be stated further that the soul is at least determined to be what it is, and that its degree of amplitude at every moment is inscribed in it and foreseen by God. What does all that change? That God foresees Adam's laziness and the narrow-mindedness of the damned does not impede the one or the other from being the motive of a free act, and not the effect of a determination. That God preordains the degrees of a soul's amplitude does not impede each one from being the entire soul at a given moment. That another degree implies another soul and another world does not hinder this degree from actualizing the liberty of a given soul in this world. The automaton is free not because it is determined from within, but because every time it constitutes the motive of the event that it produces. The automaton is programmed, but the "spiritual automaton" is programmed by motivation for voluntary acts, just as the "material automaton" is programmed by determination for mechanical actions: if things are enveloped in God's understanding, it is such as they are, "the free as free, and the blind and mechanical still as mechanical."[31]

A reader is immediately struck by the similarity of Leibniz's themes to Bergson's thesis: the same critique of illusion on motives, the same conception of the inflections of the soul, the same requirement of inherence or inclusion as a condition of the free act, the same description of the free act as what expresses the self ("it is from the entire soul that free decision emanates, and the act will be all the freer since the dynamic series to which it is attached will tend to be identified further with the fundamental self").[32] And how can we not fail to recall Leibniz again when Bergson appeals to a second problem, that does not take up the act as it is being done, but "future or past action": can a superior intelligence, apt enough to know "all antecedents," predict the act with an absolute necessity? With Leibniz that is the situation of God the reader, who reads in everyone "what is being done everywhere and even what has been done or will be," who reads the future in the past because he can "unfold all the pleats that are only sensorially developed over time."[33] Here the present seems to be losing its privilege, since determinism is being reintroduced as predestination.

But in what way? Is it because God knows everything in advance? Is it not rather because he exists forever and everywhere? The first hypothesis, in effect, is quite ambiguous: either God only knows everything about antecedents, or we are sent back to the question "Can God predict or foresee the act?" Either God knows absolutely everything, or we have to return to the second hypothesis. Now, to say that God is forever and everywhere is to strictly state that God passes through all the conditions of the monad, no matter how minute they are, and in such a way that God coincides with it at the instant of action "without any postponement."[34] Reading does not consist in concluding from the idea of a preceding condition the idea of the following condition, but in grasping the effort or tendency by which the following condition itself ensues from the preceding "by means of a natural force."

Divine reading is God's apparent passage into the monad (somewhat in the way Whitehead speaks of a "passage of Nature" into a place). Further, each monad is none other than a passage of God: each monad has a point of view, but this point of view is the "result" of God's reading or viewing, which goes through the monad and coincides with it.[35] The monad is free because its action is the result of what passes through it and is happening within it. To state that God has already passed through, by virtue of his prescience, means nothing since eternity consists, much less in forging ahead or in going backwards, than in coinciding each time with all the passages that follow in the order of time, with all the present living beings that make up the world.

Liberty is not what is threatened in the system of inclusion. Rather, it is morality. For if the free act is what expresses the entire soul at the moment it conveys its expression, what happens to the tendency to the best that has to animate every part of the world or monad inasmuch as it animates God's choice for the totality of the world or of monads? And yet no one has pondered morality—a very concrete morality—more than Leibniz himself. The amplitude of a reasonable soul is the region that it clearly expresses, that is, its living present. This amplitude is rather statistical, and subject to broad variation: the same soul does not have the same amplitude as a child, an adult, or an aging being, in good or bad health, and so on. Amplitude even has variable limits at any given moment. Morality consists in this for each individual: to attempt each time to extend its region of clear expression, to try to augment its amplitude, so as to produce a free act that expresses the most possible in one given condition or another.

That is what progress is called, and all Leibniz's morality is a morality of progress. For example, when I go to the nightclub, have I chosen the side where amplitude is maximal, the side where my region goes the furthest, even if I were unable to wait a second, with time enough to discover another means or direction that would have inclined me otherwise? Does Adam's sin not correspond to a soul, too pressed or too lazy, that has not explored everything in its subdivision or its garden? Extending its clear region, prolonging God's passage to the maximum, actualizing all the singularities that are concentrated on, and even won over to, new singularities would amount to a soul's progress. In this way we might say that it imitates God. Of course it is not only a conquest or extension that matters, but an amplification, an intensification of an elevation of power, a growth in dimensions, and a gain in distinction.

However, this possibility for progress or expansion of the soul seems to run up against the total quantity of progress in the world, this quantity being defined by the convergence of all regions that correspond to compossible monads.[36] And this would be true if time did not pertain, that is, if all existing monads were simultaneously summoned to the altitude that makes them reasonable. But things do not work that way: souls fated to become reasonable wait for their time in the world, and are first of all only sensitive souls who sleep in Adam's seed, bearing only an "official act" that marks the hour of their future elevation as on to a birth certificate. This birth certificate or act is a flame lit within the dark monad. And inversely, when we die, we fold infinitely upon ourselves; we return to the state of an animal until the bodily resurrection brings us to a second and final elevation. But further, the soul, which has for some time become sensitive again, will bring with it a new and official act, now akin to an act or certification of death, which is its last reasonable thought prior to death. More precisely, the damned are those whose last thought is a scorn of God because, when their soul vomits all and can no longer enclose clearly anything other than this hate or this rage, it is the maximum of all possible hate or the smallest amplitude of reason. Resurrection still brings them to this thought from which they forge their new present.[37] This order of time must be considered in all questions of progress: a whole dramaturgy of souls, which makes them rise, descend, and rise again.

In all cases it is true that the world only exists folded in the monads that express it, and is only unfolded virtually as the common horizon of all monads, or as the outer law of the series they include. But in a more restricted sense, in an intrinsic way, it can be said that when a monad is summoned to "live"—yet more when it is called to reason—it unfolds in itself this region of the world that corresponds to its enclosed enlightened zone: it is called upon to "develop all its perceptions," and therein its task resides. Then, at the same time, an infinity of monads has not yet been called and remains folded; another infinity of them has fallen or falls in the night, folded onto themselves; while another infinity has been damned, hardened in a single fold that it will not unfurl. It is due to these three involutions that a soul-monad can amplify and deepen the region that it unfolds during the course of its reasonable life; it can bring it to the region of the highest degree of evolution, of development, of distinction, and reflection: an infinite progress of the conscience that exceeds the statistical variations of which we were speaking not long ago. It has often been said that this progress of a soul could only be accomplished to the detriment of others. But this is not true. Except for the damned, others can do just as much. It is only to the detriment of the damned, who are freely cut away. Their worst punishment may be that of serving the progress of others, not by the negative example that they offer, but through the quantity of positive progress that they involuntarily leave to the world when they renounce their own clarity. In this sense, despite themselves, the damned could be attached in no better way to the best of all possible worlds.

Leibniz's optimism is based on the infinity of the damned as the foundation of the best of all worlds: *they liberate an infinite quantity of possible progress.* That is what multiplies their rage, and thus they make possible a world of progress. We could never think of the best of all worlds without hearing the scornful shrieks of Beelzebub make the lower level tremble. The Baroque house divides its two floors between the world of the damned and that of the saved, in the fashion of Tintoretto's *Last Judgment*. There again God does not determine the total quantity of progress either beforehand or afterwards, but eternally, in the calculus of the infinite series that moves through all increased magnitudes of consciousness and all the subtractions of the damned.[38]

Chapter 6
What Is an Event?

Whitehead is the successor, or *diadoche,* as the Platonic philosophers used to say, of the school's leader.[1] The school is somewhat like a secret society. With Whitehead's name there comes for the third time an echo of the question, *What is an event?*[2] He takes up the radical critique of the attributive scheme, the great play of principles, the multiplications of categories, the conciliation of the universal and the individual example, and the transformation of the concept into a subject: an entire hubris. He stands provisionally as the last great Anglo-American philosopher before Wittgenstein's disciples spread their misty confusion, sufficiency, and terror. An event does not just mean that "a man has been run over." The Great Pyramid is an event, and its duration for a period of one hour, thirty minutes, five minutes . . . , a passage of Nature, of God, or a view of God. What are the conditions that make an event possible? Events are produced in a chaos, in a chaotic multiplicity, but only under the condition that a sort of screen intervenes.

Chaos does not exist; it is an abstraction because it is inseparable from a screen that makes something — something rather than nothing — emerge from it. Chaos would be a pure *Many,* a purely disjunctive diversity, while the something is a *One,* not a pregiven unity, but instead the indefinite article that designates a certain singularity. How can the Many become the One? A great screen has to be placed in between them. Like a formless elastic membrane, an electromagnetic field, or the receptacle of the *Timaeus,* the screen makes something issue from chaos, and *even if this something differs only slightly.* In this way Leibniz had long been able to ascribe several approximations to chaos. According to a cosmological approximation, chaos would be the sum of all possibles, that is, all individual essences insofar as each tends to existence on its own account; but the screen only allows compossibles — and only the best combination of compossibles — to be sifted through.

Following a physical approximation, chaos would amount to depthless shadows, but the screen disengages its dark backdrop, the "fuscum subnigrum" that, however little it differs from black, nonetheless contains all colors: the screen is like the infinitely refined machine that is the basis of Nature. From a psychic point of view, chaos would be a universal giddiness, the sum of all possible perceptions being infinitesimal or infinitely minute; but the screen would extract differentials that could be integrated in ordered perceptions.[3] If chaos does not exist, it is because it is merely the bottom side of the great screen, and because the latter composes infinite series of wholes and parts, which appear chaotic to us (as aleatory developments) only because we are incapable of following them, or because of the insufficiency of our own screens.[4] Even the cavern is not a chaos, but a series whose elements remain caverns filled with an increasingly rarefied matter, each of which is extended over the following ones.

That is clearly the first component or condition of both Whitehead's and Leibniz's definition of the event: extension. Extension exists when one element is stretched over the following ones, such that it is a whole and the following elements are its parts. Such a connection of whole-parts forms an infinite series that contains neither a final term nor a limit (the limits of our senses being excepted). The event is a vibration with an infinity of harmonics or submultiples, such as an audible wave, a luminous wave, or even an increasingly smaller part of space over the course of an increasingly shorter duration. For space and time are not limits but abstract coordinates of all series, that are themselves in extension: the minute, the second, the tenth of a second. . . . Then we can consider a second component of the event: extensive series have intrinsic properties (for example, height, intensity, timbre of a sound, a tint, a value, a saturation of color), which enter on their own account in new infinite series, now converging toward limits, with the relation among limits establishing a conjunction. Matter, or what fills space and time, offers characters that always determine its texture as a function of different materials that are part of it. No longer are these extensions but, as we have seen, intensions, intensities, or degrees. It is something rather than nothing, but also this rather than that: no longer the indefinite article, but the demonstrative pronoun. How remarkable that Whitehead's analysis, based on mathematics and physics, appears to be completely independent of Leibniz's work even though it coincides with it!

Then comes the third component, which is the individual. There the confrontation with Leibniz is the most direct. For Whitehead the individual is creativity, the formation of a New. No longer is it the indefinite or the demonstrative mood, but a personal mood. If we call an element everything that has parts and is a part, but also what has intrinsic features, we say that the individual is a "concrescence" of elements. This is something other than a connection or a conjunction. It is, rather, a *prehension*: an element is the given, the "datum" of another element that prehends it. Prehension is individual unity. Everything prehends its antecedents and its concomitants and, by degrees, prehends a world. The eye is a prehension of light. Living beings prehend water, soil, carbon, and salts. At a given moment the pyramid prehends Napoleon's soldiers (forty centuries are contemplating us), and inversely. We can say that "echoes, reflections, traces, prismatic deformations, perspective, thresholds, folds" are prehensions that somehow anticipate psychic life.[5] The vector of prehension moves from the world to the subject, from the prehended datum to the prehending one (a "superject"); thus the data of a prehension are *public* elements, while the subject is the intimate or *private* element that expresses immediacy, individuality, and novelty.[6] But the prehended, the datum, is itself a preexisting or coexisting prehension, such that all prehension is a prehension of prehension, and the event thus a "nexus of prehensions." Each new prehension becomes a datum. It becomes public, but for other prehensions that objectify it; the event is inseparably the objectification of one prehension and the subjectification of another; it is at once public and private, potential and real, participating in the becoming of another event and the subject of its own becoming.

Beyond the prehending and the prehended, prehension offers three other characteristics. First, the subjective form is the way by which the datum is expressed in the subject, or by which the subject actively prehends the datum (emotion, evaluation, project, conscience . . .). It is the form in which the datum is folded in the subject, a "feeling" or manner, at least when prehension is positive. For there are negative prehensions that exist as long as the subject excludes certain data from its concrescence, and is thus only filled by the subjective form of this exclusion. Second, the subjective aim assures the passage from one datum to another in a prehension, or from one prehension to another in a becoming, and places the past in a present portending the future. Finally, satisfaction as a final phase, as *self-enjoyment,* marks the way by which the subject is filled with itself and attains a richer and richer private life, when prehension is filled with its own data. This is a biblical — and, too, a neo-Platonic — notion that English empiricism carried to its highest degree (notably with Samuel Butler). The plant sings of the glory of God, and while being filled all the more with itself it contemplates and intensely contracts the elements whence it proceeds. It feels in this prehension the *self-enjoyment* of its own becoming.

These traits of prehension also belong to Leibniz's monad. And, initially, perception is the datum of the prehending subject, not in the sense that the latter would undergo a passive effect, but, on the contrary, to the degree it fulfills a potential or objectifies it by virtue of its spontaneity: thus perception is the active expression of the monad, as a function of its own point of view.[7] But the monad has several forms of active expression that make up its ways or manners, according to the ways in which its perceptions are sensitive, active, or conceptual.[8] In this sense appetite designates the movement from one perception to another as being constitutive of a becoming. Finally, this becoming is not completed without the sum of perceptions tending to be integrated in a great pleasure, a Satisfaction with which the monad fills itself when it expresses the world, a musical Joy of contracting its vibrations, of calculating them without knowing their harmonics or of drawing force enough to go further and further ahead in order to produce something new.[9] For with Leibniz the question surges forth in philosophy that will continue to haunt Whitehead and Bergson: not how to attain eternity, but in what conditions does the objective world allow for a subjective production of novelty, that is, of creation? The best of all worlds had no other meaning: it was neither the least abominable nor the least ugly, but the one whose All granted a production of novelty, *a liberation of true quanta of "private" subjectivity,* even at the cost of the removal of the damned. The best of all worlds is not the one that reproduces the eternal, but the one in which new creations are produced, the one endowed with a capacity for innovation or creativity: a teleological conversion of philosophy.[10]

There are no fewer eternal Objects. It is even the fourth and last component of Whitehead's definition of the event: extensions, intensities, individuals or prehensions, and, finally, eternal objects or "ingressions." Extensions effectively are forever moving, gaining and losing parts carried away in movement; things are endlessly being altered; even prehensions are ceaselessly entering and leaving variable components. Events are fluvia. From then on what allows us to ask, "Is it the same flow, the same thing or the same occasion? It's the Great Pyramid . . ." A permanence has to be born in flux, and must be grasped in prehension. The Great Pyramid signifies two things: a passage of Nature or a flux constantly gaining and losing molecules, but also an eternal object that remains the same over the succession of moments.[11] While prehensions are always current forms (a prehension is a potential only in respect to another current prehension), eternal objects are pure Possibilities that are realized in fluvia, but also pure Virtualities that are actualized in prehensions. That is why a prehension does not grasp other prehensions without apprehending eternal objects (properly, conceptual *feeling*). Eternal objects produce ingression in the event. Sometimes these can be Qualities, such as a color or a sound that qualifies a combination of prehensions; sometimes Figures, like the pyramid, that determine an extension; sometimes they are Things, like gold or marble, that cut through a matter. Their eternity is not opposed to creativity. Inseparable from the process of actualization or realization into which they enter, they gain permanence only in the limits of the flux that creates them, or of the prehensions that actualize them. An eternal object can thus cease becoming incarnate, just as new things — a new shade of color, or a new figure — can finally find their conditions.

With Leibniz the situation hardly differs. For if monads or simple substances are always current forms, they not only arch back to virtualities that they actualize in themselves, as innate ideas demonstrate, but yet again to possibilities that are realized in composite substances (thus perceived qualities), or in aggregate materials (things), or in extended phenomena (figures). Everything flows down below, "in a perpetual flux, with bits and pieces continually entering and exiting."[12] From that moment permanency is not reduced to monads that actualize the virtual, but is extended to the possibilities that they seize in their acts of reflection, and that are born in the extended composite materials. Reflexive objects are correlative to reasonable monads, just as in Whitehead, where eternal objects are correlative to thinking prehensions. Figures, things, and qualities are schema of permanence that are reflected or actualized in monads, but that are realized in flux; even composite substances, as we shall observe, need an ultimate quality that marks every one of them.

A concert is being performed tonight. It is the event. Vibrations of sound disperse, periodic movements go through space with their harmonics or submultiples. The sounds have inner qualities of height, intensity, and timbre. The sources of the sounds, instrumental or vocal, are not content only to send the sounds out: each one perceives its own, and perceives the others while perceiving its own. These are active perceptions that are expressed among each other, or else prehensions that are prehending one another: "First the solitary piano grieved, like a bird abandoned by its mate; the violin heard its wail and responded to it like a neighboring tree. It was like the beginning of the world. . . ."

The origins of the sounds are monads or prehensions that are filled with joy in themselves, with an intense satisfaction, as they fill up with their perceptions and move from one perception to another. And the notes of the scale are eternal objects, pure Virtualities that are actualized in the origins, but also pure Possibilities that are attained in vibrations or flux. "As if the instrumentalists played the little phrase far less than they were performing the rites it required in order to appear . . ." But then, in the midst of this totality, Leibniz adds the conditions of a Baroque concert. If we suppose that the concert is divided into two sources of sound, we are positing that each hears only its own perceptions but is harmonized with those of the other even better than if it had perceived them, because of the vertical rules of harmony that happen to be enveloped in their respective spontaneity. These are the harmonies that replace horizontal connections.[13]

There is a great difference that depends on Leibniz's Baroque condition. For

Whitehead it involves prehensions being directly connected to each other, either because they draw on others for data and form a world with them, or because they exclude others (negative prehensions), but always in the same universe in process. For Leibniz, to the contrary, monads exclude only universes that are incompossible with their world, and all those that exist express the same world without exclusion. As this world does not exist outside of the monads that express it, the latter are not in contact and have no horizontal relations among them, no intraworldly connections, but only an indirect harmonic contact to the extent they share the same expression: they "express one another" without harnessing each other. We might say that in the two instances monadic or prehensive units have neither doors nor windows. But for Leibniz, it is because the monads' being-for the world is submitted to a condition of closure, all compossible monads including a single and same world. Now for Whitehead, to the contrary, a condition of opening causes all prehension to be *already* the prehension of another prehension, either to control it or to exclude it. Prehension is naturally open, open onto the world, without having to pass through a window.[14] A difference of this kind must surely have a reason.

For Leibniz, as we have seen, bifurcations and divergences of series are genuine borders between incompossible worlds, such that the monads that exist wholly include the compossible world that moves into existence. For Whitehead (and for many modern philosophers), on the contrary, bifurcations, divergences, incompossibilities, and discord belong to the same motley world *that can no longer be included in expressive units,* but only made or undone according to prehensive units and variable configurations or changing captures. In a same chaotic world divergent series are endlessly tracing bifurcating paths. It is a "chaosmos" of the type found in Joyce, but also in Maurice Leblanc, Borges, or Gombrowicz.[15] Even God desists from being a Being who compares worlds and chooses the richest compossible. He becomes Process, a process that at once affirms incompossibilities and passes through them. The play of the world has changed in a unique way, because now it has become the play that diverges. Beings are pushed apart, kept open through divergent series and incompossible totalities that pull them outside, instead of being closed upon the compossible and convergent world that they express from within. Modern mathematics has been able to develop a fibered conception according to which "monads" test the paths in the universe and enter in syntheses associated with each path.[16] It is a world of captures instead of closures.

We can better understand in what way the Baroque is a transition. Classical reason toppled under the force of divergences, incompossibilities, discords, dissonances. But the Baroque represents the ultimate attempt to reconstitute a classical reason by dividing divergences into as many worlds as possible, and by making from incompossibilities as many possible borders between worlds. Discords that spring up in a same world can be violent. *They are resolved in accords* because the only irreducible dissonances are between different worlds. In short, the Baroque universe witnesses the blurring of its melodic lines, but what it appears to lose it also regains in and through harmony. Confronted by the power of dissonance, it discovers a florescence of extraordinary accords, at a distance, that are resolved in a chosen world, even at the cost of damnation.

This reconstitution could only be temporary. With the neo-Baroque, with its unfurling of divergent series in the same world, comes the irruption of incompossibilities on the same stage, where Sextus will rape *and* not rape Lucretia, where Caesar crosses *and* does not cross the Rubicon, where Fang kills, is killed, and neither kills nor is killed. In its turn harmony goes through a crisis that leads to a broadened chromatic scale, to an emancipation of dissonance or of unresolved accords, accords not brought back to a tonality. The musical model is the most apt to make clear the rise of harmony in the Baroque, and then the dissipation of tonality in the neo-Baroque: from harmonic closure to an opening onto a polytonality or, as Boulez will say, a "polyphony of polyphonies."

Part III
Having a Body

Chapter 7
Perception in the Folds

I *must* have a body, it's a moral necessity, a "requirement." And in the first place, I must have a body because an obscure object lives in me. But, right from this first argument, Leibniz's originality is tremendous. He is not saying that only the body explains what is obscure in the mind. To the contrary, the mind is obscure, the depths of the mind are dark, and this dark nature is what explains and requires a body. We can call "primary matter" our passive power or the limitation of our activity: we say that our primary matter requires extension, but also resistance or antitype, and yet an individuated requirement to possess a body that belongs to us.[1] It is because there is an infinity of individual monads that each one requires an individuated body, this body resembling the shadow of other monads cast upon it. Nothing obscure lives in us because we have a body, but we must have a body because there is an obscure object in us. In the place of Cartesian physical induction Leibniz substitutes a moral deduction of the body.

But this first argument gives way to another, which seems to contradict it, and which is even more original. This time, we must have a body because our mind possesses a favored—clear and distinct—zone of expression. Now it is the clear zone that is the requirement for having a body. Leibniz will go as far as stating that what I express clearly is what "relates to my body."[2] And in effect, if the monad Caesar clearly expresses the crossing of the Rubicon, is it not because the river maintains a relation of proximity with his body? The same holds for all other monads whose zone of clear expression coincides with the body's immediate environment.

There we nonetheless find an inversion of causality—justifiable in certain respects—that must not impede our putting together the real order of deduction: (1) each monad condenses a certain number of unique, incorporeal, ideal events that do not yet put bodies in play, although they can only be stated in the form, "Caesar crosses the Rubicon, he is assassinated by Brutus . . ."; (2) these unique events included in the monad as primary predicates constitute its zone of clear expression, or its "subdivision"; (3) they necessarily relate to a body that belongs to this monad, and are incarnated in bodies that act immediately upon it. In brief, it is *because* every monad possesses a clear zone that it must have a body, this zone constituting a relation with the body, not a given relation, but a genetic relation that engenders its own "relatum." It is because we have a clear zone that we must have a body charged with traveling through it or exploring it, from birth to death.

Here we confront two difficulties. Why is the requirement of having a body sometimes based on a principle of passivity, in obscurity and confusion, but at others on our activity, on clarity and distinction? And more particularly, how does the existence of the body derive from the clear and distinct? As Arnauld states, how can what I express clearly and distinctly have anything to do with my body, the sum of whose movements are known only in obscurity?[3]

Singularities proper to each monad are extended as far as the singularities of others and in all senses. Every monad thus expresses the entire world, but obscurely and dimly because it is finite and the world is infinite. That is why the lower depths of the monad are so dark. Since it does not exist outside of the monads that convey it, the world is included in each one in the form of perceptions or "representatives," *present and infinitely minute elements.*[4] Still again, since the monad does not exist outside of other monads, these are minute perceptions lacking an object, that is, hallucinatory microperceptions. The world exists only in its representatives as long as they are included in each monad. It is a lapping of waves, a rumor, a fog, or a mass of dancing particles of dust. It is a state of death or catalepsy, of sleep, drowsiness, or of numbness. It is as if the depths of every monad were made from an infinity of tiny folds (inflections) endlessly furling and unfurling in every direction, so that the monad's spontaneity resembles that of agitated sleepers who twist and turn on their mattresses.[5]

Microperceptions or representatives of the world are these little folds that unravel in every direction, folds in folds, over folds, following folds, like one of Hantaï's paintings, or one of Clérambault's toxic hallucinations.[6] And these are minute, obscure, confused perceptions that make up our macroperceptions, our conscious, clear, and distinct apperceptions. Had it failed to bring together an infinite sum of minute perceptions that destabilize the preceding macroperception while preparing the following one, a conscious perception would never happen. How could a pain follow a pleasure if a thousand tiny pains or, rather, half-pains were not already dispersed in pleasure, which will then be united in conscious pain? However abruptly I may flog my dog who eats his meal, the animal will have experienced the minute perceptions of my stealthy arrival on tiptoes, my hostile odor, and my lifting of the rod that subtend the conversion of pleasure into pain. How could a feeling of hunger follow one of satisfaction if a thousand tiny, elementary forms of hunger (for salts, for sugar, butter, etc.) were not released at diverse and indiscernible rhythms? And inversely, if satisfaction follows hunger, it is through the sating of all these particular and imperceptible hungers.

Tiny perceptions are as much the passage from one perception to another as they are components of each perception. They constitute the animal or animated state par excellence: disquiet. These are "pricklings," or little foldings that are no less present in pleasure than in pain. The pricklings are the representative of the world in the closed monad. The animal that anxiously looks about, or the soul that watches out, signifies that there exist minute perceptions that are not integrated into present perception, but also minute perceptions that are not integrated into the preceding one and that nourish the one that comes along ("so it was that!").

The *macroscopic* distinguishes perceptions, and appetites that are the passage from one perception to another. Such is the condition of great composite folds, or draped forms. But the *microscopic* level no longer distinguishes minute perceptions and minute inclinations: pricklings of anxiety render all perception unstable.[7] The theory of minute perceptions is based thus on two causes: a metaphysical cause, according to which every perceptive monad conveys an infinite world that it contains; a psychological cause, according to which every conscious perception implies this infinity of minute perceptions that prepare, compose, or follow it. *From the cosmological to the microscopic, but also from the microscopic to the macroscopic.*

The task of perception entails pulverizing the world, but also one of spiritualizing its dust.[8] The point is one of knowing how we move from minute perceptions to conscious perceptions, or from molecular perceptions to molar perceptions. Is it through a process of totalization, when for instance I grasp a whole whose parts are imperceptible to me? Thus I apprehend the sound of the sea, or of an assembly of people, but not the murmur of each wave or person who nonetheless is part of each whole. But, although Leibniz states the point in terms of totality, the question involves something other than a sum of homogenous parts.[9] We are not dealing with a relation of parts-and-wholes because the totality can be as imperceptible as the parts, as also when I *do not* sense the grinding noise of the water mill to which I am overly accustomed. And a buzzing or a deadening effect are wholes without necessarily being perceptions.

In truth, Leibniz never fails to specify that the relation of the inconspicuous perceptions to conscious perception does not go from part to whole, but from the *ordinary* to what is *notable* or *remarkable*. "There are countless inconspicuous perceptions, which do not stand out enough for one to be aware of or to remember them."[10] We have to understand literally—that is, mathematically—that a conscious perception is produced when at least two heterogenous parts enter into a differential relation that determines a singularity. It works thus in the equation of circumferences in general:

$$ydy + xdx = 0, \text{ or } \frac{dy}{dx} = -\frac{x}{y}$$

expresses a determinable magnitude. For example, the color green: yellow and blue can surely be perceived, but if their perception vanishes by dint of progressive diminution, they enter into a differential relation

$$(\frac{db}{dy})$$

that determines green. And nothing impedes either yellow or blue, each on its own account, from being already determined by the differential relation of two colors that we cannot detect, or of two degrees of chiaroscuro:

$$\frac{dy}{dx} = Y$$

Such is the case of hunger, where a lack of sugar, butter, etc., engages differential relations that determine hunger as something notable or remarkable. For example, the sound of the sea: at least two waves must be minutely perceived as nascent and heterogenous enough to become part of a relation that can allow the perception of a third, one that "excels" over the others and comes to consciousness (implying that we are near the shoreline). For example, the position of the sleeper: all the little bends and tiny creases engage relations that produce an attitude, a habitus, and a great sinuous fold as a good position that can bring all of them together. "Good" macroscopic form always depends on microscopic processes.

All consciousness is a matter of threshold. In each case we would probably have to state why the threshold is marked where it is. Yet if we take thresholds to be so many minimal units of consciousness, tiny perceptions are in each instance smaller than the virtual minimum and, in this sense, are infinitely small. *The ones selected in each order are those engaged in differential relations,* and hence they produce the quality that issues forth at the given threshold of consciousness (for example, the color green). Inconspicuous perceptions are thus not parts of conscious perception, but requisites or genetic elements, "differentials of consciousness." Even more than Fichte, Salomon Maïmon — the first post-Kantian who returns to Leibniz — draws all the consequences from this kind of psychic automatism of perception. Far from having perception presuppose an object capable of affecting us, and conditions in which we would be apt to be affected, the reciprocal determination of the differentials

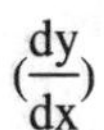

$$\left(\frac{dy}{dx}\right)$$

brings about the complete determination of the object as a perception, and the determinability of space-time as a condition. Beyond the Kantian method of conditioning, Maïmon restores an internal subjective method of genesis: between red and green there is given an empirically outer difference, but also an inner concept of difference such that "the mode of the differential makes up the particular object, and the relations of differentials the relations among different objects."[11] The physical object and mathematical space both refer to a transcendental (differential and genetic) psychology of perception. Space-time ceases to be a pure given in order to become the totality or the nexus of differential relations in the subject, and the object itself ceases to be an empirical given in order to become the product of these relations in conscious perception. Thus there exist Ideas of understanding, the color green as a quality being as much the actualization of an eternal Object or Idea in the subject as a given figure is a determination of space.

If, with Kant, it is objected that such a conception reintroduces infinite understanding, we might be impelled to remark that the infinite is taken here only as the presence of an unconscious in finite understanding, of something that cannot be thought in finite thought, of a nonself in the finite self, the presence that Kant will himself be forced to discover when he will hollow out the difference between a determinant and a determinable self. For Maïmon, as for Leibniz, reciprocal determination of differentials does not refer to a divine understanding, but to tiny perceptions as representatives of the world in the finite self (the relation with infinite understanding devolves from it, and not the inverse). The infinite present in the finite self is exactly the position of Baroque equilibrium or disequilibrium.

Now we can understand how the same argument can appeal to both obscurity and clarity. It is because for Leibniz clarity comes of obscurity and endlessly is plunging back into it. Thus the Cartesian map of darkness-clarity-confusion-distinction is redrawn with an entirely new meaning and new set of relations.

Inconspicuous perceptions constitute the obscure dust of the world, the dark depths every monad contains. There are differential relations among these presently infinitely small ones that are *drawn into clarity*; that is to say, that establish a clear perception (the color green) with certain tiny, dark, evanescent perceptions (the colors yellow and blue). And no doubt yellow and blue can themselves be clear and conscious perceptions, but only if they too are drawn into clarity, each from its own position, by differential relations among other minute perceptions, or differentials of other orders. *Differential relations always select minute perceptions that play a role in each case,* and bring to light or clarify the conscious perception that comes forth. Thus differential calculus is the psychic mechanism of perception, the automatism that at once and inseparably plunges into obscurity and determines clarity: a selection of minute, obscure perceptions and a perception that moves into clarity.

An automatism of this kind has to be taken in two ways, universally and individually. On the one hand, insofar as the same world is included in all existing monads, the latter offer the same infinity of minute perceptions, and the same differential relations that yield in them strangely similar conscious perceptions. All monads thus perceive the same green color, the same note, the same river, and in every case a single and same eternal object is actualized in them. Yet, on the other hand, actualization is different for each monad. Never do two monads perceive the same green in the same degree of chiaroscuro. It could be said that every monad favors certain differential relations that hereafter confer on it exclusive perceptions; that the monad leaves other relations below the necessary degree; or, further, that it lets an infinity of minute perceptions subsist in it without at all assuming relations. At the limit, then, all monads possess an infinity of compossible minute perceptions, but have differential relations that will select certain ones in order to yield clear perceptions proper to each. In this way every monad, as we have seen, expresses the same world as the others, but nonetheless owns an exclusive zone of clear expression that is distinguished from every other monad: its *subdivision*.

These subdivisions appear even if we adhere to orders of clarity and distinction in Leibniz's classification of ideas. Contrary to Descartes, Leibniz begins in darkness. Clarity emerges from obscurity by way of a genetic process, and so too clarity plunges into darkness, and continues to plunge deeper and deeper: it is natural chiaroscuro, a development out of obscurity, and it is *more or less* clear to the degree that sensibility reveals it as such.[12] Thus the preceding paradox is resolved: even if we grant that the same differential relations are established in all monads, not all of them will attain the same level of clarity, required by conscious perception in conformity with its threshold.

And, above all, we can clear up the two difficulties encountered at the beginning, that is, that the same requirement appeals now and again to obscurity and to clarity, and that clarity itself depends on what is only fathomed obscurely. For clarity has to emerge out of darkness, as if through a first filter that would be followed by many other filters, for what is distinct, what is confused, and so on.[13] In effect, differential relations indeed fill the role of a filter — and already of an infinity of filters — since they let through only minute perceptions that in each instance can furnish a relatively clear perception. But, because filters change their nature at each level, we must admit that clarity is relatively obscure and absolutely confused, just as what is distinct remains relatively confused and absolutely inadequate. What then is the implication of the Cartesian expression "clear and distinct," which Leibniz nonetheless retains? How can he say that the privileged zone of every monad is not only clear but also distinct, all the while it consists of a confused event? It is because clear perception as such is never distinct.

Rather, it is "distinguished," in the sense of being remarkable or notable. It is decisive in respect to other perceptions, and the first filter is obviously applied to *ordinary* perceptions in order to extract from them whatever is *remarkable* (clear and distinguished).[14] But, strictly speaking, the distinct presupposes another filter that assumes the remarkable to be *regular,* and from it extracts singularities. These are the inner singularities of the idea or of the distinct perception. Must a third filter be imagined, of the adequate or even of the complete, that draws the ordinary out of the singular, in a manner that the organization of filters would constitute a circular system, although this last filter exceeds our power of imagination? The totality would allow us to utter in the same breath, like Balthasar, "Everything is ordinary!" and "Everything is unique!"

The development of the theory of the idea pertains less here than the different meanings of the singular. We have encountered three of its meanings: singularity is above all (1) inflection, the point of inflection that is extended up to the neighborhood of other singularities, thus tracing the lines of the universe mapped according to relations of distance; and then (2) it is the axis of the curve from the concave side insofar as the monad's point of view is defined according to relations of perspective; finally, (3) it is what is remarkable, according to differential relations that in the monad are constituting perception. We shall observe that a fourth kind of singularity can be added, one that makes up maximal and minimal "extrema" in matter or extension. Already, in the deepest Baroque regions, and in the deepest Baroque knowledge of the world, this subordination of the true to what is singular and remarkable is being made manifest.

Now we can return to perception. All monads express the whole world darkly, even if not in the same order. Each one encloses in itself the infinity of minute perceptions. They cannot be distinguished by weakness or strength. What distinguishes them is their zone of clear, remarkable, or privileged expression. Ultimately, "totally naked monads" (lacking this zone of light) might be conceived. They would live in darkness or near-darkness, in the vertigo and giddiness of minute and dark perceptions. No differential mechanism of reciprocal determination would come to select a few of these tiny perceptions in order to extract a clear perception. They would have nothing remarkable about them.

A limit-condition of this kind is present only in death; everywhere else it is merely an abstraction.[15] The tiniest of all animals has glimmers that cause it to recognize its food, its enemies, and sometimes its partner. If life implies a soul, it is because proteins already attest to an activity of perception, discrimination, and distinction — in short, a "primary force" that physical impulsions and chemical affinities cannot explain ("derivative forces"). Thus there can be no reactions ensuing from excitations, but from outer organic actions that in the soul are proof of an inner perceptive activity. If life has a soul, it is because it perceives, distinguishes, or discriminates, and because a whole world of animal psychology is first of all a psychology of perception. In most cases, the soul gets along quite well with very few clear or distinguished perceptions: the soul of the tick has three, including a perception of light, an olfactory perception of its prey, and a tactile perception of the best place to burrow, while everything else in the great expanse of Nature, which the tick nevertheless conveys, is only a numbness, a dust of tiny, dark, and scattered perceptions.[16]

But if an animal scale exists, or an "evolution" in the animal series, it is insofar as increasingly numerous differential relations of a deepening order are determining a zone of clear expression that is both more extensive and increasingly hermetic. Each of the conscious perceptions that comprise the zone is associated with others in the infinite process of reciprocal determination. These are *remembering monads*. And furthermore, certain monads are endowed with the power of extending themselves and intensifying their zones, of attaining a real connection of their conscious perceptions (and not a simple associative consecution), and of surpassing clarity with what is distinctive and even with what is adequate: *reasonable or reflexive monads,* to be sure, find their condition of self-development in the sacrifice of certain ones among them — the Damned — that regress to the state of almost naked monads, their only single and clear perception being their hatred of God.

Whence the possibility for an admittedly summary classification of monads as functions of their perceptive qualities: there are almost naked monads, remembering monads, and reflexive or reasonable monads.[17] Fechner, another of the great disciples of Leibniz, and the founder of a psychophysics inseparable from the spiritual mechanisms of the monadic soul, does not hesitate to develop classifications endlessly, from vertigo or dizziness to luminous life. In them he envisions the three ages of man, with all their possibilities of regression and damnation, through which Fechner himself passes as a monad, reduced to his dark room or his somber depths, turned over to the digestive swarm of tiny perceptions, but also to the force of a resurrection, to an ascendant surge of intense and expansive light.[18] Few monads fail to believe themselves damned at certain moments of their existence. When their clear perceptions are now and again extinguished, when they recede into the night—in relation to this the tick's life appears to be singularly rich. But with freedom there also comes the moment when a soul is won over to itself and can whisper with a convalescent's astonishment, "My God, what did I do in all of these years?"

If the differential mechanisms of our clear perceptions are checked, then the minute perceptions force selection and invade consciousness, as in drowsiness or in giddiness. A dust of colored perceptions falls on a black backdrop; yet, if we look closely, these are not atoms, but minuscule folds that are endlessly unfurling and bending on the edges of juxtaposed areas, like a mist or fog that makes their surface sparkle, at speeds that no one of our thresholds of consciousness could sustain in a normal state. But when our clear perceptions are reformed, they draw yet another fold that now separates the conscious from the unconscious, that joins the tiny edges of surface to a great area, that moderates the different speeds, and rejects all kinds of minute perceptions in order to make from all the others the solid fabric of apperception: dust falls, and I see the great fold of figures just as the background is unfurling its tiny folds.

Fold over folds: such is the status of the two modes of perception, or of microscopic and macroscopic processes. That is why the unfolded surface is never the opposite of the fold, but rather the movement that goes from some to the others. Unfolding sometimes means that I am developing—that I am undoing—infinite tiny folds that are forever agitating the background, with the goal of drawing a great fold on the side whence forms appear; it is the operation of a vigil: I project the world "on the surface of a folding . . ."[19] At other times, on the contrary, I undo the folds of consciousness that pass through every one of my thresholds, the "twenty-two folds" that surround me and separate me from the deep, in order to unveil in a single movement this unfathomable depth of tiny and moving folds that waft me along at excessive speeds in the operation of vertigo, like the "enraged charioteer's whiplash . . ."[20] I am forever unfolding between two folds, and if to perceive means to unfold, then I am forever perceiving within the folds.

Every perception is hallucinatory because perception has no object. Conscious perception has no object and does not even refer to a physical mechanism of excitation that could explain it from without: it refers only to the exclusively physical mechanism of differential relations among unconscious perceptions that are comprising it within the monad.[21] And unconscious perceptions have no object and do not refer to physical things. They are only related to the cosmological and metaphysical mechanism according to which the world does not exist outside of the monads that are conveying it. The mechanism is thus inevitably folded in the monads, with unconscious perceptions comprising these minute folds as the representatives of the world (and not representations of objects).

The idea of hallucinatory perception has clearly undergone a slow degradation in psychology; but because it overlooked the properly Leibnizian conditions: that is, the double — microscopic and macroscopic — circuit, the being-for the world of unconscious or minute perceptions, and the differential relations that hold for conscious perceptions. Hallucination is always duplicitous, somewhat like what Clérambault distinguishes in the chloralic state as hallucinations of "a small area" and others of "a large area." That we were always perceiving in folds means that we have been grasping figures without objects, but through the haze of dust without objects that the figures themselves raise up from the depths, and that falls back again, but with time enough to be seen for an instant. I see the fold of things through the dust they stir up, and whose folds I cast aside. I do not see into God, but I do see into the folds. The situation of perception is not what Gestalt theory describes when it erects the laws of the "proper form" against the idea of hallucinatory perception, but what Leibniz and de Quincey describe: *When a herd or an army approaches,* under our hallucinated gaze . . . — the event:

> Through the next hour, during which the gentle morning breeze had a little freshened, the dusty vapour had developed itself far and wide into the appearance of huge aerial draperies, hanging in mighty volumes from the sky to the earth; and at particular points, where the eddies of the breeze acted upon the pendulous skirts of these aerial curtains, rents were perceived, sometimes taking the form of regular arches, portals, and windows, through which began dimly to gleam the heads of camels "indorsed" with human beings — and at intervals the moving of men and horses in tumultuous array — and then through other openings or vistas at far distant points the flashing of polished arms. But sometimes, as the wind slackened or died away, all those openings, of whatever form, in the cloudy pall would slowly close, and for a time the whole pageant was shut up from view; although the growing din, the clamours, shrieks, and groans, ascending from infuriated myriads, reported, in a language not to be misunderstood, what was going on behind the cloudy screen.[22]

The first stage of the deduction goes from the monad to what is perceived. But everything seems to stop right there, in a sort of suspense in the mode of Berkeley, and nothing authorizes us to conclude in favor of the presence of a body that might be ours, or the existence of the body that would have happened to affect it. There exists only what is perceived, interior to the monad, while the phenomenon is what is perceived.[23] However, a first great difference is marked in respect to Berkeley: the perceived as a "being of imagination" is not a given, but possesses a double structure that allows for its genesis. Macroperception is the product of differential relations that are established among microperceptions; it is thus an unconscious psychic mechanism that engenders the perceived in consciousness.[24] Thus the variable and relative unity of any given phenomenon or another can be explained: all phenomena are collective, like a herd, an army, or a rainbow.

The collection of unconscious perceptions surely has no unity (dizziness), but nonetheless it receives a mental unity from the differential relations that are being exerted, and from a degree of reciprocal determination of these relations. A collection will have as much more unity as there are "relations among the ingredients," relations carried out necessarily through thought. The whole question is of knowing if, in ascribing to itself the force to engender the perceived and the unity of the perceived in the monad, Leibniz does not also ascribe to himself the force to engender bodies outside of monads and outside of their perceptions.

Why can't we get along without bodies? What leads us to go beyond the phenomenon or the perceived? Leibniz often says that if bodies did not exist outside of perception, the only perceiving substances would be either human or angelic, to the detriment of the variety and of the animality of the universe. If bodies did not exist outside of the perceived, there would be less variety in perceivers themselves (that "must" rightly be united with bodies).[25] But the likely argument is even more bizarre and complex: it is that the perceived *resembles* something that it forces us to reflect upon. I have a white perception; I perceive white: this perceived element looks like froth, that is, an infinity of tiny mirrors that would be reflecting a ray of light beneath our eyes. I feel a tremor of pain: this pain resembles the movement of something pointed that would dig into my flesh in concentric circles.[26]

The argument appears so difficult to understand that precautions have to be multiplied. In the first place, Leibniz is not stating that perception resembles an object, but that it evokes a vibration gathered by a receptive organ: pain does not represent the needle, nor its movement from one level to another, "such as that of a wagon's wheel," but the thousands of minute movements or throbs that irradiate in the flesh: "It is true that pain does not resemble the movement of a pin; but it might thoroughly resemble the motions that the pain causes in our body, and might represent them in the soul." White does "not resemble a convex spherical mirror," but an infinity of "little convex mirrors such as there are seen in foam when we look at it closely." Here the relation of resemblance is like a "projection": pain or color are projected on the vibratory plan of matter, somewhat in the way that a circle can be projected onto a plane as a parabola or a hyperbola. Projection is the basis for a "relation of order," or analogy, which can be formulated in the following way:

$$\frac{\text{minute perceptions}}{\text{conscious perceptions}} = \frac{\text{vibrations of matter}}{\text{the organ}}$$

In the second place, that the perceived resembles something does not immediately mean that perception represents an object. Cartesians had testified to a geometrism of perception, but through which clear and distinct perceptions were apt to represent extension. As for obscure or confused perceptions, they were operating only as conventional signs stripped of their representativity, hence of resemblance. Leibniz's point of view is entirely different, since neither the geometry nor the status of resemblance is the same. These are affective qualities, confused or even obscure perceptions that resemble something by virtue of a projective geometry. From then on they are "natural signs." And what they resemble is neither extension nor even movement, but matter in extension, vibrations, elasticities, "tendencies or efforts" in motion. Pain does not represent the pin in extension, but resembles molecular movements that it produces in matter. Along with perception, geometry plunges into obscurity. Above all, it is the meaning of resemblance that entirely changes. Resemblance is equated with what resembles, not with what is resembled. That the perceived resembles matter means that matter is necessarily produced in conformity with this relation, and not that this relation conforms to a preexisting model. Or rather, it is the relation of resemblance, it is the likeness that is itself the model, that makes matter be that which it resembles.

In the third place, if we follow the preceding analogy, how then does the resembled come forward? How does the material side of the analogy get presented? Appeal cannot be made to a material physical mechanism that would remain identical to the psychical mechanism in the soul, since the latter, because it is inherent to the monad, excludes all external causality. It often happens that Leibniz puts the status of differential calculus in question. For him it is merely a convenient and well-founded fiction.[27] In this respect the question is not that of existing infinity or of the infinitesimal, which pertain as much to matter as to obscure perceptions (they are "alike").

The question is rather: Is differential calculus adequate for infinitesimal things? And the answer is negative insofar as the existing infinite comprehends neither a great whole nor the smallest parts; nor does it tend toward limits. Differential relations intervene only in order to extract a clear perception from minute, obscure perceptions. Thus the calculus is precisely a psychic mechanism, and if it is fictive, it is in the sense that this mechanism belongs to a hallucinatory perception. Calculus surely has a psychological reality, but here it is deprived of physical reality. There can be no question of assuming it in what perception resembles, that is, by turning it into a physical mechanism, except through convention and by increasing the fiction. Physical mechanisms are infinitely tiny fluvia that form displacements, crisscrossings, and accumulations of waves, or "conspiracies" of molecular movements.

When defining the essential characters of bodies, Leibniz assigns two of them, the power of diminishing infinitely (by virtue of their infinitely tiny parts), and the power of being in constant flux (to have parts that never stop coming and going).[28] Physical mechanisms do not work by differentials, which are always differentials of consciousness, but by communication and propagation of movement, "like ripples that a stone creates when it is thrown into water." It is even in this sense that matter is full of organs, or that organs fully belong to matter because they are merely the contraction of several waves or rays: the nature of a receptive organ is to contract the vibrations that it receives.[29] It is at the origin of a principle of physical causality, because it gathers together the effect of an infinity of causes ("equality of the full cause and of the entire effect").

Thus there exists a great difference between an always extrinsic physical causality, which goes from one body, to all those from which it receives the effect, to infinity in the universe (the regime of influx or of universal interaction), and an always intrinsic psychic causality, which goes from each monad on its account to effects of perception of the universe that it produces spontaneously, independently of all influx from one monad to another. To these two causalities correspond two calculations—or two aspects of the calculus that, even if they are inseparable, must be distinguished: one relates to the psycho-metaphysical mechanism of perception, and the other to the physico-organic mechanism of excitation or impulsion. And these are like two halves of each other. This does not prevent conscious perception from resembling vibrations contracted by the body, or the threshold of consciousness from corresponding to the conditions of the organ, as Fechner's psychophysics is developed on the basis of the preceding analogy. A quality perceived by consciousness resembles the vibrations contracted through the organism.[30] Differential mechanisms on the inside of the monad resemble mechanisms of communication and propagation of extrinsic movement, although they are not the same and must not be confused.

The relation of vibrations at the receiver introduces limits into matter that make possible the application of differential calculus, but this relation is not in itself differential. The application of differential calculation to matter (through resemblance) is based on the presence of receptive organs everywhere in this matter. From it we might be able to draw conclusions that pertain to the respective interpretations of calculus for Leibniz and for Newton. It is commonly known that they did not conceive it in the same way. Now, by determining magnitudes according to the speed of movements or intensities that form them ("fluxions"), Newton invents a calculus adequate to the movement of a fluid matter, and even to its effects upon an organ. But, while considering that these fluxions disappear in the growing magnitude of which they are a part, Newton leaves aside the problem of knowing where the different parts remain. To the contrary, Leibniz's calculus, based on the reciprocal determination of "differentials," is strictly inseparable from a Soul, insofar as the soul alone conserves and distinguishes the small components.[31] Leibniz's calculus is adequate to psychic mechanics where Newton's is operative for physical mechanics. The difference between the two is as much metaphysical as it is mathematical. We would not be wrong to state that Leibniz's calculus resembles Newton's. In effect, it applies to nature only by means of resemblance, but we must recall that it is the likeness that is the model, and that it determines whatever it resembles.

The deduction has two stages, the one positing the monad's requirement of having a body (primary matter or limitation-matter), the other showing how the requirement is filled (secondary matter or flux-matter). To sum up the second stage, which moves from the perceived to the body: (1) clear-obscure perception manifests a relation of resemblance with a material receptor that receives vibrations; (2) such receptors are called organs or organic bodies, and as bodies they constitute the vibrations that they receive to infinity; (3) the physical mechanism of bodies (fluxion) is not identical to the psychic mechanism of perception (differentials), but the latter resembles the former; (4) using resemblance as a model, God necessarily creates a matter in conformity with what resembles him, a presently infinite vibratory matter (of infinitely tiny parts) in which receptive organs are distributed everywhere, swarming; (5) thus we move from one aspect of perception to another, which is no longer solely the representative of the world but becomes the representation of an object in conformity with organs.

In short, God endows the monad with organs or the organic body corresponding to its perceptions. Thus we are prepared to understand the sum of the theory of the fold. The implementation of perception establishes the folds in the soul, the folds whose monad is decorated on the inside; but these are like a matter that must hereafter be organized in outer pleats. We even find ourselves in a quadripartite system of folding, to which the preceding analogy attests, because perception straddles the micro-folds of tiny perceptions and the great fold of consciousness, and matter, the tiny vibratory folds and their amplification on a receiving organ. The folds in the soul resemble the pleats of matter, and in that fashion they are directing them.

I possess a clear and distinguished zone of expression because I have primitive singularities, ideal virtual events to which I am destined. From this moment deduction unwinds: *I have a body because I have a clear and distinguished zone of expression*. In fact, that which I express clearly, the moment having come, will *concern* my body, and will act most directly on my body, surroundings, circumstances, and environment. Caesar is the spiritual monad who clearly expresses the crossing of the Rubicon. He thus has a body that the flowing waters, a given flow of water, will eventually be soaking. But up to this point, when perception has become the perception of an object, everything can be easily inverted. I can recover ordinary language, or the habitual and empirical order of resemblance: I have a clear or privileged zone of expression because I have a body. What I clearly express is what happens to my body.

The monad expresses the world "according to" its body, according to the organs of its body, according to the action of other bodies upon itself: "What happens in the soul represents what happens in bodily organs."[32] Hereafter the monad can be said to "suffer." While in truth the monad draws all perceptive traces from itself, I act as if the bodies that are acting upon itself were acting upon it and were causing its perceptions. Is this a simple manner of speaking, or a deeper problem that can be resolved only through analysis of causalities?

Chapter 8
The Two Floors

Already in a writing of his youth Leibniz reproaches nominalists for conceiving totalities only as collective and, by doing so, spoiling the concept. Comprehension of the concept is distributive and not collective. Collectively, sheep are members of a flock, but people are reasonable only on an individual basis.[1] Therefore Leibniz notices that, insofar as they are reasonable, monads stand in the same respect to the world as to the comprehension of their concept: each one on its own basis comprises the entirety of the world. Monads are each or *every* one for itself, while bodies are *one, some,* or any.[2] William James and Russell used this difference to their advantage. Monads are distributive units that follow a relation of part and whole, while bodies are collectives—flocks or aggregates—that follow a relation of the-ones-to-the-others. Division into two floors thus appears strict since, in the upper area, we have reasonable monads or the Each, like private apartments that are not connected to one another, that do not act upon each other, and that are variants of the same interior decoration.

On the floor below we find the material universe of bodies, like that of Commoners who are forever expressing movement, propagating waves, and acting upon one another. Surely there is a convergence, because each monad *expresses* the sum of the world, and because a body receives the *impression* of "all" the others up to infinity.[3] But this convergence moves along two diverging paths or according to two entirely different regimes, a regime of expression and a regime of impression, a vertical immanent causality and a transitive horizontal causality. They can be summarily opposed: in one case, concepts of liberty or grace are at stake; "free decrees," final causes and "moral necessity" (the best) are involved. In the other case, we are dealing with concepts of nature, with efficient causes, "subaltern maxims" such as physical laws, in which necessity is hypothetical (if one is . . . , so then the other . . .).

We not only have convergence, but here and there broad encroachments. Subaltern maxims are a part of free decrees, and among them a certain number concern monads directly, inasmuch as the latter already form a first "nature"; with moral necessity and hypothetical necessity lumped together, efficient causes would never exert influence if final causes did not happen to fulfill the conditions.[4]

And yet two halves are in question, as we have just seen in the case of infinitesimal calculus. In fact, if we assimilate the object (that is, the world) to the primary equation of an infinite curvature of inflection, we obtain the position or the respective point of view of monads as primitive or *primal forces,* by means of a simple rule of tangents (vectors of concavity), and from the equation we extract differential relations that are present in every monad between minute perceptions, in a way that every one of them conveys the entire curvature of its point of view. Thus we have a first part, a first moment of the object, the object as perceived or the world as expression. But there persists the question of knowing what the other part may be which now corresponds to the initial equation: pure relations are no longer at stake, but differential equations and integrations that determine the efficient causes of perception, that is, which have to do with a matter and the bodies that perception resembles. Such is the second moment of the object, no longer expression, but content.[5] These are no longer decrees, but maxims or empirical laws of second Nature.

These are no longer singularities of inflection, but *singularities of extremum,* because the curve is now related—but only now—to coordinates that allow us to determine minima or maxima. These are no longer vectors of concavity that define the position of monads in relation to inflection, but vectors of weight that define the position of a body's equilibrium and the lowest center of gravity (the catenary curve). It is no longer a reciprocal determination through differential relations, but a complete determination of the object through a maximum or minimum: finding the form of a closed line of a given length that limits the greatest possible planar surface, finding the minimal area of surface limited by a given contour. Everywhere in matter the calculus of "minimis and maximis" will allow the modification of movement to be determined in respect to action, the course of light in respect to reflection or refraction, the propagation of vibrations in respect to harmonic frequencies, but also the organization of receivers, and the general diffusion or balanced distribution of all kinds of *derivative forces,* elastic and plastic alike.[6]

It is as if the equation of the world had to be inscribed twice, once in the minds that conceive it more or less distinctly, and a second time in a Nature that makes it possible in the form of two calculi. And these two calculi probably are concatenated or are continuous, and they are probably complementary and have to be homogenized. That is why Leibniz can put forward the choice of the world or of monads as if they already operate through a calculus of minimum and maximum; the difference of the two halves nonetheless remains, since in one case the differential relations determine a maximum of quantity of being, while in the other the maximum (or minimum) determines the relations in the equation. We have seen the diversity of singulars in Leibniz's work: properties of extremum rule over the constitution of the world chosen in Nature, but the very choice goes back first of all to *other properties*—of inflection—that put the form of the whole into play at an upper level, as if it were the property of being the limit of a convergent series.[7] The great equation, the world thus has two levels, two moments, or two halves, one by which it is enveloped or folded in the monads, and the other, set or creased in matter. If the two are confused, the whole system falls apart, and no less mathematically than metaphysically.

On the upper level we have a line of variable curvature, without coordinates, a curve with infinite inflection, where inner vectors of concavity mark for each ramification the position of individual monads in suspension. But only on the lower level have we coordinates that determine extrema, extrema that define the stability of figures, figures that organize masses, masses that follow an extrinsic vector of gravity or of the greatest incline: it is already the ogive, the Gothic arch, as a symmetrical mapping of inflection, which represents the figure that meets with a minimum of resistance from a fluid.[8] This is the organization of the Baroque house with its division into two floors, one in individual weightlessness, the other in a gravity of mass. Between them a tension is manifested when the first rises up or drops down, in spiritual elevation and physical gravity.

Raymond Ruyer (the latest of Leibniz's great disciples) opposes "true forms" to figures and structures.[9] Figures are functions that refer to the axes of coordinates, and structures are functionings that refer to relative positions ordered from one to the next, according to states of equilibrium and horizontal linkages, even when there exists a relation of dominance. But the so-called substantial or individual forms are absolute vertical positions, surfaces or absolute volumes, unified areas or "overviews," unlike figures, which do not imply a supplementary dimension in order to be themselves understood, and are not dependent as are preexisting and localizable linkages. These are souls, monads, "self-surveiling" superjects.

Self-present in the vertical dimension, overseeing themselves without taking any distance, these are neither objects that can explain perception, nor subjects capable of grasping a perceived object; rather, they are absolute interiorities that take hold of themselves and everything that fills them, in a process of "self-enjoyment," by withdrawing from themselves all perceptions with which they are co-present on this one-sided inner surface, independently of receptive organs and physical excitations that do not intervene at this level. My eyes would refer to a third eye, which would in turn refer to a fourth eye, if an absolute form were incapable of seeing itself and, in that way, of seeing all the details from its domain in all the areas from which it is located at the same time: *nonlocalizable linkages*. Every time that we have attributable individual beings that are not content with merely functioning, but that are endlessly "being formed," these true forms do not only apply to living organisms, but to physical and chemical particles, to molecules, atoms, and photons. Although the inner variety of forms accounts for differences between the organic and the inorganic, the question does not thus concern a matter of vitalism. No matter what, genuine or absolute forms are primary forces, essentially individual and active primary unities, that actualize a virtuality or a potential, and that are in harmony with each other without any one being determined by the other.

Gestalttheorie believed that it attained these forms by appealing—as much for perceived figures as for physical structures—to a total action and to extreme dynamic equilibriums, a kind of "soap bubble" that would be capable of exceeding simple actions of contact, successive mechanisms, and preexisting illusions (for example, a law of minimal tension would explain foveal fixation without assuming special conductors). But perhaps *Gestalt* thus revives the great Newtonian attempts when people began to elaborate notions of force and field in order to get beyond classical mechanics. And in this respect the opposition of Leibniz to Newton is not explained merely by the critique of vacuum, but because phenomena of "attraction," in which Leibniz clearly recognizes a specificity (magnetism, electricity, volatility), do not seem to him to be of a nature that would exceed the order of mechanisms of contact or succession ("thrusts" or "impulsions").[10] A journey created from one instant to the next through an infinitesimal diminution of tension operates no less successively than a preformed road, a set of rails, or a pipeline; a progressive filling of all possible space by a sum of waves implies just as much the actions of contact in a fluid.

The laws of extremum, to which D'Arcy Thomson recently appealed in order to account for organic phenomena, still imply paths in extension that can be compared only by assuming the form that one claims to explain. In short, we are not moving thus toward active primary unities; on the contrary, we remain in an extension without any overview, and in linkages without sufficient reason. What Leibniz calls for, against Newton (as does Ruyer against Gestaltists), is the establishment of a true form that cannot be reduced to an apparent whole or to a phenomenal field, because it must retain the distinction of its details and its own individuality in the hierarchy in which it enters. To be sure, the semi-wholes have as much importance as the parts, as do attractions as much as thrusts, dynamic and mechanical equilibriums, laws of extremum and laws of contact, ways and channels, bindings and adhesions. They are indispensable but, *once they are formed,* only make up secondary horizontal linkages and follow subaltern maxims according to which structures function and figures are ordered or linked. If there is a finality here, it is only what the mechanism is producing.

All these laws are like statistics because they pertain to collections, masses, organisms, and no longer to individual beings. Thus they do not convey primary forces or individual beings, but they distribute derivative forces in masses, elastic forces, forces of attraction, and plastic forces that in each case are determining the material linkages. A great line of difference does not separate the organic from the inorganic, but crosses the one and the other by distinguishing what is individual from what is a collective or mass phenomenon, what is an absolute form and what are massive, molar figures or structures.[11] These are the two levels or two aspects of the calculus.

Above, individual beings and true forms or primal forces; below, masses and derivative forces, figures and structures. Individual beings are probably the last and sufficient reasons: their forms and primal forces are hierarchy, accord, and variety and, in the last instance, they make up collections and different types of collection. But the lower floor is no less irreducible, because it implies a loss of individuality among its components, and relates to different kinds of composite collections material or secondary forces of linkage. Clearly, one level is folded over the other, but above all each one conveys a very different kind of fold. A chain of mountains, a genetic chain, or even a gastrula will not be creased in the same way. The same example can even be applied to the organic and inorganic. What must be radically distinguished are the bends of matter, which always consist in hiding something from the relative surface that they are affecting, and the folds of form, which on the contrary reveal to itself the detail of an absolute surface that is copresent with all its modifications.

Why the lower level, which is not a simple appearance? It is because the world or the hazy line of the world resembles a virtuality that is actualized in the monads. The world has actuality only in the monads, which each convey it from each monad's own point of view and on its own surface. But the coupling of the virtual-actual does not resolve the problem. There exists a second, very different coupling of the possible-real. For example, God chooses one world among an infinity of possible worlds: the other worlds also have their actuality in monads that are conveying them, Adam who does not sin or Sextus who does not rape Lucretia. Therefore there exists an actual that remains possible, and that is not forcibly real. The actual does not constitute the real; it must itself be realized, and the problem of the world's realization is added to that of its actualization. God is "existentifying," but the Existentifying is, on the one hand, Actualizing and, on the other, Realizing.

The world is a virtuality that is actualized monads or souls, but also a possibility that must be realized in matter or in bodies. It is curious, we might argue, that the question of reality is posited in respect to bodies that, even if they are not appearances, are simple phenomena. Yet what happens to be a phenomenon

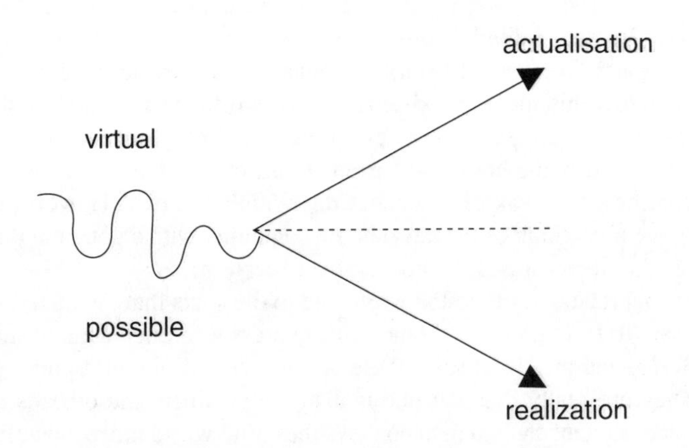

in the strict sense is what is perceived in the monad. When, by virtue of the resemblance of the perceived to something = x, we ask if bodies might not be acting upon each other in ways such that our inner perceptions correspond to them, we are thus asking the question of a realization of the phenomenon or, better, of a "realizing" of the perceived, that is, of the transformation of the currently perceived world into an objectively real world, into an objective Nature.[12] It is not the body that realizes, but it is in the body that something is realized, through which the body itself becomes real or substantial.

The process of actualization operates through distribution, while the process of realization operates by resemblance. This raises an especially delicate point. For if the world is taken as a double process — of actualization in monads and of realization in bodies — then in what does it itself consist? How can we define it as *what* is actualized and is realized? We find ourselves before events: Adam's soul is now sinning (following final causes), and thus his body is really absorbing the apple (according to efficient causes). My soul feels a current pain, my body receives a real blow. But what is it? What is this secret part of the event that is at once distinguished from its own realization, from its own actualization, even though realization does not exist on the outside? This death, for example, is neither exterior reality nor its intimacy in the soul. We have seen that it is pure inflection as ideality, a neutral singularity, incorporeal as much as impassible or, if we use Blanchot's words, "the part of the event as much as its accomplishment" can neither actualize nor realize its carrying out.[13] It is what can be conveyed by all expression, or what can be realized by all realizations, the *Eventum tantum* to which the body and soul attempt to be equal, but that never stops happening and that never ceases to await us: a pure virtuality and possibility, the world in the fashion of a Stoic Incorporeal, the pure predicate.

As the Chinese (or Japanese) philosopher would say, the world is the Circle, the pure "reserve" of events that are actualized in every self and realized in things one by one. Leibniz's philosophy, as shown in the letters written to Arnauld, as much in respect to spiritual monads as in respect to the material universe, requires this ideal preexistence of the world, this silent and shaded part of the event. We can speak of the event only as already engaged in the soul that expresses it and in the body that carries it out, but we would be completely at a loss about how to speak of it without this withdrawn part. However difficult it may be, we must think of the naval battle beginning with a potential that exceeds the souls that direct it and the bodies that execute it.

It is in its relation both to the world and to the souls that the material universe can be said to be expressive. Some souls express it through actualization, others through realization. To be sure, these are two very different regimes of expression. They are really distinct; one is distributive where the other is collective. On its own account each monad conveys the entire world independently of others and without influx, while every body receives the impression or influx of others, and that is the totality of bodies; that is the material universe that expresses the world. Preestablished harmony is thus presented first of all as an accord between the two regimes. But in turn these have a second difference: the expression of the soul goes from the whole to the part, that is, from the entire world to a designated zone, while the expression of the universe goes from part to part, from the near to the far, to the degree that a body corresponds to the designated zone of the soul and successively submits to the impression of all the others. From this point of view there always exists a *body* that expresses from its side, with its surroundings, what a soul expresses in its own region, and preestablished harmony is located between the soul and "its" body.

But what allows us to speak of "the body of a monad" or "its body," since the monad is always an Each, an *Every,* while the body, always a body, is a *One*? What founds the appurtenance of one body to each monad, despite the real distinction and the difference of level or of regime? A *One* — without ceasing to be a *One* — must belong to each *Every.* In brief, preestablished harmony is distinguished not only in itself from Malebranche's occasionalism or from Spinoza's parallelism, but also by its consequences: far from replacing the problem of the union of the soul and the body, of the incarnation or of "immediate presence," it makes it all the more necessary, even if only to move from the first to the second aspect.[14] In fact, harmony explains the correspondence between each soul and the material universe, but when it appeals to the correspondence between the soul and its body, it cannot explain it through any relation in the body simply because a relation of this kind is based on a pregiven appurtenance. It is only at the level of a theory of appurtenance that the problem will find its solution: What does it mean to belong, and in what way does *one* body belong to each soul?

In the last of his *Cartesian Meditations* Husserl goes back to Leibniz for good reason. He effectively develops an entire theory of appurtenance that takes up three great moments that Leibniz had brought to light: the monad is the Ego in its concrete plenitude, the Self is related to a "sphere of appurtenance," to the sphere of its possessions; but myself, a monad, I find in the sphere of what belongs to me the mark of something that I do not possess, something foreign to me; thus I can constitute an objective Nature to which the other in me belongs. To the first question, "What belongs to me?" Leibniz responds just as will Husserl much later: it is first of all the thought of the self, the cogito, but also the fact that I have diverse thoughts, all my changing perceptions, all my predicates included, the entire world as perceived; and yet still, this is the zone of the world that I convey clearly, it is my special possession; and then, primary matter is what I own as the requirement of having a body. And finally, the body, a body, is what I own, a body that happens to fill the requirement, as we have seen just previously: an organic body with which I am immediately "present," that I can use in an immediate fashion and with which I coordinate what is perceived (I perceive with organs, with my hands, with my eyes . . .). There is the whole list of my belongings; the last is distinguished from all the others because it is extrinsic, a body not being *in* my monad.

Now we can specify the great gap that will open between Leibniz and Husserl: at the level of the body Husserl discovers the other as being the other-self, the other monad, "through aperceptive transposition that begins with my own body." The same does not hold for Leibniz, for whom the plurality of monads was discovered at an earlier stage: indeed, everything that exceeds my clear zone or my subdivision and that nevertheless I include, everything that remains dark or obscure in me, resembles the negative image of other monads, because other monads use it to form their own clear zone. It happens then that a community of monads is already in place, and a first Nature, constituted by all their respective zones of clarity, does not need bodies in order to appear. To be sure, no monad contains others, but my intrinsic possessions sufficiently bear the mark of those foreign ones whose shadow I discover within me, since there is nothing obscure in me that might not be pulled into clarity from *another* monad. Thus for Leibniz, if a meeting with the other is produced at the level of the body, it will not be with the other-self, but with an even more unexpected element that makes up a second Nature.

I have a body, a body belongs to me: How can my monad have an extrinsic possession, outside of itself, on the lower level? One of Leibniz's essential theses consists in positing at once the real distinction and the inseparability: it is not because two things are really distinct that they are separable. In the very same way Harmony and Union discover the principle of their division: preestablished harmony of the soul and of the body rules their real distinction, while the union determines their inseparability.[15] Even when I die, my monad is not separated from a body whose parts are happy to become involuted. As we have observed, my monad does not perceive in itself without having a body in "resemblance" with what it is perceiving. By virtue of the generality of the order of resemblance, it is a generic, specific, organic body: a body of a man, or even of a horse, a dog . . . The requirement of having a body is quite individual, but not the body that happens to fill it, at least not immediately.

Leibniz often insists on this point: God does not endow the soul with a body without furnishing the given body with organs. Now what makes an organic, specific, or generic body? It is probably made of infinities of present material parts, in conformity with infinite division, in conformity with the nature of masses or collections. But these infinities in turn would not comprise organs if they were not inseparable from crowds of little monads, monads of heart, liver, knee, of eyes, hands (according to their special zone that corresponds to one infinity or another): animal monads that themselves belong to material parts of "my" body, and that are not confused with the monad to which my body belongs. These are merely the requisites of my organic, specific, or generic body; and there is no cause to ask if matter thinks or perceives, but only whether it is separable from these little souls capable of perception.[16]

Thus we see that Leibniz's theory of appurtenance leads to a fundamental inversion that will forever begin over and again. Monads that have a body must be distinguished, and monads that are the specific requisites of this body, or that belong to parts of this body. And these second monads, these monads of bodies, themselves possess a body that belongs to them, a body specifically other than that whose requisites they are, and whose parts in their turn possess crowds of tertiary monads. And these tertiary monads . . . [17] The soul and the body can always be truly distinguished, but inseparability traces a coming and going between one level and the other. My unique monad has a body; the parts of this body have crowds of monads; each one of these monads has a body . . .

If my body, the body that belongs to me, is a body according to the law of collections, it is because its parts not only grow and shorten, involve and evolve, but also never cease to move about and go away (fluxion). And, when they leave, the monads that are inseparable from either follow them or evade me. Requisites of my body, these were merely "pro tempore" requisites.[18] The theory of appurtenance thus distinguishes nonsymmetrical and inverted appurtenances (a body belongs to my monad, some monads belong to parts of my body), but also constant or temporary appurtenances (a body belongs constantly to my monad, some monads belong temporarily to my body). That is where, in the theory of appurtenance, the revelation of a half-other occurs: the animal in me as a concrete being. The great difference with Husserl is that the latter does not face any special problem in organic composition: my body does not pose any problems in my sphere of appurtenance, and the other springs up only with the other body, through which I aim at an Alter Ego that does not belong to me; as for the animal, it is only an "anomaly" of this Other.

For Leibniz, on the contrary, the alter ego has already sprung up at an earlier stage of phenomenological deduction, and is sufficiently explained through pre-established harmony. With the union of the soul and the body, the other who now springs forth amid my effects — in order to throw them topsy-turvy — is the animal, and first of all the little animals inseparable from the fluid parts of my body, insofar as they become as foreign to me as they had formerly been. "If Caesar's soul, for example, had to be solitary in nature, the author of things would have been perfectly able to get along without furnishing him with any organs; but this same author wished to make yet an infinity of other beings that are enveloped in the organs of one another; our body is a type of world full of an infinity of creatures that are also worthy of life."[19]

The animals that I meet outdoors are nothing but an enlargement of the latter. This is not only an animal psychology, but also an animal monadology. The two are essential to Leibniz's system: because my sphere of appurtenance essentially discovers me, these are inverted, temporary, or provisional appurtenances (although a body always belongs to me). In fact, it is very difficult for every one of us to make a list of our own belongings. It is not easy to know what we own, and for what length of time. Phenomenology does not suffice. The great inventory of Beckett's Malone is consummate proof. Malone is a naked monad, or almost naked, scatterbrained, degenerate, whose zone of clarity is always shrinking, and whose body folds upon itself, its requisites always escaping him. It's hard for him to tell what remains in his possession, that is, "according to his definition," what belongs to him only partially, and for what duration of time. Is he a thing or an animalcule? If he does not have belongings, then to whom does he belong? That is a metaphysical question. He needs a special hook, a sort of *vinculum* on which he can hang and sort through his different things, but he has even lost this hook.

These reincarnations of appurtenance or possession carry a great philosophical importance. It is as if philosophy were penetrating into a new element and were putting the element of Having in place of that of Being. Clearly, there is nothing new about the formula of "having a body," but what is new is that analysis bears upon species, degrees, relations, and variables of possession in order to use it to fashion the content or the development of the notion of Being. Much more than Husserl, Gabriel Tarde fully discerned the importance of this mutation, and he called in question the unjustifiable primacy of the verb "to be." "The true opposite of the self is not the non-self, it is *the mine*; the true opposite of being, that is, the having, is not the non-being, but *the had*."[20]

Already Leibniz had been erecting, on the inside of the monad, "I have diverse thoughts" in correlation with "I am thinking." Perceptions as included predicates, that is, as inner properties, were replacing attributes. Predication was of the domain of having, and was resolving the aporias of being or of attribution. This was all the more reason for the body, as an extrinsic property, to introduce into possessions factors of inversion, turnaround, precariousness, and temporalization. In fact, this new domain of having does not put us into an element of calm, which would be a relation of the proprietor and property that could be easily established once and for all. What rules in the domain of having are moving and perpetually reshuffled relations among the monads, as much from the standpoint of harmony, where they can be considered "each and every one for each other," as from the point of view of union, where they are considered "the one and the other." There again we have a casuistry. Finally, a monad has as its property not an abstract attribute — movement, elasticity, plasticity — but other monads, such as a cell, other cells, or an atom, and other atoms. These are phenomena of subjugation, of domination, of appropriation that are filling up the domain of having, and this latter area is always located under a certain power (this being why Nietzsche felt himself so close to Leibniz). To have or to possess is to fold, in other words, to convey what one contains "with a certain power." If the Baroque has often been associated with capitalism, it is because the Baroque is linked to a crisis of property, a crisis that appears at once with the growth of new machines in the social field and the discovery of new living beings in the organism.

Appurtenance and possession hark back to domination. A specific body belongs to my monad, but *as long as* my monad dominates the monads that belong to the parts of my body. As a code of correspondences, expression exceeds itself, moving toward domination as a cipher of appurtenances; each monad conveys the entire world, and therefore all other monads, but from a point of view that links each one more strictly to certain others, which they dominate or which dominate them. If a body always belongs to me, it is because the parts that go away are replaced by others whose monads in turn come to replace them under the domination of my own (there exists a periodicity of the renewal of parts, never all leaving at the same time). The body is analogous to Theseus's ship "which the Athenians were always repairing."[21] But, as no monad contains any others, domination would remain a vague notion, having only a nominal definition, if Leibniz had not succeeded in defining it exactly by means of a "substantial vinculum." It is a strange linkage, a bracket, a yoke, a knot, a complex relation that comprises variable terms and one constant term.

Because the vincular relation belongs to it or is "fixed" upon it, the constant term will be the dominant monad. Apparently we can be all the more astonished, because this relation, having other monads for its variable terms (hereafter dominated), cannot be a predicate *contained* in its subject. That is why the relation, not being a predicate, will be called "substantial." Because every relation has a subject, the dominant monad is surely the subject of the vinculum, but a "subject of adhesion," not of inherence or of inhesion.[22] As many readers have shown, this is an almost insufferable paradox in Leibnizianism. That relations are predicates is in no way paradoxical, but only if we understand what a predicate is, what makes it differ from an attribute; and the preestablished harmony implies no outer relation among the monads, but only ties regulated on the inside.

In contrast, the paradox appears insurmountable as soon as appeal is made to an extrinsic possession: that is, a relation that clearly has a subject, but that is not in its subject, and that is not a predicate. There Leibniz discovers that the monad as absolute interiority, as an inner surface with only one side, nonetheless has another side, or a minimum of outside, a strictly complementary form of outside. Can topology resolve the apparent contradiction? The latter effectively disappears if we recall that the "unilaterality" of the monad implies as its condition of closure a torsion of the world, an infinite fold, that can be unwrapped in conformity with the condition only by recovering the other side, not as exterior to the monad, but as the exterior or outside *of* its own interiority: a partition, a supple and adherent membrane coextensive with everything inside.[23] Such is the vinculum, the unlocalizable primary link that borders the absolute interior.

As far as variable terms are concerned, monads are what enter in the relation as "objects," even if for brief moments. They can exist without the relation, and the relation can exist without them. The relation is exterior to variables, as it is

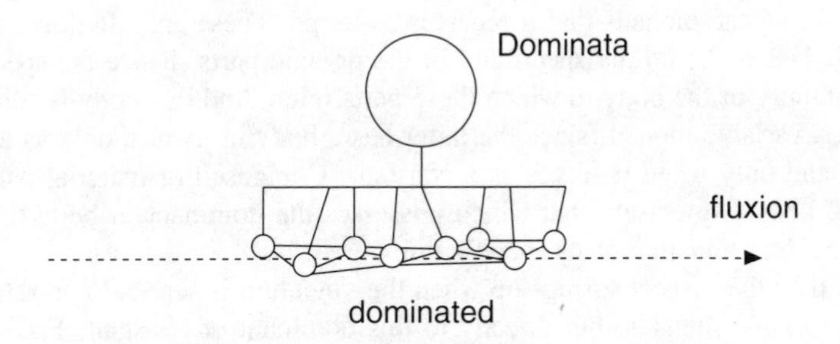

the outside of the constant.[24] It is especially complex since it acquires an infinity of variables. The latter are said to be dominated, specifically insofar as they enter into the relation attached to the dominant or constant. When they cease being submitted to this relation, they enter under another, into another vinculum attached to another dominant (unless they are not freed from every vinculum). In order to evaluate the action of the vinculum, we have to distinguish the two aspects very clearly. First, it is what acquires its variables *en masse,* and *by masses*. Not that the monads that enter under its rule in themselves lose their own individuality (which would imply a miracle). It even presupposes this individuality, and the modifications or inner perceptions of the monads, but it changes nothing and does not depend on them. From them it merely extracts a "common modification," in other words, an Echo that they all have together when they are reflected on the surface of a wall.[25]

As Yvon Belaval and Christiane Frémont have shown, the vinculum itself is a "reflecting wall," and it is so because it comprises this form of the outside that depends on the dominant or constant; variable monads, then, are "emitters," while the echo is the modification of the whole.[26] In this way the vinculum takes up its variables in a massive effect and not in their individuality: whence the passage from optics to acoustics, or from the individual mirror to the collective echo, the effects of whisper or swarming that now refer to this new acoustical register. Then, if the vinculum acquires monads en masse, it thus causes an inversion of appurtenance. As long as monads are understood in their individuality, a body belongs to each monad and is inseparable from it. It is true for the dominant monad, but equally true for every dominated monad that, taken individually, is in turn dominant and thus possesses a body. But the inverse is produced when the dominated monads are taken en masse under a vinculum. Then they are the ones belonging to infinities of material parts that are inseparable from them. They make up the specificity of these parts in general, in the double meaning of homogeneity for the parts that are endlessly being replaced and heterogeneity for the parts that are being coordinated.

In short, as a membrane, wall, or partition, the vinculum works as a sort of grid filtering the monads that it receives as terms. These are sifted masses that in each case make up the specificity of the organic parts, hence the specific or generic unity of the body to which these parts refer. And this body is surely not that of a variable monad, since the latter has a body in its turn only as an individual and only when it serves as a constant. Composed of material parts, the organic body is precisely that which possesses the dominant, *a* body that here finds the determination of its specific unity.

But the other aspect springs up when the vinculum is sent back, not to dominated variable monads, but directly to this dominant or constant. Fixed or attached to an individual dominant, the vinculum in fact determines an individual unity of the body that belongs to it: this body that I have is not only the body of a man, a horse, or of a dog, it is my own body. Further, there would be no specific unity if individual unity were not already presupposed in this first function of the vinculum. If so many material parts can at all times disperse in order to be replaced by others, it is not only because they can be specifically replaced, it is because the body to which they belong in passing remains individually one, a unified body, by virtue of the monad of which it does not cease being a part. Here is an entire cycle of the body and the soul that goes through *Every* and *One,* and returns to *Every* by way of the intermediary of appurtenances or of the "possessive": (1) *each* individual monad possesses a body that cannot be separated from it; (2) each one possesses *a* body insofar as it is the constant subject of the vinculum that is fixed to it (*its* vinculum); (3) for variables this vinculum has monads taken en masse; (4) these masses of monads are inseparable from infinities of material parts to which they belong; (5) these material parts make up the organic composition of *a* body, whose vinculum, envisioned in respect to the variables, assures its specific unity; (6) *this* body is the one that belongs to the individual monad, it is *its* body to the extent that it already avails itself of an individual unity (thanks to the vinculum now envisioned in relation to the constant).

It is even more complicated if we consider the necessary classification of monads. Taken individually, without exception all monads convey the entire world, and are distinguished only by their subdivisions, by the clear zones of their expression. Reasonable monads have a zone so wide and so intense that they lend themselves to operations of reflection or deepening that makes them tend toward God. But every animal monad also has its clear zone—no matter how reduced—including ticks, even a monad of blood, of liver . . . Taken thus in its individuality, every monad is a *simple substance,* a *primary active force,* an *inner unity of action or of change.* Clearly, it has a body, it is inseparable from a body corresponding to its clear zone, but it does not contain it, and is really distinguished from it. The monad merely requires it because of the limitation of its force that constitutes its passive power or its *initial matter* ("moles"). It is a dominant monad to the degree that it has requirements. All reasonable monads are dominant and cannot be otherwise. But even in death, when it "appears" to have lost its body, when it becomes animal again, the formerly reasonable monad does not cease to be dominant. All animal monads, all monads, no matter how dark they may be, are dominant to a certain degree—if they are considered individually, and if they have a body, even if it is infinitely involuted, crushed, or mutilated. They are immediately present in the body, but only through *projection*: active primary force is projected as dominant at a point in the body.[27]

Dominated monads form a second species (although they are dominant, or of the first species, from the preceding point of view). Reasonable monads are never dominated, whereas animal monads can always be dominated. They are so when taken en masse, and not in their individuality. When they are taken in clusters, it is not in respect to the bodies they possess, each on its own account, because they are dominant under this relation. They are taken in clusters in respect to infinite aggregates of material parts that own them, on the contrary, and that remain inseparable from them. From then on these parts clearly compose a body, but it is not the body of dominated monads, but rather the body of the dominant one, the body that their dominant monad possesses. In effect, what acquires an infinity of monads en masse is a knot, a vinculum that is fixed to an individual monad that can be determined as dominant, and that relates to the body of the latter the material aggregates corresponding to the mass in question.

In the paragraphs above we have used "clusters," "crowds," and masses or aggregates synonymously. Now we observe that they are (really) distinguished, aggregates being material, and clusters being monads; with the aggregates from which they are inseparable, under the vinculum masses make organic parts from the body of the monad that dominates them. They make an organism from masses; they organize aggregates. In that way, they are active, but *collective* and *derivative* ("plastic" forces): no longer as units of inner change, but as apparent units of generation and corruption that account for organic composition through envelopment, development, and fluxion of material parts.

And, instead of being projected in a body that belongs to them, they are collectively related to the material parts to which they belong, and they are themselves said to be material.[28] It can be concluded that the monads of the second species, the monads in clusters, constitute, in the most narrow sense of the term, *corporal or composite substances, substantials*: "a multiplicity of substances of which the mass (massa) is that of the total body," and that are "the parts of a second matter."[29] But since monads are taken in clusters only under a vinculum, corporal or composite substances require a broader definition that includes the dominant monad, of the first species, insofar as its requirement of having a body is effectively filled by the monads that it dominates. "Composite substance exists only where a dominant monad is found with a living organic body."

The same holds for what is called secondary matter. If primary or "naked" matter (moles) is the requirement for having a body, secondary or "clothed" matter (massa) is, in a broad sense, what fills the requirement, that is, the organism inseparable from a crowd of monads. Yet as there is nonetheless a real distinction, secondary matter has a narrower meaning according to which it designates only the inorganic aggregate that the mass of monads organizes.[30] We can also remark that derivative forces are exerted on secondary matter, or that they belong to it. It is because material aggregates themselves possess structures and figures that conform to statistical laws of equilibrium, of contact or of field, of thrust or of traction, as we have seen for the extrema. But such laws or secondary linkages imply that forces en masse are exerted upon the aggregates, and may be collective without being, for that, statistical. These derivative forces are effectively those of dominated monads that, however, conserve their individuality, each in respect to another body where it is projected as a primary force or a dominant monad. And further, all clusters of dominated monads, along with their derivative forces, exist only in the pure individuality of their dominant as a primary force of surveillance.

Derivative forces thus trace an entire area that can be called mixed, or rather, intermediary, between statistical collections and individual distributions, and which is made manifest in the phenomena of crowds.[31] It is still more interindividual and interactive than it is collective. It is in this aspect that derivative forces belong, as organic matter, to secondary or clothed matter. They are exerted upon the aggregates but belong to the organisms. Then matter has not only structures and figures but also *textures,* insofar as it comprises these masses of monads from which it cannot be detached. A Baroque conception of matter, in philosophy as in science or in art, has to go up to that point, to a texturology that attests to a generalized organicism, or to a ubiquitous presence of organisms (such as Caravaggio's paintings?).[32] Secondary matter is clothed, with "clothed" signifying two things: that matter is a buoyant surface, a structure endowed with an organic fabric, or that it is the very fabric or clothing, the texture enveloping the abstract structure.

This area of interindividual, interactive clustering is quite agitated, because it is an area of temporary appurtenances or of provisional possessions. At all times aggregates of parts (never all at once) are leaving my body, and thus crowds of monads that my monad was dominating enter under another vinculum, under a new domination. It will no longer be the same cluster, since the vinculum has changed, but neither will these be the same specific parts, since the new vinculum implements another selection that breaks down and recomposes specified aggregates. To be sure, for Leibniz there exists no place for a transformation of species, but everywhere there are places available for mutations, explosions, abrupt associations and dissociations, or reconcatenations. What Leibniz calls metamorphosis or metaschematism not only involves the initial property of bodies—in other words, their capacity to envelop infinitely and, up to a certain point, develop their specific parts—but also the second property, the fluxion that causes parts endlessly to leave their specified aggregate in order to enter into entirely different aggregates that are differently specified.

However, does it not also happen that material aggregates leave an organic body without entering into another? Or that their monads escape the domination where they were, without for all that entering under another vinculum? They remain in the state of unlinked monads, without a vinculum. Material aggregates seem to have nothing more than secondary linkages. No longer are they fabrics, but a felt that is obtained by simple pressing. Surely these inorganic, disorganized aggregates of felt continue to have organisms in their subaggregates. Every body has organisms in its folds; organisms are everywhere . . . It remains the case that not everything is organic. We might say that these inorganic bodies are less composite or corporal substances than *substantial components, semisub-*

stances, or sorts of *substantiats.*[33] In the style in which the question is put forward, we clearly see that any response is impossible, just as we might have wished in order to move ahead more quickly: these bodies are purely mechanical (even with laws of extrema taken into account), these bodies do not or no longer have any monads. For they would not be bodies. They would only be "phenomena," and yet in this fashion they would be "perceived" by a monad. But, insofar as they are bodies, or actualized phenomena, they "have" monads. They follow secondary mechanical linkages, but organisms were already doing that. Every material particle has monads and derivative forces (although these are no longer plastic forces), without which it would not heed any maxim or law.

And Leibniz will never hesitate to remind us of it: organic *or no,* no body can follow a law if it does not have an *inner nature* that enables it to do so. It would be stupid to believe that the law acts on one occasion or another: as if the law of gravitation "were acting" in order to make things fall. That is the fundamental point that opposes preestablished harmony to occasionalism. Leibniz reproaches Malebranche for having submitted bodies (and souls) to general laws that—in order to be general—remain not in the least miraculous, since no force in the individual nature of things fails to enable it to follow them.[34] In short, inorganic bodies have forces, monads, and *a third species of monad.*

These are neither dominant nor dominated monads. They might be called defective monads, in the way that one speaks of defective conic sections. Every monad is an inner unity, but what it is a unit of is not forcibly inside the monad. Monads of the first species are unities of inner change. Monads of the second species are units of organic generation and corruption (composition). Degenerated or defective monads are themselves units of outer movement. The extrinsic character of movement is mixed up in the very condition of bodies or of material parts, as a relation with a surrounding, a successive determination, a mechanical linkage. But all movement that goes, according to the law, to infinity under the force of exterior bodies nonetheless possesses an inner unity without which it could not be ascribed as movement, discerned as inertia.

As we have seen, the same holds for Leibniz as for Bergson: there is a determination inevitably extrinsic to the course, but which supposes an inner unity of the trajectory, in relation to which the extrinsic determination is now only an obstacle or a means, or an obstacle and a means together. Elasticity is what is determined from without, but not the inner force exerted upon it. This force becomes only "living" or "dead" in a proportion that conforms to the extrinsic state. There exists an active elastic force, not only for the sum of movement in the universe, but for each discernible movement in a determined aggregate, and that, in this last case, can only be impeded or released by other aggregates.[35] These forces or inner units of movement belong to aggregates as such, and are defective monads that lack a vinculum. They are "tendencies." In effect, Leibniz proposes to surpass all duality of force and of action, but according to several levels.

Monads of the first species are actions, *powers in action,* since they are inseparable from an actualization that they are implementing. But monads of the second species are not "bare" powers either; they are as much *dispositions,* or *habitus,* inasmuch as they are arranged beneath a vinculum. And those of the third species are tendencies to the degree that what they await on the outside is not a movement toward action, but the "sole suppression of impediment."[36] It is true that the tendency is extinguished in a flash. This seems to contradict the eternity of the monad and the unity of the trajectory. But the instantaneity of the tendency only means that the instant itself is a tendency, not an atom, and that it does not disappear without passing into the other instant: that is why it is up to the tendency, or the inner unity of movement, to be recreated or reconstituted at each and every instant, in accord with a particular mode of eternity. Tendency is not instantaneous unless the instant is a tendency to the future. Tendency dies ceaselessly, but it is only dead in the time during which it dies, that is, instantaneously, in order to be recreated in the following instant.[37] Monads of the third species are flashing, twinkling in a way, through the difference of the illuminators and the illuminated.

Would it not be a misreading to identify derivative forces—whether elastic or plastic—with species of monads? Every monad is an individual, a soul, a substance, a primal force, endowed with a solely inner action, while derivative forces are said to be material, accidental, modal, "states of a substance" that are exerted on bodies.[38] But the issue involves knowing what is meant by state, and if it is reducible to a predicate. If derivative forces cannot be substances by virtue of their recognizable characters, it is impossible to see how they could ever be predicates contained in a substance. We believe that the terms "state" or "modification" must be understood in the sense of predicate, but as a status or a (public) aspect. *Derivative forces are none other than primary forces,* but they differ from them in status or in aspect. Primary forces are monads or substances in themselves or of themselves. Derivative forces are *the same,* but under a vinculum or in the flash of an instant. In one case, they are taken in multitudes and become plastic, while in the other they are taken in a mass and become elastic, because masses are what change at every instant (they do not go from one instant to another without being reconstituted). Derivative force is neither a substance nor a predicate, but several substances, because it exists only in a crowd or in a mass.[39] They might be called mechanical or material forces, but in the sense in which Leibniz also speaks of "material souls," because in the two cases they belong to a body, they are present to a body, an organism or an aggregate.

They are no less really distinct from this body, and they do not act upon it any more than they act upon one another. If they are present to the body, it is *by requisition,* in the name of requisites. And this body to which they belong is not their own, but a body that on its account belongs to a monad removed from its status, from a multitude, and from a mass, in and by itself, as a primary force. The latter is also present to its body, and without acting upon it, but in a different way. It is present *by projection.* Now, in their turn, derivative forces have a body that belongs to them, but insofar as they abandon their status in order to return in and of themselves, each one becomes the primal force that it never ceased to be. We have seen how Whitehead, by way of Leibniz, had developed the public and the private as phenomenological categories.

For Leibniz the public means the status of monads, their requisition, their in-multitude or in-mass, their derivative state. But the private means their in-themselves of-themselves, their points of view, their primitive condition and their projections. In the first aspect they belong to a body that cannot be dissociated from them. In the other aspect, a body belongs to them from which they are indissociable. It is not the same body, but these are the same monads—except for the reasonable ones, whose basis is only private, that have no public status, and that cannot be derived. Or at least, reasonable monads own a "public" status only by private means, as distributive members of a society of spirits for whom God is the monarch.[40]

Leibniz often happens to distinguish three classes of monads: bare entelechies or substantial forms that only have perceptions; animal souls that have memory, feeling, and attention; and, finally, reasonable minds. We have seen the direction that this classification follows. But what relation exists among these "degrees" in the monads given the fact that "some more or less dominate over the others"?[41] It is that the reasonable monads are always dominant and that the animal monads are sometimes dominated and sometimes dominant: *dominant* insofar as they individually own a body, and *dominated* to the extent that they are related massively to another body that a dominant, or a reasonable, monad may or may not possess. Now entelechies are still souls, but are *degenerate*; that is, they are no longer either dominant or dominated since they are tied to a body, in a heap, and at all times. That is why, in the distinction of classes of monads, another must be joined that is coinciding only partially, a distinction of aspects such that a same class (animal souls) can take on several states, sometimes by acceding to the role of dominants and sometimes degenerating.

A real distinction holds between souls and matter and between the body and the soul. One never acts upon the other, but each operates according to its own laws, one by inner spontaneity or action, the other by outer determination or action. In other words, there exists no influence, action, or even infrequent interaction between the two.[42] There is, however, an "ideal action," as when I assign something bodily to be the cause of what happens in a soul (a suffering), or when I assign to a soul the cause of what happens to a body (a movement taken as voluntary). But this ideal action merely implies this: that the soul and the body, each in its fashion or following its own laws, expresses a single and same thing, the World. Therefore we have two really distinct expressions, expressants of the world. One actualizes the world, the other realizes it. In respect to a singular event of the world, in each case an "ideal cause" will be called the best expressant (if we can determine what "the best" means).

Yet we realize that two worlds do not exist especially because there are not three: there exists only one and the same world, conveyed on the one hand by the souls that actualize it and, on the other, by the bodies that realize it; this world does not itself exist outside of its expressants. We are dealing with two cities, a celestial Jerusalem and an earthly one, but with the rooftops and foundations of a same city, and the two floors of a same house. Thus the allotment of the two worlds, the in-itself and the for-ourselves, gives way to an entirely different division of the rooms of the house: private apartments are on top (individual ones) and the common rooms below (the collectives or the totalities). Kant will derive a great deal from Leibniz, most notably the respective autonomy of the two floors; but at the same time Kant turns the upper floor into something empty or inhabited, and he isolates the two floors such that in his own way he refashions two worlds, one now having nothing more than a regulatory value. Leibniz's solution is entirely different.

For Leibniz, the two floors are and will remain inseparable; they are really distinct and yet inseparable by dint of a presence of the upper in the lower. The upper floor is folded over the lower floor. One is not acting upon the other, but one belongs to the other, in a sense of a double belonging. The soul is the principle of life through its presence and not through its action. *Force is presence and not action.* Each soul is inseparable from a body that belongs to it, and is present to it through projection. Every body is inseparable from the souls that belong to it, and that are present to it by requisition. These appurtenances do not constitute an action, and even the souls of the body do not act upon the body to which they belong. But the belonging makes us enter into a strangely intermediate, or rather, original, zone, in which every body acquires individuality of a possessive insofar as it belongs to a private soul, and souls accede to a public status; that is, they are taken in a crowd or in a heap, inasmuch as they belong to a collective body. Is it not in this zone, in this depth or this material fabric between the two levels, that the upper is folded over the lower, such that we can no longer tell where one ends and the other begins, or where the sensible ends and the intelligible begins?[43]

Many different answers can be made to the question, *Where is the fold moving?* As we have seen, it moves not only between essences and existences. It surely billows between the body and the soul, but already between the inorganic and the organic in the sense of bodies, and still between the "species" of monads in the sense of souls. It is an extremely sinuous fold, a zigzag, a primal tie that cannot be located. And there are even regions in this zone where the vinculum is replaced by a looser, instantaneous linkage. The vinculum (or its replacement) only binds souls to souls. But that is what inaugurates the inverse double belonging by which it ties them together. It links to a soul that possesses a body other souls that this body possesses. Having jurisdiction only over souls, the vinculum thus engages a movement going to and from the soul to the body and from bodies to souls (whence the perpetual overlappings of the two floors). If, now, we can find in the body an "ideal cause" for what happens in the soul and, then, find in the soul an ideal cause of what happens to the body, it works only by virtue of this coming-and-going. Furthermore, souls can be said to be material—or forces can be said to be mechanical—not because they act upon matter, but inasmuch as they belong to it. Matter is what continues to make syntheses in accord with its laws of exteriority, while souls make up units of synthesis, under the vinculum or instantaneously, in the flash of an instant. Inversely, bodies can be not only animal but also animated: not because they act upon souls, but to the extent they belong to them; only souls have an inner action that follows their own laws, while bodies are forever "realizing" this action in accord with their own laws.

Thus we see exactly how the two floors are allotted in relation to the world they are conveying. The world is actualized in souls, and is realized in bodies. It is therefore folded over twice, first in the souls that actualize it, and again folded in the bodies that realize it, and each time according to a regime of laws that corresponds to the nature of souls or to the determination of bodies. And between the two folds, in the in-between of the fold, the *Zweifalt,* the bending of the two levels, the zone of inseparability that produces the crease or seam. To state that the bodies realize is not to say that they are real: they become real with respect to what is actual in the soul (inner action or perception). *Something completes or realizes it in the body.* A body is not realized, but what is realized in the body is currently perceived in the soul. The reality of the body is the realization of phenomena in the body. What is realized is the fold of the two levels, the vinculum itself or its replacement.[44] A Leibnizian transcendental philosophy, which bears on the event rather than the phenomenon, replaces Kantian conditioning by means of a double operation of transcendental actualization and realization (animism and materialism).

Chapter 9
The New Harmony

If the Baroque is defined by the fold that goes out to infinity, how can it be recognized in its most simple form? The fold can be recognized first of all in the textile model of the kind implied by garments: fabric or clothing has to free its own folds from its usual subordination to the finite body it covers. If there is an inherently Baroque costume, it is broad, in distending waves, billowing and flaring, surrounding the body with its independent folds, ever-multiplying, never betraying those of the body beneath: a system like *rhingrave-canons* — ample breeches bedecked with ribbons — but also vested doublets, flowing cloaks, enormous flaps, overflowing shirts, everything that forms the great Baroque contribution to clothing of the seventeenth century.[1]

Yet the Baroque is not only projected in its own style of dress. It radiates everywhere, at all times, in the thousand folds of garments that tend to become one with their respective wearers, to exceed their attitudes, to overcome their bodily contradictions, and to make their heads look like those of swimmers bobbing in the waves. We find it in painting, where the autonomy conquered through the folds of clothing that invade the entire surface becomes a simple, but sure, sign of a rupture with Renaissance space (Lanfranc, but already Il Rosso Fiorentino). Zurburán adorns his Christ with a broad, puffy loincloth in the rhingrave style, and his Immaculate Conception wears an immense mantle that is both open and cloaked. And when the folds of clothing spill out of painting, it is Bernini who endows them with sublime form in sculpture, when marble seizes and bears to infinity folds that cannot be explained by the body, but by a spiritual adventure that can set the body ablaze. His is not an art of structures but of textures, as seen in the twenty marble forms he fashions.

This liberation of folds that are no longer merely reproducing the finite body is easily explained: a go-between — or go-betweens — are placed between clothing and the body. These are the Elements. We need not recall that water and its rivers, air and its clouds, earth and its caverns, and light and its fires are themselves infinite folds, as El Greco's painting demonstrates. We have only to consider the manner by which the elements are now going to mediate, distend, and broaden the relation of clothing to the body. It may be that painting needs to leave the frame and become sculpture in order fully to attain these effects. A supernatural breeze, in Johann Joseph Christian's *Saint Jerome,* turns the cloak into a billowing and sinuous ribbon that ends by forming a high crest over the saint. In Bernini's bust of Louis XIV the wind flattens and drapes the upper part of the cloak in the image of the Baroque monarch confronting the elements, in contrast to the "classical" sovereign sculpted by Coysevox. And especially, is it not fire that can alone account for the extraordinary folds of the tunic of Bernini's Saint Theresa? Another order of the fold surges over the Blessed Ludovica Albertoni, this time turning back to a deeply furrowed earth. Finally, water itself is creased, and closely woven, skintight fabric will still be a watery fold that reveals the body far better than nudity: the famous "wet folds" flow over Jean Goujon's bas-reliefs to affect the entire volume, to create the envelope and the inner mold and the spiderweb of the whole body, including the face, as in Spinazzi's and Corradini's late masterpieces, *Faith* and *Modesty.*[2] In every instance folds of clothing acquire an autonomy and a fullness *that are not simply decorative effects.* They convey the intensity of a spiritual force exerted on the body, either to turn it upside down or to stand or raise it up over and again, but in every event to turn it inside out and to mold its inner surfaces.

The great elements thus intervene in many ways: as whatever assures the autonomy of folds of fabric in relation to the finite wearer; as themselves raising the material fold up to infinity; as "derivative forces" that materialize an infinite spiritual force. It is seen not only in the masterworks of the Baroque period, but also in its stereotypes, in its standard formulas or its everyday productions. In fact, if we want to test the definition of the Baroque — the fold to infinity — we cannot be limited to masterpieces alone; we must dig into the everyday recipes or modes of fashion that change a genre. For example, the object of the *still life* is the study of folds. The usual formula of the Baroque still life is: drapery, producing folds of air or heavy clouds; a tablecloth, with maritime or fluvial folds; jewelry that burns with folds of fire; vegetables, mushrooms, or sugared fruits caught in their earthy folds. The painting is so packed with folds that there results a sort of schizophrenic "stuffing." They could not be unraveled without going to infinity and thus extracting its spiritual lesson. It seems that this ambition of covering the canvas with folds is discovered again in modern art, with the *all-over* fold.

The law of extremum of matter entails a maximum of matter for a minimum of extension. Thus, matter tends to flow out of the frame, as it often does in trompe l'oeil compositions, where it extends forward horizontally. Clearly some elements, such as air and fire, tend to move upward, but matter generally always tends to unfold its pleats at great length, in extension. Wölfflin underscored this "multiplication of lines in width," this taste for masses and this "heavy broadening of mass," this fluidity or viscosity that carries everything along an imperceptible slope, in a great conquest of abstraction. "The Gothic underlines the elements of construction, closed frames, airy filling; Baroque underlines matter: either the frame disappears totally, or else it remains, but, despite the rough sketch, it does not suffice to contain the mass that spills over and passes up above."[3]

If the Baroque establishes a total art or a unity of the arts, it does so first of all in extension, each art tending to be prolonged and even to be prolonged into the next art, which exceeds the one before. We have remarked that the Baroque often confines painting to retables, but it does so because the painting exceeds its frame and is realized in polychrome marble sculpture; and sculpture goes beyond itself by being achieved in architecture; and in turn, architecture discovers a frame in the façade, but the frame itself becomes detached from the inside, and establishes relations with the surroundings so as to realize architecture in city planning. From one end of the chain to the other, the painter has become an urban designer. We witness the prodigious development of a continuity in the arts, in breadth or in extension: an interlocking of frames of which each is exceeded by a matter that moves through it.

This extensive unity of the arts forms a universal theater that includes air and earth, and even fire and water. In it sculptures play the role of real characters, and the city a decor in which spectators are themselves painted images or figurines. The sum of the arts becomes the Socius, the public social space inhabited by Baroque dancers. Perhaps we rediscover in modern abstract art a similar taste for a setting "between" two arts, between painting and sculpture, between sculpture and architecture, that seeks to attain a unity of arts as "performance," and to draw the spectator into this very performance (*minimal* art is appropriately named following a law of extremum).[4] Folding and unfolding, wrapping and unwrapping are the constants of this operation, as much now as in the period of the Baroque. This theater of the arts is the living machine of the "new system" as Leibniz describes it, an infinite machine of which every part is a machine, "folded differently and more or less developed."

Even compressed, folded, and enveloped, elements are powers that enlarge and distend the world. It hardly suffices to speak of a succession of limits or of frames, for every frame marks a direction of space that coexists with the others, and each form is linked to unlimited space in all directions at once. It is a broad and floating world, at least on its base, a scene or an immense plateau. But this continuity of the arts, this collective unity in extension, goes out and beyond, toward an entirely different unity that is comprehensive and spiritual, punctual, is indeed *conceptual*: the world as a pyramid or a cone, that joins its broad material base, lost in vapors, to an *apex,* a luminous origin or a point of view. Leibniz's world is one that encounters no difficulty in reconciling full continuity in extension with the most comprehensive and tightly knit individuality.[5] Bernini's Saint Theresa does not find her spiritual unity in the satyr's little arrow, that merely spreads fire, but in the upper origin of the golden rays above.

The law of the cupola, a Baroque figure par excellence, is double: its base is a vast ribbon, at once continuous, mobile, and fluttering, that converges or tends toward a summit as its closed interiority (Lanfranc's cupola, for Sant'Andrea della Valle). The apex of the cone is probably replaced by a rounded point that inserts a concave surface in the place of an acute angle. It is not only in order to soften the point, but also because the latter must still be in an infinitely folded form, bent over a concavity, just as the base is of a matter that can be unwrapped and folded over again. This law of the cupola holds for all sculpture; it shows how all sculpture amounts to architecture, and to city planning. The sculpted body, taken in an infinity of folds of marble cloth, goes back, on the one hand, to a base made of personages or powers, genuine elements of bronze that mark not so much limits as directions of development. On the other, it refers to the upper unity, the obelisk, the monstrance or stucco curtain, from which falls the event that affects it. Thus the derivative forces are allotted to the lower area and primal force to the upper reaches.

It even happens that an organized group that follows the vertical tends to topple in an optical sense, and to place its four powers on a fictive horizontal plan, while the sculpted body appears to be inclined by half of a right angle, in order to acquire height in relation to this base (the tomb of Gregory XV). The world as cone brings into coexistence, for the arts themselves, the highest inner unity and the broadest unity of extension. It is because the former could not exist without the latter. For some time now the idea of an infinite universe has been hypothesized, a universe that has lost all *center* as well as any figure that could be attributed to it; but the essence of the Baroque is that it is given unity, through a projection that emanates from a *summit* as a point of view. For some time the world has been understood on a theatrical basis, as a dream, an illusion—as Harlequin's costume, as Leibniz would say.

But the essence of the Baroque entails neither falling into nor emerging from illusion but rather *realizing* something in illusion itself, or of tying it to a spiritual *presence* that endows its spaces and fragments with a collective unity.[6] The prince of Hamburg, and all of Kleist's characters, are not so much Romantic as they are Baroque heroes. Prey to the giddiness of minute perceptions, they endlessly reach presence in illusion, in vanishment, in swooning, or by converting illusion into presence: Penthesilea-Theresa? The Baroque artists know well that hallucination does not feign presence, but that presence is hallucinatory.

Walter Benjamin made a decisive step forward in our understanding of the Baroque when he showed that allegory was not a failed symbol, or an abstract personification, but a power of figuration entirely different from that of the symbol: the latter combines the eternal and the momentary, nearly at the center of the world, but allegory uncovers nature and history according to the order of time. It produces a history from nature and transforms history into nature in a world that no longer has its center.[7] If we consider the logical relation of a concept to its object, we discover that the linkage can be surpassed in a symbolic and an allegorical way. Sometimes we isolate, purify, or concentrate the object; we cut all its ties to the universe, and thus we raise it up, we put it in contact no longer with its simple concept, but with an Idea that develops this concept morally or esthetically.

Sometimes, on the contrary, the object itself is broadened according to a whole network of natural relations. The object itself overflows its frame in order to enter into a cycle or a series, and now the concept is what is found increasingly compressed, interiorized, wrapped in an instance that can ultimately be called "personal." Such is the world as cone or cupola, whose base, always in extension, no longer relates to a center but tends toward an apex or a summit. The world of allegory is especially projected in devices and emblems; for example, a porcupine is drawn to illustrate the inscription "From near and afar" because the porcupine stands its quills on end when near, but it also shoots them from afar. Devices or emblems have three elements that help us understand the basis of allegory: images or figurations, inscriptions or maxims, and personal signatures or proper names of owners. Seeing, reading, dedicating (or signing).

First, *basic images* tend to break their frames, form a continuous fresco, and join broader cycles (either of other aspects of the same animal, or aspects of other animals) because the pictured form—an animal or whatever—is never an essence or an attribute, as in a symbol, but an event, which is thus related to a history or to a series. Even in the worst of representations, "Fidelity Crowns

Love," we find the charm of allegory, the presence of the event that makes an appeal to an antecedent and a sequel. Second, *inscriptions,* which have to keep a shrouded relation with images, are themselves propositions akin to simple and irreducible acts, which tend toward an inner concept, a truly propositional concept. A judgment is not broken down into a subject and an attribute; rather, the whole proposition is a predicate, as in "From near and afar." Finally, the many inscriptions or propositions — that is, the propositional concept itself — is related to an individual subject who envelops it, and who allows himself or herself to be determined as the owner: allegory offers us Virtues, but these are not virtues in general. They belong to Cardinal Mazarin and figure among his effects. Even the Elements are put forth as belongings pertaining to Louis XIV or to someone else.

The concept becomes a "concetto," or an apex, because it is folded in the individual subject just as in the personal unity that amasses for itself the many propositions, but that also projects them in the images of the cycle or the series.[8] Although practicians and theorists of concettism had rarely been philosophers, they developed rich materials for a new theory of the concept reconciled with the individual. They fashioned the world in the shape of a cone that becomes manifest and is imposed in the Baroque world. This world even appears — in the frontispiece to Emmanuel Tesauro's *La lunette d'Aristote* (1655) — as an allegory of allegory. "At the center of this frontispiece we find a conical anamorphosis, that is, an image projected in the shape of a cone. The maxim 'Omnis in unum' has thus become legible; this deformed moral is written by an allegorical figure who represents Painting. According to Tesauro, Painting would have the power of transforming the real into figured shapes, but the cone is what allows the real to be recovered."[9]

How much Leibniz is part of this world, for which he provides the philosophy it lacks! The principal examples of this philosophy are shown in the transformation of the perceptible object into a series of figures or aspects submitted to a law of continuity; the assignation of events that correspond to these figured aspects, and that are inscribed in propositions; the predication of these propositions to an individual subject that contains their concept, and is defined as an apex or a point of view, a principle of indiscernibles assuring the interiority of the concept and the individual. Leibniz occasionally sums it up in the triad, "scenographies-definitions-points of view."[10] The most important consequence that ensues concerns the new relation of the one and the multiple. Always a unity *of* the multiple, in the objective sense, the one must also have a multiplicity "of" one and a unity "of" the multiple, but now in a subjective sense. Whence the existence of a cycle, "Omnis in unum," such that the relations of one-to-multiple and multiple-to-one are completed by a one-to-one and a multiple-to-multiple, as Michel Serres has shown.[11] This square finds its solution in the distributive

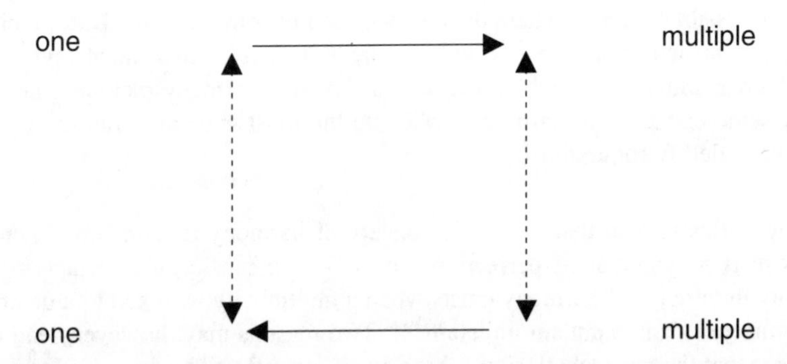

character of the one and an individual unit or Every, and in the collective character of the multiple as a composite unit, a crowd or a mass. The belonging-to and its inversion show how the multiple belongs to a distributive unity, but also how a collective unity pertains to the multiple.

And if it is true that appertaining — belonging to — is the key to allegory, then Leibniz's philosophy must be conceived as the allegory of the world, the signature of the world, but no longer as the symbol of a cosmos in the former manner. In this respect the formula of the *Monadologie,* that "components symbolize with simple units," far from marking a return to the symbol, indicates the transformation or translation of the symbol into allegory. The allegory of all possible worlds appears in the story of the *Théodicée* — which might be called a pyramidal anamorphosis — which combines figures, inscriptions or propositions, individual subjects or points of view with their propositional concepts (thus, "to violate Lucretia" is a proposition-predicate, this Sextus is its subject as a point of view, and the inner concept contained in the point of view is the "Roman Empire," whose allegory Leibniz is thus puts before us).[12] The Baroque introduces a new kind of story in which, following the three traits above, description replaces the object, the concept becomes narrative, and the subject becomes point of view or subject of expression.

The basic unity, the collective unity in extension, the horizontal material process that works by exceeding the frame, the universal theater as a continuity of the arts, tends toward another, now a private, spiritual, and vertical unity of the summit. And a continuity exists not only at the base, but all the way from the base to the summit because it cannot be said where one begins and the other ends. Perhaps Music is at the apex, while the theater that moved in that direction is revealed as opera, carrying all the arts toward this higher unity. Music is in fact not without ambiguity — especially since the Renaissance — because it is at once the intellectual love of an order and a measure beyond the senses, and an affective pleasure that derives from bodily vibrations.[13] Furthermore, it is at once the horizontal melody that endlessly develops all of its lines in extension, and the vertical harmony that establishes the inner spiritual unity or the summit, but it is impossible to know where the one ends and the other begins. But, precisely, Baroque music is what can *extract harmony from melody,* and can always restore the higher unity toward which the arts are moving as many melodic lines: this very same elevation of harmony makes up the most general definition of what can be called Baroque music.

Many critics reckon that Leibniz's concept of harmony remains quite general, almost as a synonym of perfection, and refers to music only metaphorically: "unity in variety," "harmony exists when a multiplicity is linked to a determinable unity," "ad quamdam unitatem."[14] Two reasons may, however, lead us to believe that the musical allusion is both exact and reflective of what is happening in Leibniz's time. The first is that harmony is always thought to be *preestablished,* which specifically implies a very new state of things. And if harmony is so strongly opposed to occasionalism, it is to the degree that occasion plays the role of a sort of counterpoint that still belongs to a melodic and polyphonic conception of music. It is as if Leibniz were attentive to the innovations happening in Baroque music all the while his adversaries remained attached to older conceptions.

The second reason stands because harmony does not relate multiplicity to some kind of unity, but to "a certain unity" that has to offer distinctive or pertinent traits. In effect, in a programmatic text that appears to take up in detail a writing by the neo-Pythagorean Nicolas of Cusa, Leibniz suggests three traits: Existence, Number, and Beauty. Harmonic unity is not that of infinity, but that which allows the existant to be thought of as deriving from infinity; it is a numerical unity insofar as it envelops a multiplicity ("to exist means nothing other than to be harmonic"); it is extended into the affective domain insofar as the senses apprehend it aesthetically, in confusion.[15] The question of harmonic unity becomes that of the "most simple" number, as Nicolas of Cusa states, for whom the number is irrational. But, although Leibniz also happens to relate the irrational to the existant, or to consider the irrational as a number of the existant, he feels he can discover an infinite series of rationals enveloped or hidden in the incommensurable, in a particular form. Now this form in its most simple state is that of the *inverse or reciprocal number,* when any kind of denominator shares a relation with the numerical unity as a numerator:

$$\frac{1}{n} \text{ the inverse of n.}$$ [16]

We can consider the different appearances of the word "harmonic." They constantly refer to inverse or reciprocal numbers: the harmonic triangle of numbers that Leibniz invented to complete Pascal's arithmetical triangle; the harmonic mean that retains the sums of inverses; but also harmonic division, harmonic circulation, and what will later be discovered as the harmonics of a periodic movement.[17]

However simple these examples, they allow us to understand certain traits of the theory of monads, and first of all why we go, not from monads to harmony, but from harmony to monads. Harmony is monadological, but because monads are initially harmonic. The programmatic text states the point clearly: when the infinite Being judges something to be harmonic, it conceives it as a monad, that is, as an intellectual mirror or expression of the world. Thus the monad is the existant par excellence. It is because, conforming to Pythagorean and Platonic traditions, the monad is clearly a number, a numerical unit. For Leibniz the monad is clearly the most "simple" number, that is, the inverse, reciprocal, harmonic number. It is the mirror of the world because it is the inverted image of God, the inverse number of infinity,

$$\frac{1}{\infty}$$

instead of

$$\frac{\infty}{1}$$

(even though sufficient reason is the inverse of infinite identity). God thinks the monad as his own inverse, and the monad conveys the world only because it is harmonic. From then on preestablished harmony will be an original proof of the existence of God, to the degree that the divine formula,

$$\frac{\infty}{1}$$

can be found: it is a proof by the inverse.[18]

The inverse number has special traits: it is infinite or infinitely small, but also, by opposition to the natural number, which is collective, it is individual and distributive. Units taken as numerators are not identical among each other because they receive from their respective denominators a distinctive mark. That is why harmony does not at all confirm the hypothesis of a soul of the world or of a universal spirit but, to the contrary, attests to the irreducibility of "particular breezes" distributed through many pipes; the world's soul implies a confusion that belongs to pantheism, between the number and its inverse, between God and the monad.[19] The mathematician Abraham Robinson has proposed considering

Leibniz's monad as an infinite number quite different from transfinites, as a unit surrounded by a zone of infinitely small numbers that reflect the convergent series of the world.[20] And the point is effectively that of knowing how the unit of a numerator is at once combined with the infinite of the denominator,

$$\left(\frac{1}{\infty}\right)$$

but with a distinctive variable value

$$\left(\frac{1}{n}, \text{ necessarily holding for } \frac{1}{2}, \frac{1}{3}, \text{ or } \frac{1}{4} \ldots\right):$$

each monad expresses the world, but "cannot equally well express everything; for otherwise there would be no distinction between souls."[21] We have seen how Leibniz was able to implement the conciliation on his own account: each monad expresses the world

$$\frac{1}{\infty},$$

but clearly expresses only one particular zone of the world

$$\frac{1}{n}$$

(with *n* in each case having a specific value). Each monad includes the world as an infinite series of infinitely small units, but establishes differential relations and integrations only upon a limited portion of the series, such that the monads themselves enter in an infinite series of inverse numbers. In its own portion of the world or in its clear zone, each monad *thus presents accords,* inasmuch as an "accord" can be called the relation of a state with its differentials, that is, with the differential relations among infinitely small units that are integrated into this state. Whence the double aspect of the accord, insofar as it is the product of an intelligible calculus in an affective state. To hear the noise of the sea is tantamount to striking a chord, and each monad is intrinsically distinguished by its chords.[22] Monads have inverse numbers, and chords are their "inner actions."

Conveying the entire world, all monads include it in the form of an infinity of tiny perceptions, little solicitations, little springs or bursts of force: the presence of the world within me, my being-for the world, is an "anxiousness" (being on the lookout). *I produce an accord* each time I can establish in a sum of infinitely tiny things differential relations that will make possible an integration of the sum — in other words, a clear and distinguished perception. It is a filter, a selection. Now, on the one hand, I am not always capable of doing so at all times, but only in a particular zone that varies with each monad, and such that, for each monad, the greatest part remains in a state of detached dizziness, undifferentiated, unintegrated, in an absence of accord. All that can be said, to the contrary, is that no part of the world can be taken in the zone of *a* determinable monad, and that does not carry accords produced by this monad. But on the other hand especially, the linkages produced by a monad can be very different. Leibniz's writings clearly guarantee a classification of accords.

It would be wrong to seek a direct transposition of musical chords in the way they are developed in the Baroque; and yet it would also be erroneous to conclude with Leibniz's indifference in respect to the musical model: the question, rather, involves analogy. And we know that Leibniz was always trying to bring it to a new rigor. At its highest degree, a monad produces *major and perfect accords*: these occur where the small solicitations of anxiety, far from disappearing, are integrated in a pleasure that can be continued, prolonged, renewed, multiplied; that can proliferate, be reflexive and attractive for other accords, that give us the force to go further and further. This pleasure is a "felicity" specific to the soul; it is harmonic par excellence, and can even be felt in the midst of the worst sufferings, such as in the joy of martyrs. In this sense the perfect accords are not pauses, but, on the contrary, dynamisms, which can pass into other accords, which can attract them, which can reappear, and which can be infinitely combined.[23] In the second place, we speak of minor accords when the differential relations among the infinitely small parts only allow integrations or instable combinations, simple pleasures that are inverted into their contrary, unless they are attracted by a perfect accord. For, in the third place, integration can be made in pain. That is the specific character of *dissonant accords,* the accord here consisting in preparing and resolving dissonance, as in the double operation of Baroque music. The preparation of dissonance means integrating the half-pains that have been accompanying pleasure, in such ways that the next pain will not occur "contrary to all expectations." Thus the dog was musical when it knew how to integrate the almost imperceptible approach of the enemy, the faint hostile odor and the silent raising of the stick just prior to its receiving the blow.[24] The resolution of dissonance is tantamount to displacing pain, to searching for the major accord with which it is consonant, just as the martyr knows how to do it at the highest point and, in that way, not suppress pain itself, but suppress resonance or resentment, by avoiding passivity, by pursuing the effort to suppress causes, even if the martyr's force of opposition is not attained.[25] All of Leibniz's theory of evil is a method to prepare for and to resolve dissonances in a "universal harmony." A counterexample would be furnished by the damned, whose souls produce a dissonance on a unique note, a breath of vengeance or resentment, a hate of God that goes to infinity; but it is still a form of music, a chord—though diabolical—since the damned draw pleasure from their very pain, and especially make possible the infinite progression of perfect accords in the other souls.[26]

Such is the first aspect of harmony, which Leibniz calls *spontaneity.* The monad produces accords that are made and are undone, and yet that have neither beginning nor end, that are transformed each into the other or into themselves, and that tend toward a resolution or a modulation. For Leibniz even the diabolical accord can be transformed. It is because the monad is expression; it expresses the world from its own point of view (and musicians such as Rameau forever underscore the expressive character of the chord). Point of view signifies the selection that each monad exerts on the whole world that it is including, so as to extract accords from one part of the line of infinite inflection that makes up the world.

Thus the monad draws its accords from its own depths. It matters little if for Leibniz the inner selection is still not made through the first harmonics, but through differential relations. In any event the soul sings of itself and is the basis of *self-enjoyment.* The line of the world is inscribed vertically upon the unitary and inner surface of the monad, that then extracts the accords that are superimposed. That is why it can be said that harmony is a vertical writing that conveys the horizontal line of the world: the world is like the book of music that is followed successively or horizontally by singing. But the soul sings of itself because the tablature of the book has been engraved vertically and virtually, "from the beginning of the soul's existence" (the first musical analogy of Leibnizian harmony).[27]

There exists a second aspect of harmony. Monads are not only expressions, but they also express the same world that does not exist outside of its expressions. "All simple substances will always have a harmony among each other because they always represent the same universe"; monads have no reason to be closed; they are not monastic, and they are not the cells of monks because they include the same—solidary but not solitary—world.[28] We can call *concertation* this second aspect. Many musicologists prefer to speak of the "concertant" style instead of Baroque music. This time, insofar as what is expressed is a single and same world, the issue concerns an accord of spontaneities themselves, an accord among accords. But among what, in fact, is there accord? For Leibniz preestablished harmony has many formulas, each in respect to the spot through which the fold is passing: sometimes it is among principles, mechanism, or finality, or even continuity and indiscernibles; at others, between the floors, between Nature and Grace, between the material universe and the soul, or between each soul and its organic body; and at others again, among substances, simple substances and corporal or composite substances. But it is easy to see that in every event harmony is always between souls themselves or monads.

Organic bodies are inseparable from monads taken in crowds, and harmony appears between the inner perceptions of these monads and those of their dominant monad. And even inorganic bodies are inseparable from monads made instantaneous, among which harmony exists.[29] But, if there is a preestablished accord among all these monads that express a single and same world, it is no longer in the way that the accords of the one might be transformed into the accords of another, or that one monad might produce accords in the other. Accords and their transformations are strictly on the inside of every monad; vertical, absolute "forms" that make up the monads remain disconnected, and thus we do not go from one to the other one after the other by resolution or modulation. Following a second and strictly Baroque analogy, Leibniz appeals to the conditions of a choir in which two monads each sing their part without either knowing or hearing that of the other, and yet they are "in perfect accord."[30]

Of what does this concertation consist? We know that the bottom of a monad resembles a lapping of the infinitely little things that it cannot clarify, or from which it cannot extract accords. Its clear region is effectively quite selective and partial, and only constitutes a small zone of the world that it includes. However, since this zone varies from one monad to another, there is nothing obscure in a given monad about which it cannot be said: that it is taken in the clear region of another monad, that it is taken in an accord inscribed on another vertical surface. Thus we have a sort of law of the inverse: there exists for monads that convey obscurely at least one monad that conveys clearly. Since all monads convey the same world, we could state that the one that clearly expresses an event is a *cause*, while the one that expresses it obscurely is an *effect*: the causality of one monad upon another, but a purely "ideal" causality, without real action, since what each of the two monads is expressing only refers to its own spontaneity.

In any event this law of the inverse would have to be less vague; it would have to be established among monads that are better determined. If it is true that each monad is defined by a clear and distinguished zone, this zone is not unchanging, but has a tendency to vary for each monad, in other words, to increase or diminish according to the moment: in every flash of an instant, the privileged zone offers spatial vectors and temporal tensors of augmentation or diminution. A same event can thus be expressed clearly by two monads, but the difference nonetheless subsists at every instant, for the one expresses the event *more* clearly or with *less* confusion than the other, following a vector of augmentation, while the other expresses it following a vector of diminution.

Now we can return to the level of bodies or of corporal substances: when a boat moves ahead on the water, we say the vessel's movement is the cause for the movements of the water that fills the area it has just passed through. That is only an ideal cause, because the proposition, "the prow cuts the water," is clearer than the proposition, "the water pushes the stern." Causality always moves not just from the clear to the obscure, but from the clearer (or more-clear) to the less-clear, the more-confused. It goes from what is more stable to what is less. Such is the requirement of sufficient reason: clear expression is what increases in the cause, but also what diminishes in the effect.[31] When our soul feels pain, we say that what happens in the body is the cause, because it is a clearer and stable expression that pain in the soul can only resemble. Inversely, it is the soul that is the cause when our body makes what is called a voluntary movement. Concertation is the sum of ideal relations of causality. Ideal causality is concertation itself, and therefore is perfectly reconciled with spontaneity: ideal causality goes from the more-clear to the less-clear, but what is clearer in a substance is produced by that substance by virtue of its own spontaneity, and the same holds for the less-clear in the other, when the other substance produces it by virtue of its own.[32]

The two aspects of harmony are perfectly linked. Spontaneity is tantamount to the production of each monad's inner accords on its absolute surface. Concertation amounts to the correspondence according to which *there can be no major and perfect accord in a monad unless there is a minor or dissonant accord in another,* and inversely. All combinations are possible without there ever being same accord in two monads. Each monad spontaneously produces its accords, but in correspondence with those of the other. Spontaneity is the inner or sufficient reason applied to monads. And concertation is this same reason applied to spatiotemporal relations that follow from the monads. If space-time is not an empty area, but the order of coexistence and the succession of monads themselves, the order has to be marked out, oriented, vectored; in the instance of each monad movement has to go from the more-clear monad to the less-clear monad, or from the perfected accord to the less-perfected accord, for the clearest or the most perfected is reason itself. In the expression "preestablished harmony," "preestablished" is no less important than "harmony." Harmony is twice preestablished: by virtue of each expression, of each expressant that owes only to its own spontaneity or interiority, and by virtue of the common expression that establishes the concert of all these expressive spontaneities. It is as if Leibniz were delivering us an important message about communication: don't complain about not having enough communication, for there is always plenty of it. Communication seems to be of a constant and preestablished quantity in the world, akin to a sufficient reason.

The most general given has vertical harmony in accords in a position subordinate to horizontal melody, to the horizontal lines of melody. These lines do not disappear, obviously, but they do submit to a harmonic principle. It is true that this subordination implies something other than preestablished harmony: it is the vinculum that acts as a "continuous bass" and prepares a tonality. Thus it can be stated that each dominant monad has a vinculum, a continuous bass, as well as a tonality that carries its inner chords. But, as we have seen, under every vinculum infinities of "dominated" monads begin to group into clusters that can organize material aggregates (these aggregates can move from one tonality to another, from one vinculum to another, while reorganizing, or even reproducing themselves from one instant to another). In short, the continuous bass does not impose a harmonic law upon the lines of polyphony without having the melody retrieve a new freedom and unity, or a flux.

In effect, in polyphony lines were as if screwed down by points, and as if counterpoint only affirmed bi-univocal correspondences among points on diverse lines: Malebranche's occasionalism remains precisely a philosophical polyphony, in which occasion plays the role of counterpoint, in a perpetual miracle or a constant intervention of God. In the new system, on the contrary, melody, freed of this modal counterpoint, gains a force of variation that consists in introducing all kinds of foreign elements in the realization of the accord (delays, interweavings, appoggiaturas, etc., whence ensues a new tonal or "luxuriant" counterpoint), but also a force of continuity that will develop a unique motif, even across eventual tonal diversities ("continuo homophone").[33] At its limit the material universe accedes to a unity in horizontal and collective extension, where melodies of development themselves enter into relations of counterpoint, each spilling over its frame and becoming the motif of another such that all of Nature becomes an immense melody and flow of bodies.[34] And this collective unity in extension does not contradict the other unity, the subjective, conceptual, spiritual, harmonic, and distributive unity.

To the contrary, the former *depends upon* the latter by furnishing it with a body, exactly in the way the monad requires a body and organs, without which it would have no inkling of Nature. The "conformity of the senses" (melody) indicates where I recognize harmony in the real.[35] There is not only harmony in harmony, but harmony between harmony and melody. In this sense harmony goes from the soul to the body, from the intelligible to the sensible, and extends into the sensible. Rameau will say that it goes by principle and by instinct. When the Baroque house becomes musical, the upper floor includes vertical harmonic monads, inner accords that each one produces in its respective chamber, and the correspondence or concertation of these accords; the lower floor stretches out along an infinity of horizontal melodic lines drawn into each other, where at the same time it embroiders and develops its sensible variations and continuity. Yet, because the upper floor is folded over the lower floor, following tonality, the accords are realized. It is in melody that harmony is achieved.

It seems difficult not to be moved by the totality of exact analogies between Leibnizian harmony and the harmony on which, at the same time, Baroque music is based. Even the concert of monads, which Leibniz invokes in his second analogy, not only brings in harmony but also a state of inexplicable melody lacking any Baroque reference. Such are the principal traits by which musicologists have been able to define a Baroque music: music as expressive representation, expression here referring to feeling as if to an affect of accord (for example, an unprepared dissonance, an expression of despair and of fury); vertical harmony, the first in line in respect to horizontal melody, insofar as it is in chords, but no longer in intervals, and treats dissonance as a function of chords themselves; the concertant style that moves by contrasts among voices, instruments or groups of different density; melody and counterpoint that change their nature (luxuriant counterpoint and continuo homophone); continuous bass, preparing or consolidating a tonality that the accords include and in which they are resolved, but also submitting the melodic lines to the harmonic principle.[36]

Every one of these traits that does not fail to attest to a "preestablishment" of harmony also has its analogy in Leibnizian harmony. Leibniz loves to compare diverse conceptions of the body-and-soul to modes of correspondence between two clocks that include influx, chance, or even harmony (that he judges to be superior). These too are the three "ages" of music, which go from monody, to unison, to harmonic polyphony or counterpoint in accords — in other words, the Baroque.

We could hardly be satisfied in establishing binary relations between the text and music that would inevitably be arbitrary. How to fold the text so that it can be enveloped in music? This problem of expression is not fundamental to opera alone. Baroque musicians count among the first, perhaps, to propose a systematic answer: accords are what determine the affective states that conform to the text, and that furnish voices with the necessary melodic inflections. Whence Leibniz's idea that our souls sing of themselves — spontaneously, in chords — while our eyes read the text and our voices follow the melody. The text is folded according to the accords, and harmony is what envelops the text. The same expressive problem will animate music endlessly, from Wagner to Debussy and now up to Cage, Boulez, Stockhausen, and Berio.

The issue is not one of relation, but of "fold-in," or of "fold according to fold." What has happened to cause the answer — or rather, the quite diverse range of answers — to change since the Baroque musicians? Solutions no longer pass through accords. It is because the conditions of the problem itself have changed: we have a new Baroque and a neo-Leibnizianism. The same construction of the point of view over the city continues to be developed, but now it is neither the same point of view nor the same city, now that both the figure and the ground are in movement in space.[37] Something has changed in the situation of monads, between the former model, the closed chapel with imperceptible openings, and the new model invoked by Tony Smith, the sealed car speeding down the dark highway. In summary we can attribute what has changed to two principal variables.

Leibniz's monads submit to two conditions, one of closure and the other of selection. On the one hand, they include an entire world that does not exist outside of them; on the other, this world takes for granted a first selection, of convergence, since it is distinguished from other possible but divergent worlds, excluded by the monads in question; and it carries with it a second selection of consonance, because each monad in question will fashion itself a clear zone of expression in the world that it includes (this is the second selection that is made by means of differential relations or adjacent harmonics). Now the selection is what tends to be disappearing, first of all and in every way. If harmonics lose all privilege of rank (or relations, all privilege of order), not only are dissonances excused from being "resolved," divergences can be affirmed, in series that escape the diatonic scale where all tonality dissolves. But when the monad is in tune with divergent series that belong to incompossible monads, then the other condition is what disappears: it could be said that the monad, astraddle over several worlds, is kept half open as if by a pair of pliers.

To the degree that the world is now made up of divergent series (the chaosmos), or that crapshooting replaces the game of Plenitude, the monad is now unable to contain the entire world as if in a closed circle that can be modified by projection. It now opens on a trajectory or a spiral in expansion that moves further and further away from a center. A vertical harmonic can no longer be distinguished from a horizontal harmonic, just like the private condition of a dominant monad that produces its own accords in itself, and the public condition of monads in a crowd that follow lines of melody. The two begin to fuse on a sort of diagonal, where the monads penetrate each other, are modified, inseparable from the groups of prehension that carry them along and make up as many transitory captures.

The question always entails living in the world, but Stockhausen's musical habitat or Dubuffet's plastic habitat do not allow the differences of inside and outside, of public and private, to survive. They identify variation and trajectory, and overtake monadology with a "nomadology." Music has stayed at home; what has changed now is the organization of the home and its nature. We are all still Leibnizian, although accords no longer convey our world or our text. We are discovering new ways of folding, akin to new envelopments, but we all remain Leibnizan because what always matters is folding, unfolding, refolding.

Notes

A Note on References

When referring to Leibniz and other works, Deleuze can appear cryptic or allusive. To make his references clear for readers of English, I have arranged the bibliographical materials in an order that can be conceived as being arranged in three tiers.

The first includes the works of Leibniz to which Deleuze refers. We know that Leibniz developed his philosophy in fragments, in private correspondence, in transit, and in the toss of circumstance between the end of the seventeenth century and the early years of the Enlightenment; that he worked with ease in Latin, German, and French; and that he never intended to finish a complete work. Further, the heritage of his writing is affected by the tumultuous relations that France and Germany have experienced since the eighteenth century. Wars have interrupted completion of any final critical edition. For Deleuze, the history and condition of writing bear resemblance to fragmentary activity that characterizes the oeuvre of Balzac and Proust, for whom, as he explained in *Proust et les signes* ([Paris: PUF, 1979 reed.], 197) a "work" amounts to an *effect* that exceeds the material totality of a body.

Readers of Leibniz are thus required to consult a variety of editions published over the last two centuries. Deleuze uses many of them, but he ostensibly prefers to consult, where possible, current and readily available reprints. For French readers these include:

Nouveaux essais sur l'entendement humain. Ed. Jacques Brunschwig. Paris: Garnier/Flammarion, 1966.

Essais de théodicée sur la bonté de Dieu, la liberté de l'homme et l'origine du mal . . . suivi de la Monadologie. Ed. Jacques Brunschwig. Paris: Garnier/Flammarion, 1969.

Deleuze often cites the number of the paragraph (indicated by §) to allow for cross-reference with other editions. French editions of Leibniz often include numerical ciphers for each movement or paragraph. Some English translations (such as *New Essays on Human Understanding* and the *Monadology*) are thus equipped, but others are not (*On Liberty, The Correspondence with Arnauld,* etc.). Wherever Deleuze quotes the principal texts of Leibniz, for sake of clarity and thoroughness I refer to the most current and definitive English versions. I have chosen G. H. R. Parkinson's carefully selected anthology of Leibniz's philosophical writings to serve as an accompaniment to *The Fold*. It is easily obtained and modestly priced. I also refer to H. T. Mason's concise translation of the *Leibniz/Arnauld Correspondence,* as well as Peter Remnant and Jonathan Bennett's translation of the *New Essays on Human Understanding*. Both works are prepared with equal precision and elegance. The translators provide indications of volume, book, page, and paragraph that concur with Deleuze's French editions. Whenever Deleuze cites texts that can be located in these editions, I refer to them and cite their English translations. The following abbreviations and sources are used:

Mason	H. T. Mason, ed. and trans., *The Leibniz/Arnauld Correspondence*. New York: Garland, 1985.
Parkinson	G. H. R. Parkinson, ed., and trans. (with Mary Morris), *Gottfried Wilhelm Leibniz: Philosophical Writings*. London: J. M. Dent and Sons (Everyman Library), 1973 (1990 reprint).
Remnant/Bennett	Peter Remnant and Jonathan Bennett, ed. and trans., *Leibniz: New Essays on Human Understanding*. Cambridge: Cambridge University Press, 1981.

In each instance where material is quoted, the appropriate abbreviation and page number can be found in the notes. They follow the citation and are set between brackets.

The second tier involves works of Leibniz that are not easily correlated with English translations. *La théodicée,* for example, is often abridged or fragmented in English anthologies. Other important pieces — the letters to Des Bosses or Lady Masham, *The Clarification of Difficulties that Bayle found in the New System,* etc. — are available in works that constitute the primary bibliography of Leibniz's writings. Deleuze refers to them often and consistently. They are as follows:

GPh	*Die philosophischen Schriften von G. W. Leibniz.* Ed. C. I. Gerhardt. 7 vols. Berlin, 1875–90.
C	Louis Couturat, ed., *Opuscules et fragments inédits de Leibniz.* Paris, 1903.
Dutens	Louis Dutens, ed., *Gothofredi Guillelmi Leibnitii . . . opera omnia.* 6 vols. Geneva, 1768.
GM	*Leibnizens mathematische Schriften.* 7 vols. Berlin and Halle, 1849–63.
F	Foucher de Careil, ed., *Nouvelles lettres et opuscules inédits de Leibniz.* Paris: 1857–75.
J	I. Jagodinsky, ed., *Leibnitiana: Elementa philosophiae arcanae de summa rerum.* Kazan, 1913.
P	Yvan Belaval, ed., *Leibniz: Profession de foi du philosophe.* Paris: Vrin, 1961.

I have directly translated Deleuze's quotations or translations of material taken from these texts. Because no handy edition of *La théodicée* is available in English (except for E. M. Huggard's translation, London, 1952), I have taken the liberty of translating Deleuze's quotations from his French copies. Other materials from other sources, both primary and secondary, in French, or in non-English sources, are translated directly from Deleuze's citations. Wherever Deleuze refers to French translations of works in English, I cite the original. Rather than retranslating the titles of many of Leibniz's works back into English, because they are clear, I have retained them in the way he notes them. The French titles convey well, it seems, the spirit of Deleuze's relation with Leibniz.

Finally, on a third tier, are placed other significant materials that belong to contemporary sources. These often include the fine arts, mathematics, logic, literature, military strategy, music, and philosophy. Deleuze refers to many works that circulate in these contexts — often in Parisian editions, gallery catalogues, brochures, or in works pertaining to the French academic system — but are not easily located in libraries elsewhere. I have attempted to provide additional information concerning date and place of the publication of these works. Some items have not been located in American libraries and, therefore, must be taken on faith. For these and other inconsistencies in the notes below, the translator begs the reader's indulgence and generosity.

Translator's Foreword: A Plea for Leibniz

1. *The Art of the West,* 2 vols. (London: Phaidon, 1970 reprint), first appeared in 1933, without its now-familiar title, as the third part of a work entitled *Histoire du moyen age,* whose first two sections included, first, economic and social history (by Henri Pirenne) and, second, intellectual, moral, and literary movements (by Gustave Cohen). Focillon's section went under the title of "Les mouvements artistiques." The compendium was the eighth volume of an *Histoire générale* under the direction of Gustave Glotz (Paris: PUF). *Vie des formes* was published in 1934 (Paris: PUF). Charles Beecher Hogan and George Kubler's translation, *The Life of Forms in Art,* appeared in 1942 (New Haven: Yale University Press).

2. The development of the historical "grid" of literature, or the adjacent lists of dates and significant events in the life of given authors, the concurrent political spheres, and in international history parallels that of the educational mission of "surveillance" that Michel Foucault studies in *Surveiller et punir* (Paris: Gallimard, 1975). For Foucault a key term is *quadrillage,* or gridding; its meaning, developed through a history of incarceration, shares traits with traditions in the pedagogy of literature, art, and philosophy. See also note 11 below.

3. Included are profusions of moving shapes, the loss of function, search for picturesque effect, the mix of architecture, and a proclivity for anecdote. Sculpture of the twelfth century, he notes, dessicates "through an excess of confidence in formulas, through a necessary consequence of *serial production,* and industrial fabrication" (*Histoire générale,* 514, stress added). For Focillon, what would be mistaken as impoverishment is, on the contrary, a sign of living form (515).

4. *The Life of Forms in Art,* 15.

5. Michel de Certeau, "Mystique," in *Encyclopaedia universalis,* vol. 12 (Paris: Encyclopaedia Universalis, 1985), 873–78. [English translation by Marsanne Brammer, forthcoming in *Diacritics*].

6. Gilles Deleuze, *Proust et les signes* (Paris: PUF, 1979 reedition), 185 (Deleuze's emphasis).

7. *Qu'est-ce que la philosophie? [What is Philosophy?]* (Paris: Minuit, 1991), 91.

8. A more complete explanation of Deleuze's theory of music is found in Ronald Bogue, "Rhizomusicology," *Substance,* 20:3 (1991), 89–101. The entire issue, edited by Charles Stivale, offers an excellent introduction and overview of Deleuze and Guattari's writings of the last decade. It also deals extensively with *A Thousand Plateaus,* a work that inspires much of the work on the fold.

9. David Harvey calls the idealization of nature and invention of the world-picture (in the aftermath of Descartes) crucial for the beginnings of compression of time and space in our time, in *The Condition of Postmodernity* (London: Blackwell, 1989). It could be said that the "deterritorializing" effects of monadic philosophy are also apt to be co-opted. Deleuze notes that the Baroque has been linked with capitalism because it is associated with "a crisis of property, a crisis that appears at once with the growth of new machines in the social field and the discovery of new living beings in the organism" (p. 110).

10. *Qu'est-ce que la philosophie,* 95–96.

11. As Samuel Y. Edgerton, Jr., notes about the quincunx in designs of the body and the world, in "From Mental Matrix to Mappamundi to Christian Empire: The Heritage of Ptolemaic

Cartography in the Renaissance," in David Woodward, ed., *Art and Cartography: Six Historical Essays* (Chicago: University of Chicago Press, 1987), 12–13.

12. *The Life of Forms in Art,* 15.

1. The Pleats of Matter

1. *Système nouveau de la Nature et de la communication des substances,* § 7 [Parkinson, 119].

2. *Monadologie,* § 61 [Parkinson, 189]. And *Principes de la Nature et de la Grâce fondés en raison,* § 13 [Parkinson, 201].

3. *De la liberté* (*Nouvelles lettres et opuscules*) [Parkinson, 112–14].

4. On cryptography as an "art of inventing the key to an enveloped thing," see Fragment, *Un livre sur l'art combinatoire . . .* (*C, Opuscules*). And the *Nouveaux essais sur l'entendement humain,* IV, chap. 17, § 8: the fold of Nature and the "summaries."

5. *Nouveaux essais,* II, chap. 12, § 1. In this book Leibniz "refashions" Locke's *Essays*; thus the camera obscura was clearly invoked by Locke, but its curtains were not.

6. See Wölfflin, *Renaissance et Baroque,* trans. Guy Ballangé (Paris: Poche, 1967).

7. *Nouveaux essais,* preface [Remnant/Bennett, 59].

8. Letter to Des Billettes, December 1696 (GPh, VII, 452).

9. Table de définitions (C, 486). And *Nouveaux essais,* II, chap. 23, § 23.

10. *Pacidus Philalethi* (C, 614–15).

11. Letter to Des Billettes, 453.

12. *Protogaea* (Dutens II). On veins and conical forms, see chap. 8.

13. William Gibbs will develop this theme. Leibniz supposes that God does not trace "the first lineaments of the still-tender globe" without producing "something analogous to the structure of the animal or plant" (*Protogaea,* chap. 8).

14. Letter to Des Billettes; and his Letter to Bayle, December 1698 (GPh, III, 57). See Gueroult, *Dynamique et métaphysique leibniziennes* (Paris: Les Belles Lettres, 1934), 32: "How can we conceive the *motivating force* if we fail to suppose that the body is composite, and that thus it can be shrunk in flushing out of its pores the subtle particles of matter that penetrate it, and that in turn this more refined matter must be capable of expulsing from its pores another, even more refined matter, etc., ad infinitum?"

15. On elasticity and detonation, which inspire the concept that Willis (1621–1675) proposes for reflexivity, and on how this model differs from that of Descartes, see Georges Canguilhem, *La formation du concept de réflexe aux XVIIe et au XVIIIe siècles* (Paris: PUF,), 60–67.

16. Letter to Lady Masham, July 1705 (GPh, III, 368). And *Considérations sur les principes de vie et sur la natures plastiques* (GPh, VI, 544 and 553): principles of life are immaterial, but "plastic faculties" are not. See *Protogaea,* chap. 28, on fossils.

17. See *Système nouveau de la Nature,* § 10. *Monadologie,* § 64: "The tooth of a metal wheel has parts or fragments which as far as we are concerned are not artificial and which have about them nothing of the character of a machine, in relation to the use for which the wheel was intended. But machines of nature, that is to say, living bodies, are still machines in the least of their parts *ad infinitum*" [Parkinson, 189]. And the letter to Lady Masham, 374: "Plastic force is in the machine."

18. On Leibniz's technological conception, its modernity, and its opposition to Descartes, see Michel Serres, *Le système de Leibniz,* 2 (Paris: Seuil, 1982), 491–510, 621 (2d ed.).

19. Letter to Arnauld, April 1687 (GPh, II, 99) [Mason, 125].

20. *Nouveaux essais,* III, chap. 6, § 23 [Remnant/Bennett, 314–17]. Consequently, in *Palingénésie philosophique,* Bonnet wrongly reproaches his teacher, Leibniz, for holding to variations of size.

21. *Monadologie,* § 67 [Parkinson, 190].

22. See Serres, I, 371.

23. Letter to Arnauld, September 1687 [Mason, 144 (October 9, 1687)].

24. In the name of epigenesis Albert Dalcq can state, "A caudal fin can be obtained from a system of action and reaction . . . where nothing caudal is a prior," in *L'oeuf et son dynamisme organisateur* (Paris: Albin Michel, 1941), 194.

25. Geoffroy Saint-Hilaire, a partisan of epigenesis, remains one of the greatest philosophers of organic folding. Given the modifications of a same Animal, he esteems that one can still move from one to the other by way of folding (a unity of the plan of composition). If a vertebrate is folded "in such a fashion that the two parts of its spinal column are turned toward each other, its head goes toward its feet, the lower area toward the neck, and its viscera arranged as they are in a cephalopod." This is what prompts Baër's opposition in the very name of epigenesis, and already the anger of Cuvier, who posits the diversity of axes of development or of plans of organization (see Geoffroy, *Principes de philosophie zoologique*). Despite his monism, in every event Geoffroy can be called Leibnizian in other respects: he explains the organism in terms of a material force that does not change the nature of bodies, but adds to them new forms and new relations. It is an impulsive or tractive electric force in the style of Kepler. It can refold elastic fluids, and it operates in very short distances in the "world of details" or in infinitely small areas, no longer by the summation of homogenous parts, but by the confrontation of homologous parts (*Notions synthétiques et historiques de philosophie naturelle*).

26. Letter to Des Bosses, March 1706, in Christiane Frémont, *L'être et la relation* (Paris: Vrin, 1981). And the letter to Arnauld, April 1687: "As regards an insect which one cuts in two, the two parts do not necessarily have to remain animate, although a certain movement remains in them. At least the soul of the whole insect will remain only in one part. . . . It will also remain after the destruction of the insect in a certain part that is still alive, which will always be as small as is necessary to be sheltered from whoever tears or scatters the body of this insect" [Mason, 125–26].

27. Letter to Lady Masham, June 1704 (357).

28. *Principes de la Nature et de la Grâce,* § 4: "infinite degrees" in souls [Parkinson, 196], and in the *Système nouveau de la Nature,* § 11.

29. *Monadologie,* § 74 [Parkinson, 191].

30. *La cause de Dieu plaidée par sa justice,* §§ 81–85. And the *Theodicée,* § 91, 397.

31. *Eclaircissement des difficultés que M. Bayle a trouvées dans le système nouveau . . .* (GPh, IV, 544, 558). Gueroult has shown how external determinism and internal spontaneity are already perfectly reconciled in respect to physical bodies ("elasticity is now considered as the expression of the first spontaneity, of the active primitive force," 203–7 and 163).

32. *Système nouveau de la Nature,* § 18; *De la réforme de la philosophie première et de la notion de substance.*

2. The Folds in the Soul

1. Paul Klee, *Théorie de l'art moderne* (Paris: Gonthier, 1963), 73.

2. Letter to Arnauld, September 1687 (GPh, II, 119) [Mason, 152 (October 9, 1687)].

3. Bernard Cache, *L'ameublement du territoire* (forthcoming). Inspired by geography, architecture, and the decorative arts, in my view this book seems essential for any theory of the fold.

4. On the relation between catastrophe theory and an organic morphogenesis, see René Thom, *Morphologie et imaginaire,* Circé 8–9, and the presentation of the seven singularities or catastrophe-events, (Paris: Lettres modernes, 1978) 130.

5. [Homothesis (*homothétie*), a term belonging to geometry, indicates a similarity of form and position between two figures in respect to a given point. Homothesis is said to be *direct* if

two figures are in the same direction at a given point, and *inverse* when on either side of that point. The given point is the center of homothesis.—Trans.]

6. Mandelbrot, *Fractals: Form, Chance, and Dimension* (San Francisco: W. H. Freeman, 1977). On the porous or cavernous qualities, see Jean Perrin's text, cited by Mandelbrot, pp. 4–9. From different points of view, both Mandelbrot and Thom are strongly influenced by Leibniz.

7. Hocquenghem and Scherer thus describe the Baroque spiral, according to Permozer's statue, in the "Apotheosis of Prince Eugene" (1718–1721), in *L'âme atomique* (Paris: Albin Michel, 1986), 196–97.

8. From inflection to turbulence, see Mandelbrot, chap. 8, and Cache, who emphasizes the phenomena of differences.

9. *Justification du calcul des infinitésimales par celui de l'algèbre ordinaire,* GM, IV, 104.

10. Michel Serres, I, 197. Leibniz's two principal texts are GM, V: *D'une ligne issue de lignes* and *Nouvelle application du calcul différentiel* ("by comparing the curves of a series among each other, or by considering the crossing of one curve on another curve, certain coefficients are quite constant or permanent, that do not remain solely on one but on all the curves of the series, the others being variable. And clearly, so that the law of the series of curvatures can be given, a unique variability has to subsist in the coefficients, to such a point that, if several variables appear for all the curves in a principal equation explaining their common nature, other accessory equations are needed to express the dependency of variable coefficients, by which all the variables could be removed from the principal equation, except one," tr. Jean Peyroux, *Oeuvre mathématique de Leibniz autre que le calcul infinitésimal* (Paris: Blanchard, 1986).

11. Gilbert Simondon, *L'individu et sa genèse physico-biologique* (Paris: PUF, 1964), 41–42.

12. On anamorphosis see the *Theodicée,* § 147; *Nouveaux essais,* II, chap. 29, § 8 [Remnant/Bennett, 257–58]. [*Anamorphosis* pertains to distorted projections of images that are seen correctly from an oblique point of view or in reflection on a mirror placed at an indicated area. Anamorphic perspective characterizes the celebrated death's head that Hans Holbein inserts in a diagonal fashion in *The Ambassadors.* It became, as Jurgis Baltrušaitis has noted, a field of experiment in perspective in early seventeenth-century France, and a mode of visual trickery that can be seen in pictures that constitute "parlor games" in French society of the same period, in *Anamorphoses* (Paris: Musée des Arts Decoratifs, 1976). Anamorphosis is synonymous with Baroque art and literature.—Trans.]

13. Following Russell, Gueroult has often insisted on a so-called contradiction of continuity-indiscernibles (cf. *Descartes selon l'ordre des raisons,* vol. 1 [Paris: Aubier] 284). Even more curiously, elsewhere he takes up Russell's thesis, according to which Leibniz would have sketched the notion of distance as a relation indivisible, irreducible to length and measure: space is made of relations of distance, while extension consists of measurable sizes. Thus this thesis assures a perfect conciliation of points of view with the continuous (see Gueroult, "Espace, point et vide chez Leibniz," *Revue philosophique,* 1946, and already Russell himself, in *The Philosophy of Leibniz* (London: Allen and Unwin, 1937), 124–30.

14. *Entretien de Philarète et d'Ariste*: "Thus extension, *when it is the attribute of Space,* is the diffusion or continuation of the situation or locality, as the extension of the body is the diffusion of the antitype or of materiality" (GPh, VI, 585).

15. On the equation with an ambiguous sign that includes the different cases of the conic section, see *De la méthode de l'universalité,* C, 97 sq.

16. See René Taton, *L'oeuvre mathématique de Desargues* (Paris: Vrin), 110. Yvonne Toros comments on Desargues's notion of involution, not only in respect to Leibniz but also to Spinoza, by which she proves all the interest that he had for the theory of conic sections. New light is cast on Spinozism and "parallelism" (*L'optique de Spinoza,* forthcoming).

17. Serres, I, 156–63; II, 665–67, 690–93.

18. Letter to Princess Sophie, June 1700 (GPh, VII, 554). The *Justification du calcul* would even show point A contained and held the relation

$$\frac{c}{e}$$

19. This is how Leibniz distinguishes: virtuality or idea; modification, disposition, or habit, which resembles the act of force in the soul; the tendency to action and action itself as the ultimate actualization of the act. One could say, following the sculptural metaphor: the figure of Hercules; the veins of the marble; labor exerted on the marble to bring out these veins. See the preface and part II, chap. 1, § 2 ("beyond disposition, there is a tendency to action . . .") in the *Nouveaux essais*.

20. *Système nouveau de la Nature,* § 11 [Parkinson, 120–21]. On the scholastic conceptions of the point, and of the different cases that inspire Leibniz, see Boehm, *Le vinculum substantiale chez Leibniz* (Paris: Vrin, 1962), 62–81.

21. Letter to Lady Masham, June 1704: "The soul must be placed in the body where its point of view is located, according to which the soul presently represents the universe to itself. . . . To wish for something more and to enclose souls within the dimensions is to desire to imagine souls as bodies" (GPh, III, 357).

22. See Proclus, *Eléments de théologie* (Paris: Aubier, n.d.), 204, § 21.

23. Giordano Bruno, *De triplici minimo.* The theory of "complicatio" had already been developed by Nicolas of Cusa. See Maurice de Gandillac, *La philosophie de Nicolas de Cues* (Paris: Aubier-Montaigne, 1941).

24. *Considérations sur la doctrine d'un esprit universel* (GPh, VI). That is why Leibniz does not take up the term "complicatio" despite the attraction he has for words and notions that translate the fold.

25. Cf. Plotinus's concise sentence: "We multiply the city without its founding this operation" (*Enneades,* VI, 6, 2).

26. *Discours de métaphysique,* § 15 and 16 [Parkinson, 146]. *Monadologie,* § 60, 61, 83 ("each mind being as it were a little divinity in its own department") [Parkinson, 193].

27. *Monadologie,* § 37 [Parkinson, 185]. On the "law of curvatures" see *Eclaircissement des difficultés que M. Bayle a trouvées dans le système nouveau* (GPh, IV, 544): surely we can say that the law of seriality is enveloped in the soul in confusion; but what is in the soul in this sense is less the law than the "means of executing it."

28. Heidegger: "As monad, *Dasein* does not require a window to see what is outside, not, as Leibniz believes, because everything that is is already accessible inside the box . . . but because the monad, the *Dasein,* is already outside, in conformity with its own being," in *Les problèmes fondamentaux de la phénoménologie* (Paris: Gallimard, 1985), 36. Merleau-Ponty has a much stronger understanding of Leibniz when he merely posits that "our soul does not have windows, which means *In der Welt Sein* . . ." in *Le visible et l'invisible* (Paris: Gallimard, 1966), 264 and 276. As of *La phénoménologie de la perception* Merleau-Ponty invoked the fold in order to oppose it to Sartrian holes; and in *Le visible et l'invisible,* his task is one of interpreting the Heideggerian fold as a "chiasm or interlace" between the visible [*visible*] and the seeing [*voyant*].

3. What Is Baroque?

1. *Monadologie,* § 7 [Parkinson, 179]; Letter to Princess Sophie, June 1700 (GPh, VII, 554).

2. Leo Steinberg, "The Flatbed Plan of the Painting," in *Other Criteria* (New York: Oxford University Press, 1972).

3. For the Baroque city and the importance of the urban world in the Baroque, see Lewis Mumford, *The City in History* (New York, 1961), and Severo Sarduy, "Le Caravage, la ville bourgeoise," in *Barroco,* trans. Jacques Henric (Paris: Seuil, 1975), 61–66.

4. See Gravesande's "Use of the camera obscura" that Sarah Kofman takes up in her *Camera obscura* (Paris: Galilée, 1978), 79–97.

5. Michel Serres, II, 762.

6. Jean Rousset, *La littérature de l'âge baroque en France* (Paris: Corti, 1953), 168–71. And, by the same author, *L'intérieur et l'extérieur* (Paris: Corti, 1968).

7. Régis Debray, "Le Tintoret ou le sentiment panique de la vie," in *Eloges* (Paris: Gallimard, 1986), 13–57. (Debray takes Sartre to task for having seen only the lower level in Tintoretto.) Also Jean Paris, *L'espace et le regard* (Paris: Seuil, 1963), on the analysis of "ascensional space" in El Greco ("like Cartesian divers, men thus balance earthly gravity and divine attraction"), 226–28.

8. André Scala has studied this in *La genèse du pli chez Heidegger* (forthcoming). The notion springs up between 1946 and 1953, especially in "Moira," in *Essais et conférences* (Paris: Gallimard, 1980); it follows the *entre-deux* or the incident, the *Zwischen-fall,* that had rather marked a thing fallen. This is the "Greek" fold, especially related to Parmenides. Scala notes one of Riezler's comments that, as of 1933, he found in Parmenides "a pleat of being," "a fold of one in being and non-being, the two being narrowly stretched into each other" (*Faltung*); when Kurt Goldstein discovers that he is Parmenidian when he comprehends the living, appeals to Riezler [*La structure de l'organisme* (Paris: Gallimard), 325–29]. According to Scala another source puts in play the stakes of new perspective, and the projective method that already appeared in Dürer, in the name of "zweifalten cubum." Cf. Erwin Panofsky on Dürer's treatment of solids: "Instead of representing the solids in perspective or stereographic images, he devised the apparently original and, if one may say so, proto-topological method of developing them on the plane surface in such a way that the facets form a coherent 'net' which, when cut out of paper and properly folded where the two facets adjoin, will form an actual, three-dimensional model of the solid in question" *The Life and Art of Albrecht Dürer* (Princeton: Princeton University Press, 1955), 259.

9. "Every body is sensitive to everything which is happening in the universe, so much so that one who saw everything could read in each body what is happening everywhere. . . . But a soul can read in itself only what is distinctly represented there," *Monadologie,* § 61 [Parkinson, 189].

10. On Leibniz's invention of binary arithmetic, on its two characters, 1 and 0, light and shadow, on the analogy with "Fohy's Chinese figures," see the *Invention de l'arithmétique binaire, Explication de l'arithmétique binaire* (GM, VII). Reference can be made to Christiane Frémont's annotated edition, *Leibniz, Discours sur la théologie naturelle des Chinois* (Paris: L'Herne).

11. Cf. Goethe, *Traité des couleurs* (Paris: Editions Triades, 1983), § 902–9.

12. *Préceptes pour avancer les sciences* (GPh, VII, 169). And *Nouveaux essais* II, chap. 9, § 8 [Remnant/Bennett, 134–38].

13. Black, the dark background (*fuscum subnigrum*), colors, white and light are defined in the *Table de définitions,* C, 489.

14. Nietzsche, *Beyond Good and Evil,* chap. 8, § 244.

15. Cited by Ernst Bertram, in *Nietzsche* (Paris: Rieder, 1932), 233.

16. Herbert Knecht, *La logique de Leibniz, essai sur le rationalisme baroque* (Lausanne: L'Age d'homme, 1982); Christine Buci-Glucksmann, *La folie du voir, De l'esthétique baroque* (Paris: Galilée, 1987). The author develops a conception of the Baroque that appeals to Lacan and Merleau-Ponty.

17. Marcel Schwob, *Vies imaginaires* (Paris: Union générale d'éditions 10/18), 229–31.

18. Jurgis Baltrusaitis, *Formations, déformations* (Paris: Editions Flammarion, 1986), chap. 9.

19. Bernard Cache, *L'ameublement du territoire* [see chap. 2, n. 3 —Tr.]

20. On the "two orders," the material and the immaterial, see Jean Dubuffet, *Prospectus et tous écrits suivants,* II (Paris: Gallimard, 1967), 79–81.

21. On Hantaï and his method of folding, see Marcelin Pleynet, *Identité de la lumière,* catalogue of the Arca Marseille. And also Dominique Fourcade, *Un coup de pinceau c'est la pensée,* catalogue of the Pompidou Center; Yves Michaud, *Métaphysique de Hantaï,* catalogue of Venice; Geneviève Bonnefoi, *Hantaï* (Abbaye Beaulieu, coll. Artistes d'aujourd 'hui, 1973).

22. Leibniz counted on his binary arithmetic for the discovery of a periodicity in numerical series. Nature would perhaps hide this periodicity "in its foldings," as in the instance of first numbers (*Nouveaux essais,* IV, chap. 17, § 13).

23. For textures see the letter to Des Bosses, August 1715. Leibniz's physics attests to a constant interest in the problems of the resistance of materials.

24. [*Hysteresis,* which literally means a lagging, or deficiency, is used in describing magnetic fields (and in electronics) to denote the lapse of magnetic effects after their causes. —Trans.]

25. *Jeanclos-Mossé, sculptures et dessins,* Maison de la culture d'Orléans.

26. See *De la liberté* (F, 178) for the presence or absence of a "common measure."

27. Cf. Papetti, Valier, Fréminville and Tisserson, *La passion des étoffes chez un neuropsychiatrie, G. G. de Clérambault* (Paris: Editions Solin, 1981), with its photographic reproductions and two lectures on drapery (49–57). A reader might be led to believe that these photos of overabundant folds refer to pages chosen by Clérambault himself. But the postcards at the time of the colonial empire also reveal these systems of folds, which dictate all the clothing of Moroccan women, including that of the face: an Islamic Baroque.

4. Sufficient Reason

1. Letter to Arnauld, July 14, 1686 [Mason, 67–72].

2. *Discours de métaphysique,* § 14 [Parkinson, 27].

3. Cf. *Discours de métaphysique,* § 8 and 13 [Parkinson, 18, 24].

4. "Instead, the analysis proceeds to infinity, God alone seeing—not, indeed, the end of the analysis, since it has no end—but the connexion of terms or the inclusion of the predicate in the subject, for he sees whatever is in the series," *De la liberté* (F, 180–81) [Parkinson, 109].

5. See *De la liberté* (F, 183) [Parkinson, 109], but also *Sur le principe de raison* (C, 11), *Vérités nécessaires et vérités contingentes* (C, 17–18), or Fragment X (GPh, VII, 300). These texts invoke analogous arithmetical examples and use synonymous terms ("latebat" or "tecte" as well as "virtualiter"). Couturat is thus correct in stating, "*Necessary* truths are identical, some explicitly . . . , the others virtually or implicitly," in *La logique de Leibniz,* 206.

6. *Nouveaux essais,* IV, chap. 7, § 10 [Remnant/Bennett, 414].

7. Ortega y Gasset, *L'évolution de la théorie déductive, l'idée de principe chez Leibniz* (Paris: Gallimard, 1970), 10–12.

8. On this criterion or this proof of elevation to infinity, and on the condition of "neither whole nor part," cf. *Nouveaux essais,* II, chap. 17, § 2–16 [Remnant/Bennett, 159]. And *Méditations sur la connaissance, la vérité et les idées.* The two texts admit an absolute extension, "extensio absoluta," as an infinite absolute form. But it is in a very special sense, because at stake is neither space, which is relative, nor properly Leibnizian extension, which enters into relations of the wholes and parts: in question is *immensity,* which is the "idea of the absolute, with reference to space" [Remnant/Bennett, 159].

9. On the impossibility of being contradicted, for absolutely simple forms that are neces-

sarily "compatible," cf. the Letter to Princess Elisabeth, 1678, and especially *Qu'il existe un Etre infiniment parfait* (GPh, VIII, 261–62). In the latter writing Leibniz claims having taught this demonstration to Spinoza. This is questionable, since it also belongs to the first ten propositions of the *Ethics*: it is because attributes have nothing in common that they can be said to be of a sole and same Being . . . And all the more in that Spinoza and Leibniz have a same source in Duns Scotus, who showed that formally distinct quiddities compose a sole and same Being. Cf. Etienne Gilson: "The formal distinction of essences is not an obstacle for the perfect ontological unity of infinity," in *Jean Duns Scot* (Paris: Vrin, 1952), 243–54.

10. *Recherches générales sur l'analyse des notions et vérités* (C, 358–59). On the "vinculum" as a relation among the definers of a magnitude, see *De la méthode de l'universalité* (C, 101).

11. See the early work, *Sur l'art combinatoire,* along with Couturat's commentary, in *La logique de Leibniz* (560). We have simplified the example of the line that in fact belongs to level IV.

12. Spinoza also distinguishes three infinities in Letter XII, one by itself, the other by its cause, the third finally understood within limits. Leibniz congratulates Spinoza in this respect although, on his account, he conceives otherwise the relation of the limit and infinity. Cf. GPh, I, 137.

13. For the texture of gold or the connection of its characters, see the *Nouveaux essais,* II, chap. 31, § 1; III, chap. 3, § 19 [Remnant/Bennett, 266; 295–96].

14. *Nouveaux essais,* IV, chap. 2, § 7: on the category of problem.

15. *Nouveaux essais,* I, chap. 1, § 4 and 19. On the enthymeme, see Aristotle, *First Analytics,* II, 27 ("If a single premise is uttered, only one sign is obtained").

16. On the question of attaining (or not) the connection of characters (the case of gold): see the *Nouveaux essais,* III, chap. 4, § 16; III, chap. 11, § 22–24; IV, chap. 6, § 8–10.

17. *Nouveaux essais,* IV, chap. 17, § 4 (theory of the "fabric"). [With enthymemes, "the inference lies partly in what is being suppressed," 79, 479; "it is therefore only too necessary that they should have a strict logic, though of a different type from the scholastic one," Remnant/Bennett, 482].

18. *Nouveaux essais,* III, chap. 3, § 6.

19. *Nouveaux essais,* III, chap. 4, § 16.

20. Cf. the beginning of *L'origine radicale des choses* [*On the Ultimate Origination of Things*]. And the *Monadologie,* § 36–37: "Ultimate reason . . . must certainly be greater, higher and prior to the world itself" [Parkinson, 140]. The latter text has the advantage of moving through souls or monads, that contain final reason no more than the states of the world. If serial reason is outside of the series, it appears to us that in this instance it has to be taken literally. Here is one of the few points on which we do not concur with Michel Serres (I, 262). An argument often invoked by Leibniz is that a "series enclosing sin" cannot have its reason in the monad.

21. *De la liberté*: "For demonstration consists simply in this: by the analysis of the terms of a proposition, and by substituting for a defined term a definition or part of a definition, one shows a certain equation or coincidence of predicate with subject in a reciprocal proposition, or in other cases at least the inclusion of the predicate in the subject, in such a way that what was latent in the proposition and as it were contained in it virtually is rendered evident and express[ed] by the demonstration" [Parkinson, 108].

22. "The concept of an individual, regarded as possible (*sub ratione possibilitatis*), contains what in fact exists or what is related to the existences of things and to time," in the correspondence with Arnauld, "Remarks on M. Arnauld's letter" (May 13, 1686). [Mason, 41.]

23. Arnauld and Nicole, *La logique ou l'art de penser,* II (Paris: Flammarion, 1970 reprint), chap. 2.

24. See the texts quoted by Couturat in *La logique de Leibniz* (Hildesheim: Olms, 1961), 70.

25. Letter to Arnauld, July 1686: inclusion is offered as a direct connection "between me, I who am the subject, and the accomplishment of the journey, which is the predicate" [Mason, 58].

26. On the first Stoics' conception of the event, Emile Brehier, *La théorie des incorporels dans l'ancien stoïcisme* (Paris: Vrin, 1970), chaps. 1 and 2, is still a basic study. And on the substitution of "to follow" for "to be," see Brochard, *Etudes de philosophie ancienne et de philosophie moderne* (Paris: Vrin, 1974), 226–27. This substitution is found in Leibniz.

27. "The kinds and degrees of perfection vary up to infinity, but as regards the foundation of things. The foundations are everywhere the same; this is a fundamental maxim for me, which governs my whole philosophy. But if this philosophy is the simplest in resources it is also the richest in kinds [of effects]," *Nouveaux essais,* IV, chap. 17, § 16 [Remnant/Bennett, 490].

28. That is why, sometimes, Leibniz briefly presents the inherence of the predicate in conformity with opinion in general ("ut aiunt"), or to Aristotle in particular.

29. Cf. the letter to Arnauld (March 4, 1687), and the letter to Arnauld dated April 30 [Mason, 105–29]. André Robinet shows that for a long time, up to 1696, Leibniz avoids speaking of "simple substance," in *Architectonique disjonctive, automates systémiques et idéalité transcendantale dans l'oeuvre de Leibniz* (Paris: Vrin, 1986), 355, and Anne Becco's study, *Du simple selon Leibniz* (Paris: Vrin, 1975).

30. On local movement and qualitative change, see *De la nature en elle-même,* § 13.

31. "If separability is a consequence of the real distinction," Letter to Malebranche (GPh, I, 325–26).

32. On Leibniz against the Cartesian attribute, see the Correspondence with De Volder (GPh, II), especially June 30, 1703.

33. *Eclaircissement des difficultés que M. Bayle a trouvées dans le système nouveau* (GPh, IV, 532, 546–47).

34. *Addition à l'explication du système nouveau* (GPh, IV, 586).

35. Whence the *Monadologie,* § 36: "Sufficient reason has a duty also to find in contingent truths . . ." [Parkinson, 140], which implies that it already held for necessary truths. And the *Théodicée,* "Remarques sur le livre de l'origine du mal," § 14.

36. "The principle of identity affirms that every identical proposition is true, while the principle of reason affirms to the contrary that every true proposition is analytical, that is, virtually identical," notes Couturat (in *La logique de Leibniz,* 215).

5. Incompossibility, Individuality, Liberty

1. Fragment *Vingt-quatre propositions,* GPh, VII, 289–91), and the fragment *Les vérités absolument premières,* 195). Couturat (*La logique de Leibniz,* 219) and Gueroult (*Dynamique et métaphysique leibniziennes,* 170) believe that incompossibility implies a negation or an opposition that Leibniz was unable to discern among positive notions like monads: he would thus have been led to declare that the origin of incompossibility cannot be known. But it seems to us that for Leibniz the incompossible is an original relation irreducible to any form of contradiction. It is a difference and not a negation. That is why in the following pages we are proposing an interpretation based only on divergence or convergence of series. The reading has the advantage of being "Leibnizian." But why then does Leibniz declare the origin unknowable? On the one hand, it is because divergence is still not understood very well in serial theory in the seventeenth century. On the other and, more generally, at the level of incompossible worlds, we are reduced to supposing that series diverge but without comprehending why they do.

2. "For anything which is noticeable must be made up of parts which are not," *Nouveaux essais,* II, chap. 1, § 18 [Remnant/Bennett, 117].

3. *Théodicée,* § 413–17. In *Figures II* (Paris: Seuil, 1966), 195 sq., Gérard Genette provides criteria allowing us to observe how much the text of the *Théodicée* follows a model of Baroque narrative.

4. Jorge-Luis Borges, "Le jardin aux sentiers qui bifurquent," in *Fictions* (Paris: Gallimard, 1974).

5. Maurice Leblanc, *La vie extravagante de Balthazar* (Paris: Livre de Poche, 1979).

6. Letter to Bourget, December 1714 (GPh, III, 572).

7. "Remarques sur la lettre de M. Arnauld," Correspondence with Arnauld, letter of May 13, 1686. "Primary predicates" are obviously not reserved for Adam, since every individual has his or her own. Are they for everyone in a finite number? No, because we can always multiply singular points between two singular points. The question is moot since what counts is that two individuals do not share the same primitive attributes. On the themes that we take up later—"vague Adam," Adam common to incompossible worlds, primitive predicates grasped "sub ratione generalitatis"—see the same text [Mason, 24–34].

8. For this hypothesis see Gueroult, "La constitution de la substance chez Leibniz," *Revue métaphysique et de morale* (1947).

9. *Nouveaux essais,* II, 1, § 2; *Eclaircissement des difficultés que M. Bayle a trouvées dans le système nouveau* (GPh, IV, 566). In other writings, Leibniz brings together the individual with a last species; but he makes it clear that the comparison holds for only a mathematical and not a physical species. Cf. *Discours de métaphysique,* § 9; Letter to Arnauld, GPh, II, 131.

10. On the difference between the two types of species, see the *Nouveaux essais,* III, chap. 6, § 14.

11. *Nouveaux essais,* II, chap. 27, § 4–5.

12. *Justification du calcul des infinitésimales par celui de l'algèbre ordinaire* (GM, IV, 104): how difference or reason of two lengths subsists in a point when these lengths vanish and when their relation tends toward

$$\frac{0}{0}$$

13. " "Tis an hard matter to say where the sensible and the rational begin," *Nouveaux essais,* IV, chap. 16, § 12 [Remnant/Bennett, 471]. Kant is the one who claims to denounce the conciliation of indiscernibles and continuity because a confusion of phenomena with things in themselves would be implied; it is thus the distinction of the two worlds (such as Kant restores it) that gives birth to a contradiction; and with Kant we know in fact where the sensible ends and the intelligible begins, which amounts to stating that the principles of indiscernibles and the law of continuity are opposed, but in a Kantian type of system. We often see the distinction among authors who assume a contradiction: Gueroult (*Descartes selon l'ordre des raisons,* 1 [Paris: Aubier, 1953], 284) and even Philonenko, in "La loi de continuité et le principe des indiscernables," *Revue de métaphysique et de morale* (1967), appeal to the ideal and the real in Leibniz as two worlds. But the two worlds do not exist, and for Leibniz the break is never a gap or a discontinuity.

14. *Principes de la Nature et de la Grâce,* § 4.

15. *De l'origine radicale des choses.*

16. Eugen Fink, *Le jeu comme symbole du monde* (Paris: Minuit, 1966), 238–39.

17. Cf. Gaston Grua, *Jurisprudence universelle et théodicée selon Leibniz* (Paris: PUF, 1953).

18. Tibor Klaniczay, "La naissance du Maniérisme et du Baroque au point de vue sociolo-

gique," in *Renaissance, Maniérisme, Baroque* (Paris: Vrin, 1972), 221. The author paints a picture of the great crisis that brings about the decline of the Renaissance and of the two attitudes, Mannerism and Baroque, that are related to this crisis.

19. Cf. the letter to Rémond (January 1716), in GPh, III, 668–69, in which Leibniz rejects each in its turn: chance, for the sake of chess and checkers, games of position; void, for the purpose of inverted solitaire; the model of battle, for the sake of a Chinese game of nonbattle, or the Roman game of Brigands. On nonbattle as a paradigm of current strategy, see Guy Brossolet, *Essai sur la non-bataille* (Paris: Bélin, 1975), in which the author appeals to the Baron of Saxony, but in reality proposes very Leibnizian schemes, "a modular type of combat based on light, numerous, but independent cells" (113).

20. Georges Friedmann, in *Leibniz et Spinoza* (Paris: Gallimard, 1975), insists on Leibniz's philosophy as the thinking of universal anxiety: the Best is not a "vote of confidence in God; on the contrary, Leibniz seems to be defying God himself" (218).

21. Jacques Brunschwig has underscored this theme of the lawyer: the *Théodicée* can be understood "in a prudent sense (doctrine of God's justice) as it also can in an audacious sense (justification, or a trial for the justification of God)," that conforms to the treatise *La cause de Dieu plaidée par sa justice*: "The business of God, one of the *perplexing cases* to which as a young man he had devoted his doctoral thesis," in the Introduction to *La Théodicée* (Paris: Garnier/Flammarion, 1969).

22. "The smallest parts of the universe are ruled according to the order of the greatest perfection; the whole would not be," *Essai anagogique* (GPh, VII, 272).

23. "Mannerism" is one of the most pathetic traits of schizophrenia. In two different ways Blankenburg (in *Tanz in der Therapie Schizophrener* [Psych. Psychosom., 1969]), and Evelyn Sznycer ("Droit de suite baroque," in Navratil, *Schizophrénie et art* [Paris: Complexe, 1978]) compare schizophrenia to Baroque dances (the German dance, the pavane, the minuet, the running dance, etc.). Sznycer recalls Freud's theses on the reconstruction of the world and the schizophrenic's inner modifications. She engages a function of excess that she calls "hypercritical."

24. On the old problem of future contingents as an essential part of the logic of events, see Schuhl, *Le dominateur et les possibles* (Paris: PUF, 1960), and Jules Vuillemin, *Nécessité ou contingence: L'aporie de Diodore et les systèmes philosophiques* (Paris: Minuit, 1984). One of the basic propositions is that the impossible does not proceed from the possible. But Leibniz is able to consider that the incompossible can proceed from the possible.

25. Correspondence with Clarke, Leibniz's fifth piece of writing, § 14–15; *Nouveaux essais,* II, chaps. 20 and 21.

26. *Discours de métaphysique,* § 30 [Parkinson, 40–41].

27. "There is an infinity of present and past figures and movements that play in the efficient cause of my present writing, and there is an infinity of my soul's minute inclinations and dispositions, both present and past, that play a role in the final cause," *Monadologie,* § 36 [Parkinson, 185].

28. "Reason counsels us to expect ordinarily that what we find in the future will conform to a long experience in the past," Preface to the *Nouveaux essais* [Remnant/Bennett, 51]. On movement that is being made, see *De la Nature en elle-même*: "In the present moment of its movement, the body is not only what occupies a place equal to itself, but it also comprehends an effort or drive to change position so that, through a natural force, the following state will issue from itself in the present" (§ 13).

29. *Théodicée,* § 269–72. And especially *Profession de foi du philosophe,* ed. Y. Belaval, in which Leibniz compares damnation to movement that is taking place: "Just as what has changed never remains in one place, but always tends toward a place, and just as they are never damned and powerless, so then they would desire to cease forever being damnable, that is, to

cease damning themselves over and again forever" (Paris: Vrin, 1970), 85, 95, and 101 (where Beelzebub's beautiful song is written in Latin verse).

30. Cf. Quevedo's text, quoted by Jean Rousset, *La littérature de l'âge baroque en France* (Paris: Corti, 1953), 116–17. Rousset speaks of "death in movement."

31. Letter to Jaquelot (September 1704), GPh, VI, 559.

32. Bergson, *Essai sur les données immédiates de la conscience* (Paris: PUF, Ed. du centenaire, 1982), 105–20. Readers can take note of the scheme of inflection that Bergson advances (117).

33. *Monadologie,* § 61, and *Principes de la Nature et de la Grâce,* § 13 [Parkinson, 188–89, 201].

34. Cf. Bergson, 123–26, and the second schema of inflection.

35. *Discours de métaphysique,* § 14 [Parkinson, 26].

36. Cf. the letter to Bourguet (August 5, 1715), that defines the quantity of progress by the "outcome" of the world as being "the most perfect of all possible outcomes," although no condition can be the most perfect.

37. On the "official act bearing a later effect," in sensitive souls called upon to become reasonable, cf. *La cause de Dieu plaidée par sa justice,* § 82. On the return to a sensitive state after death, while waiting for the resurrection: *Considérations sur la doctrine d'un esprit universel,* § 12–14. On the case of the damned, from the points of view both of the last thought and the resurrection, *Profession de foi du philosophe,* pp. 37–93.

38. In *Le système de Leibniz* (I, 233–86) Michel Serres analyzes the physical and mathematical implications of Leibniz's schemes of progress in detail, especially through the correspondence with Bourguet. It appears to us that the damned play an indispensable physical role in these schemes (somewhat like "demons").

6. What Is an Event?

1. [*Diadoche* means what succeeds, or is in succession. The term derives from the Diadochi, the Macedonian generals under Alexander the Great who divided up their leader's empire immediately after his death.—Trans.]

2. Here we refer to Whitehead's three principal works: *The Concept of Nature* (Cambridge: Cambridge University Press, 1920) for extensions and intensities, the first two components of the event; for the third, prehensions, we refer to *Process and Reality* (New York: Macmillan, 1941) and *Adventures of Ideas* (New York: Macmillan, 1933). For the totality of Whitehead's philosophy readers can consult Wahl, *Vers le concret* (Paris: Vrin); Cesselin, *La philosophie organique de Whitehead* (Paris: PUF, 1950); Dumoncel, *Whitehead ou le cosmos torrentiel,* in *Archives de philosophie* (December 1984 and January 1985).

3. Michel Serres has analyzed the process of screening, the grid, or "cribratio" in Leibniz. "There would be two infraconsciences: the deeper would be structured as any given totality, a pure multiplicity or general possibility, a haphazard mixture of signs; the shallower would be covered by combinatory schemas of this multiplicity. It would be already structured like a complete mathematics, arithmetic, geometry, infinitesimal calculus (I, 111, and also 107–27). Serres shows the profound opposition between this method and the Cartesian method. There exists an infinity of filters or superimposed grids, from our senses themselves up to the final filter, beyond which chaos would exist. The paradigm of the filter is the key to *Méditations sur la connaissance, la vérité et les idées.*

4. Letter to Bourguet, March 1714: "When I maintain that chaos does not exist, I do not at all mean that our globe or other bodies have never been in a state of outer apparent confusion . . . but I do mean that whoever would have sensitive organs discerning enough to notice the

smallest parts of things would find that everything is organized. . . . For it is impossible for a creature to be capable of delving at once into the smallest parcel of matter because the actual subdivisions go up to infinity" (GPh, III, 565).

5. Dumoncel, 1985, 573.

6. *Process and Reality* constantly appeals to the "public-private" pair. The origin of this distinction is found in *Discours de métaphysique,* § 14 [Parkinson, 26–27]; we shall discover the importance of this theme.

7. "Action belonging to the soul is perception," letter to Des Bosses (April 1709).

8. Letter to Arnauld, September 1687, GPh, II, 112.

9. *Principes de la Nature et de la Grâce,* § 17 [Parkinson, 203].

10. The *Profession de foi du philosophe* will go the furthest in its analysis of subjective "satisfaction," and in the conciliation of "novelty" with totality (87–89).

11. "The event which is the life of nature in the Great Pyramid yesterday and today is divisible into two parts, namely the Great Pyramid yesterday and the Great Pyramid to-day. But the object recognizable which is also called the Great Pyramid is the same object to-day as it was yesterday," notes Whitehead in *The Concept of Nature* (77).

12. *Monadologie,* § 71 (and on "reflexive acts," § 30).

13. Cf. the conditions of the choir in the Letter to Arnauld (April 1687), GPh, II, 95 [Mason, 119].

14. Such was Heidegger's remark: the monad does not need a window because it is "already outside, conforming to its own being"; in *Les problèmes fondamentaux de la phénoménologie* (Paris: Gallimard, 1986), 361.

15. See especially the play of divergent series in Gombrowicz's *Cosmos* (Paris: Denoël, 1966).

16. On the new monadology in mathematics since Riemann, see Gilles Chatelet, "Sur une petite phrase de Riemann," *Analytiques* 3 (May 1979).

7. Perception in the Folds

1. Letter to Des Bosses (March 1706, October 1706), in which a primal matter "belongs to" or is "fixed" in each entelechia. The letters to Des Bosses are translated with commentary by Christiane Frémont in *L'être et la relation* (Paris: Vrin, 1981); see especially the remarks on the notion of exigency.

2. This is constant in his letters to Arnauld (especially in April 1687) [Mason, 113–29].

3. Arnauld, Letter to Leibniz (August 28, 1687) [Mason, 132ff].

4. "Because the universe being ruled is a perfect order, there must also exist an order in a representative, that is, in the soul's perceptions." In the *Monadologie,* § 63 [Parkinson, 189].

5. On minute perceptions and little pricklings, see the *Nouveaux essais,* II, chap. 1, § 9–25; chap. 20, § 6–9; chap. 21, § 29–36 [Remnant/Bennett, 78–86; 163–67; 183–91].

6. Gaëtan Clérambault, guided by his love of folds, analyzed the so-called Lilliputian hallucinations marked by striations, trellises, and interweavings. The chloralic's mind is "surrounded by a veil [where] the play of folds gives an uneven transparency," in the *Oeuvre psychiatrique,* 1 (Paris: PUF, 1942), 204–50.

7. For the distinction of a microscopic process and a macroscopic process in prehension, see Whitehead, *Process and Reality,* 129.

8. With these terms Gabriel Tarde appeals to and defines "monadology" in "Monadologie et sociologie," in *Essais et mélanges sociologiques* (Lyon: Storck, 1895), 335.

9. On this problem—that includes the example of the sound of the sea—the principal texts are: *Discours de métaphysique,* § 33 [Parkinson, 43]; Letter to Arnauld (April 1687) [Mason, 114ff]; *Considération sur la doctrine d'un Esprit universel,* § 14; *Monadologie,* § 20–25 [Par-

kinson, 182–83]; *Principes de la Nature et de la Grâce,* § 13 [Parkinson, 201]. Elias Canetti has recently taken up the theory of pricklings, but he treats it as a simple reception, accumulation, and propagation of commands coming from without, in *Masse et puissance* (Paris: Gallimard, 1966), 321.

10. *Nouveaux essais,* II, chap. 1, § 10 [Remnant/Bennett, 112].

11. Salomon Maïmon, *Versuch über Transzendantalphilosophie* (Berlin, 1790), 33. Kant will state his critique in a letter to Marcus Herz, in which he reproaches Maïmon for restoring infinite understanding. Martial Gueroult has reviewed the sum of Maïmon's work by underscoring the "differentials of consciousness" and their principal of reciprocal determination, in *La philosophie transcendantale de Salomon Maïmon* (Paris: Alcan, 1929), chap. 2.

12. This "expression, albeit obscure and confused, which the soul possesses of the future in advance, is the true cause of what will happen to it, and of the clearer perception that it will have afterwards when obscurity will have developed," in a letter to Arnauld (April 30, 1687) [Mason, 114]. See also the *Nouveaux essais,* II, chap. 29, § 2 [Remnant/Bennett, 254].

13. On filters or the scale of graduation, and on Leibniz's opposition to Descartes on this point, see Yvon Belaval, *Leibniz critique de Descartes* (Paris: Gallimard, 1978), 164–67; Michel Serres, *Le système de Leibniz,* I (Paris: Seuil, 1982), 107–26. Belaval's study is a profound analysis of Leibniz's logic of the idea.

14. In the same way Leibniz remarks, "Bear in mind that we do think of many things at once, but pay heed only to the thoughts that stand out most distinctly," in the *Nouveaux essais,* II, chap. 1, § 11 [Remnant/Bennett, 113]. Such thoughts are distinct only because they are relatively the most clear and the least obscure. Hence Leibniz can write, " 'the soul expresses more distinctly what pertains to its body'" (Letter to Arnauld, April 30, 1687) [Mason, 113]. Or: "The soul represents the whole universe also in representing the body that belongs to it in a particular way" (*Monadologie,* § 62) [Parkinson, 189], although the question is only one of clarity.

15. "For we experience within ourselves a state, in which we remember nothing and have no distinguishable perception; as when we fall in a swoon, or when we are overcome by a deep dreamless sleep. . . . And this is the state of bare monads," *Monadologie,* § 20–24 [Parkinson, 182]. And the letter to Hartsoeker (October 30, 1710): "It is true that there is no soul that sleeps all the time" (GPh, III, 508).

16. "In the gigantic world that surrounds the tick, three stimulants shine like luminous signals in the shadows, and they serve as signposts that would guide it unflinchingly to its goal," notes Jacob von Uexküll, in *Mondes animaux et monde humain* (Paris: Gonthier), 24.

17. *Principes de la Nature et de la Grâce,* § 4 [Parkinson, 196–97].

18. "Le petit livre de la vie après la mort" (1836), in *Patio VIII* (Paris: l'Eclat, 1987), with Claude Rabant's commentary, which especially treats of Fechner's great crisis of photophobia, his digestive problems and his loss of ideas (21–24).

19. Jean Cocteau, *La difficulté d'être* (Paris: Rocher, 1983), 79–80.

20. Henri Michaux, "Les 22 plis de la vie humaine," in *Ailleurs* (Paris: Gallimard, 1948), 172. The theme of the fold haunts all of Michaux's work—writing, drawings, paintings—as demonstrated by the collection *La vie dans les plis* (Paris: Gallimard, 1949), or the poem "Emplie de": "Emplie de voiles sans fin de vouloirs obscurs. Emplie de plis, Emplis de nuit. Emplie des plis indéfinis, des plis de ma vigie . . . [Filled endlessly with folds of dark desires. Filled with folds, Full of night. Filled with vague folds, folds of my vigil . . .]." Leibnizian memories are frequent in Michaux: fog and giddiness, Lilliputian hallucinations, minute perceptions speeding over a tiny surface, spontaneity: "une vague toute seule une vague à part de l'océan . . . c'est un cas de spontanéité magique [a wave all alone a wave apart from the ocean . . . it's a case of magical spontaneity]." Cocteau's text above (n. 19) itself resonates with those of Michaux because Cocteau also goes from waking to dream, and from conscious perception to minute per-

ceptions: "The folding, through whose intervention eternity becomes livable and is not done in dream as in life. Something of this folding is unfolding within." Finally, Fernando Pessoa has developed a conception of metaphysical, psychological, and esthetic perception that is quite original and yet close to Leibniz. It is based on minute perceptions and "maritime series"; a remarkable analysis can be found in José Gil, *Pessoa et la métaphysique des sensations* (Paris: Différence, 1988).

21. "*Perception* and that which depends upon it and *cannot be explained mechanically*. . . . The explanation of perception must therefore must be sought in simple substance, and not in a compound or a machine" *Monadologie,* § 17 [Parkinson, 181].

22. Thomas de Quincey, *The Revolt of the Tartars,* in *The Collected Writings,* vol. 7 (Edinburgh: Adam and Charles Black, 1890), 411–12.

23. "I think that for the fundamental examination of things it is useful to explain all phenomena by the sole perceptions of monads," Letter to Des Bosses (June 1712).

24. Cf. André Robinet, "Leibniz: lecture du *Treatise* de Berkeley," in *Etudes philosophiques* (1983).

25. Letters to Arnauld, November 1686 (GPh, II, 77) and April 1687 (98) [Mason, 92–94 and 114].

26. The two basic texts are *Addition à l'explication du système nouveau* (GPh, IV, 575–76) and *Nouveaux essais,* II, chap. 8 § 13–15 [Remnant/Bennett, 131–32].

27. The letters to Varignon (February, April, and June 1702, in GM, IV) display the complexity of Leibniz's position.

28. *Nouveaux essais,* II, chap. 27, § 4 [Remnant/Bennett, 231–32]. There is transformation, envelopment, or development, and, finally, a fluxion of the body of this soul. On "the movement of fluids" and stones thrown into water, see the letter to Princess Sophie (February 1706), in GPh, VII, 566–67. For "conspiring movements," see the Letters to Hartsoeker, GPh, III.

29. "Nature takes care to provide [animals] with organs which collect several rays of light, or several undulations of the air," *Monadologie,* § 25 [Parkinson, 183].

30. Bergson will rediscover this idea of a resemblance through the perceived quality by consciousness and tiny movements "contracted" by a receptive organ (in the resumé and conclusion to *Matière et mémoire*).

31. "Nature alone effectively receives all the impressions and comprises one of them, but without the soul the order of impressions that matter has received could not be sorted out, and impressions would only be confused. . . . The soul is located exactly at the point where the preceding impressions are distinguished and held," letter to Princess Sophie (570).

32. *Monadologie,* § 25; and the *Nouveaux essais,* II, chap. 21, § 72 [Remnant/Bennett, 210–11].

8. The Two Floors

1. [*Every, one,* and *some* are in English in the original. —Trans.]

2. *Du style philosophique de Nizolius* (GPh, IV), § 31, on collective totalities and distinctive or distributive totalities.

3. *Monadologie,* § 61–62 [Parkinson, 188–89].

4. Effectively God's first free decrees concern the whole world (moral necessity); but the particular nature of each monad, its clear region, obeys subaltern maxims (hypothetical necessity: if such is the sum, then the parts . . .). Cf. *Discours de métaphysique,* § 16 [Parkinson, 29], and *Remarques sur la lettre de M. Arnauld* (May 1686) [Mason, 39–52]. In this sense hypothetical necessity is firmly grounded in moral necessity, as is shown by *L'origine radicale des choses* [*On the Ultimate Origination of Things,* Parkinson, 136–44]; and inversely, moral

necessity and final causes are everywhere in the concatenations of hypothetical necessity (*Discours de métaphysique,* § 19).

5. Hegel shows that the application of infinitesimal calculus implies the distinction of two parts or moments of the "object." He admires Lagrange for having brought it forward, in *Science de la logique,* II (Paris: Aubier, 1981), 317–37.

6. *Essai anagogique dans le recherche des causes* (GPh, VIII). Maurice Janet analyzes the principal qualities of extremum in *La finalité en mathématiques et en physique* (*Recherches philosophiques,* II). The problem of the "brachystochrone" that Leibniz often studies happens to be a problem of extremum ("minimal descent"). So too is the question of the gothic arch (the best form of a projectile in a liquid) in Newton's *Principia mathematica.*

7. After having analyzed Janet's themes, Albert Lautman clearly marks the limit of extrema, or the difference of nature between two kinds of properties. "Insofar as properties that make selection possible are properties of maximum or minimum, they confer the obtained being with an advantage of simplicity as if it were an appearance of finality, but this appearance disappears when we realize that what assures the passage to existence is not the fact that the properties in question are extremal properties, but that the selection they determine is implied through the totality of the structure in question. . . . The exceptional property that marks it is no longer a property of extremum, but the property of being the limit of a convergent series," in *Essai sur les notions de structure et d'existence en mathématiques,* chap. 6 (Paris: Hermann, 1938; reprint, Union générale d'editions 10/18, 1977), 123–25. It is true that in the *Origine radicale des choses* [Parkinson, 136–44], Leibniz likens the selection of the best world to a property of extremum; but it is at the cost of a fiction that consists in considering space as an empty "receptivity," common to all possible worlds, that must be filled with a maximum number of places. In fact, we have observed that the distinction of incompossible wholes was not based on properties of extremum but on serial properties.

8. See Bernard Cache, *L'ameublement du territoire* (forthcoming), in which the two levels are clearly distinguished (inflection-extrema, vector of concavity-vector of gravity).

9. Raymond Ruyer, especially *La conscience et le corps* (Paris: PUF, 1950); *Eléments de psychobiologie, Néofinalisme* (Paris: PUF, 1952); and *La genèse des formes vvantes* (Paris: Flammarion, 1958).

10. Leibniz announces his agreement with Newton on the law of gravitation inverse to squares, but thinks that attraction is sufficiently explained with the special case of fluids and "their impulsions" (harmonic circulation of planets whence originates a centripetal force). Here we have an entire theory of the formation of a vector of gravity, in the *Essai sur les causes des mouvements célestes,* GM, VI; and on magnetism, Ed. Dutens, II. On the alternative of "attraction-impulsion" (even for Newton), see Koyré, *Etudes newtoniennes* (Paris: Gallimard, 1968), 166–97. With a tinge of irony Koyré underscores the importance of the *Essai* for a conciliation of Newtonian gravity with the action of succession. "Leibniz did what Huygens did not succeed in achieving . . ." (166 and 179).

11. Ruyer, *La genèse des formes vivantes,* 54, 68.

12. Leibniz's correspondence with Des Bosses begs this question of the "realization" of phenomena or of the perceived outside of the souls. On "Realizing," see the letter of April 1715.

13. The theme is frequent in Blanchot, especially in *L'espace littéraire* (Paris: Gallimard, 1955), 160–61 [tr. Ann Smock, *Literary Space* (Lincoln: University of Nebraska Press, 1988)]. This conception of the event can be compared to a Chinese or Japanese tradition, such as what René de Ceccatty and Nakamura translate and comment in *Shôbôgenzô, La réserve visuelle des événements dans leur justesse,* by Dôgen, the thirteenth-century monk (Paris: Editions de la Différence). [See also *La vision immédiate: nature, éveil et tradition selon le Shôbôgenzô,* trans. Bernard Faure (Paris: Le Mail, 1987), or Kosen Nirhiyama and John Stevens, trans., *A Complete*

English Translation of Dôgen Zenji's Shôbôgenzô, 4 vols. (Sendai, Japan: Daihokkaikaku, and Tokyo: Nakayama Shobo, 1975–83). —Trans.]

14. Leibniz often underlines that the union of the soul and the body, defined by an "immediate presence," cannot be confused with harmony, in the *Théodicée,* discourse § 55; *Remarque . . . sur un endroit des mémoires de Trévoux* (GPh, VI, 595–96); Letter to Rémond, November 1715 (GPh, III, 658). See Christiane Fremont's commentary in *L'Etre et la relation* (Paris: Vrin, 1981), 41. The *Système nouveau de la Nature* (§ 14) [Parkinson, 121] marks the linkage of the two problems, and the passage from one to the other. Clearly Malebranche's occasionalism also appeals to incarnation, but as a mystery of faith. Although he tends to express himself in the same way, Leibniz sometimes takes up the problem of incarnation as something intelligible and resolvable, at least at the human level.

15. "Although I do hold neither that the soul changes the laws of the body, nor that the body changes the laws of the soul, and that I may have introduced preestablished harmony in order to avoid this trouble, I am not willing to admit a true union between the soul and the body that makes a supposition of it," *Théodicée,* discourse § 55.

16. End of the preface to the *Nouveaux essais* [Remnant/Bennett, 65–68].

17. *Monadologie,* § 70 [Parkinson, 190]; letter to Des Bosses (June 1712).

18. Letter to Arnauld, September 1687 (GPh, II, 120) [Mason, 143ff (October 9, 1687]. And: "But we must not imagine, as some have done who have misunderstood my view, that each soul has a mass or portion of matter appropriate or attached to itself forever, and that it consequently possesses other inferior living things, forever destined to its service," *Monadologie,* § 71 [Parkinson, 190].

19. Letter to Lady Masham, June 1704 (GPh, III, 356).

20. In his groundbreaking article "Monadologie et sociologie," Gabriel Tarde puts forth this substitution of having for being, as a true inversion of metaphysics that issues directly from the monad; in *Essais et mélanges sociologiques* (Lyon: Storck, 1895). Jean Milet has commented on this theme and proposes naming "echology" this discipline that replaces ontology, in *Gabriel Tarde et la philosophie de l'histoire* (Paris: Vrin), 167–70.

21. *Nouveaux essais,* II, chap. 27, § 4–6 [Remnant/Bennett, 231]. The theme is constant in his correspondence with Des Bosses.

22. On this distinction in scholastic theories of the vinculum, see Léonore Boehm, *Le vinculum substantiale chez Leibniz* (Paris: Vrin, 1962), 77–98; see also the letter to Des Bosses, April 1715: "This link will always be tied to the dominant monad."

23. Buffon develops a paradoxical idea that is very close to the vinculum: an "inner mold" is imposed upon variable organic molecules, in *Histoire des animaux,* chap. 3. See also Georges Canguilhem, *Connaissance de la vie* (Paris: Vrin, 1975), 63–67 and 215–17, on the use of the word "monad"—according to Leibniz—in natural history.

24. The vinculum is "as such naturally, but not essentially, for it requires monads, but does not basically envelop them, since it can exist without them and they can exist without it," in a letter to Des Bosses (May 1716).

25. Letters to Des Bosses (April and August 1715).

26. The theory of the vinculum comes late in Leibniz's work, appearing in the correspondence with Des Bosses (1706–1716). Two of Belaval's commentaries have especially enlightened its problems, in Leibniz, *Initiation à la philosophie* (Paris: Vrin), 244–52; also, Christiane Frémont, *L'être et la relation* (Paris: Vrin, 1981), 31–42. Frémont shows that the vinculum is crucial to Leibniz's theory of relation; she renews our knowledge of this theory.

27. The soul of the insect that is cut in two, up to infinity, or the soul of the goat in ashes, remains in an area, no matter how small, where they are projected (letter to Arnauld, April 1687) [Mason, 125ff]; the soul's "point of view" is in the body (*Nouveaux essais,* II, chap. 8, § 13–

15) [Remnant/Bennett, 131–32]: through a relation of projection we are able to locate a pain, for example, in the body.

28. To be sure, there is strictly speaking neither generation nor corruption of organisms, but only composition. Leibniz nonetheless retains the category of *generation-corruption* in order to have it distinguished from the two other categories of "kinesis"; *inner change* and *outer local movement.* But if the change is of a psychical nature, organic composition is as much material as it is movement. Cf. the letter to Lady Masham (July 1705), 368. Plastic forces are in themselves "mechanical."

29. Letter to Arnauld (October 1687) [Mason, 153]. And his letter to Des Bosses (May 1716): "I limit corporal, that is, composite, substance to living beings alone, that is to say, solely to organic machines."

30. "Secondary matter is an aggregate," letter to Des Bosses (May 1716); it is "only piled up," in the *Nouveaux essais,* IV, chap. 3, § 4. To the contrary, in a broad sense, see the preceding letter to Arnauld, and *De la Nature en elle-même,* § 12 ("secondary matter is a complete substance"). On the meanings of secondary and primary matter, and on the terminology of "massa" and "moles," see Christiane Frémont's remarks (n. 25 above), 103 and 132–33.

31. Raymond Ruyer has marked very well this mixed area, either in Markov's chains (*La genèse des formes vivantes,* chap. 8), or in atomic phenomena (*Néo-finalisme,* 218–20).

32. As a painter of textures, Caravaggio modulates dark matter with colors and forms that act as forces. See Françoise Bardon, *Caravage ou l'expérience de la matière* (Paris: PUF, 1978), 68–71. See also the comparison with Giordano Bruno.

33. "Semi-beings, that are not upheld by a vinculum," in his Letter to Des bosses (August 1715).

34. *Addition à l'explication du Système nouveau* (GPh, IV, 587); Letter to the Abbé de Conti (Dutens III, 446).

35. For these inner unities and external determination, see *Eclaircissement des difficultés de la philosophie première et de la notion de substance; De la Nature en elle-même ou de la force immanente,* § 14.

36. On the need to recast the Aristotelian coupling of power and action, see the Letter to Des Bosses (February 1706); *De la réforme de la philosophie première et de la notion de substance.* And on force-disposition-tendency, see the preface to the *Nouveaux essais*; II, chap. 1, § 2, and chap. 21, § 1. In the latter passage, monads of the first species are said to be "primary acting forces" [Remnant/Bennett, 170–71]. That is literally true to the extent that they "have impenetrability."

37. In addition to the writings of his youth, the basic text is Leibniz's letter to De Volder (in response to that of August 1699, GPh, II, 191). Gueroult demonstrates that the two models of movement, free action and labor, are united in this respect. "We obtain a succession of pulsations, each having a distinct reality in that each time marks a different instant," and not at all because of a discontinuity of time, but for the reason that its very continuity implies the change of what fills it in two instants, no matter how frequent they are. Cf. Leibniz: *Dynamique et métaphysique leibniziennes* (Paris: Aubier-Montaigne, 1978), 148–49.

38. Letter to Jaquelot, March 1703 (GPh, III, 457); letters to De Volder (June 1703, June 1704). See Gueroult's commentary and his interpretation of derivative force as "predicate" (193–94).

39. "Matter (I mean the secondary or mass) is not one substance, but made of substances . . ." in his Letter to Jaquelot, November 1715; "Secondary matter is not a substance, but . . . a mass of several substances," in his letter to Rémond, November 1715 (GPh, III, p. 657). The *Système nouveau de la Nature* speaks of "brute souls" (§ 6) [Parkinson, 118].

40. *Discours de métaphysique,* § 35–36; *Monadologie,* § 83–86 [Parkinson, 192–93]. At the

end of his letter to Arnauld in April 1687, Leibniz appeals to a "right of the bourgeoisie" that must be reserved for true substances [Mason, 127–29]. See André Robinet's remarks in *Architectonique disjonctive* (Paris: Vrin, 1986), 51.

41. *Principes de la Nature et de la Grâce,* § 4. The other texts on classes of monads are notably his letter to Wagner of June 1710 (GPh, VII, 529), and the *Monadologie,* § 18 ff. [Parkinson, 181ff].

42. The theme is constant in Leibniz and is especially developed in his polemics with the physician Stahl (*Remarques et exceptions,* Dutens II). Leibniz contends at once against mechanism, that souls exist in Nature; and against "paganism," that they do not act outside of themselves or upon bodies. It is clear that Leibniz is not satisified with a vitalism or an organicism. He sticks to an animism for which he refuses an exterior efficacity. It is quite different from a vitalism in the manner of Kant or of Claude Bernard. It breaks with animism, all the while keeping two levels, the one being mechanical and the other only regulatory or directive, in a word, "ideal" without being active. The difficulty of Kant's solution is that we cannot be sure if the organic or vital idea is a force, that is, a soul.

43. " 'Tis an hard matter to say where sensible and rational begin, and . . . which is the lowest species of living things . . . and that the only difference is that between the large and the small, between sensible and insensible," *Nouveaux essais,* IV, chap. 16, § 12 [Remnant/Bennett, 471 and 474].

44. Letter to Des Bosses (April 1715): "hoc realisans . . ."

9. The New Harmony

1. Rhingrave means "breeches of extreme breadth, up to a yard and a half per leg, with folds so abundant that they absolutely look like a skirt and impede the eye from seeing where the legs begin to separate," in François Boucher, *Histoire du costume* (Paris: Flammarion, 1965), 256–59.

2. See Bresc-Bauteir, Ceysson, Fagiolo dell'Arco, and Souchal, *La grande tradition de la sculpture du XVe au XVIIIe siècle* (Geneva: Skira, 1987). Fagiolo dell'Arco has excellent remarks on Baroque sculpture, and so does Souchal for the "Rococo." The examples raised here are all reproduced and analyzed in this book (191, 224, 231, 266, 270).

3. Heinrich Wölfflin, *Renaissance et Baroque,* trans. Guy Ballangé (Paris: Poche, 1987), 73 (and all of chap. 3).

4. Carl Andre's planar sculptures, and also the conception of "rooms" (in the sense of the rooms of an apartment) would not only illustrate the passages of painting and sculpture, or of sculpture and architecture, but also the extensive unity of minimal art, in which form no longer contains a volume but embraces a limitless space in all directions. One is struck perhaps by the properly Leibnizian position to which Tony Smith appeals: a closed car going along an interstate highway that only the headlights are illuminating, and on whose windshield asphalt streams past at top speed. *It is a monad,* with its privileged zone (if we object that the closure is not in fact absolute, since the asphalt is on the outside, then we must recall that neo-Leibnizianism requires a condition of capture rather than one of absolute closure; and even here closure can be considered to be perfect insofar as the asphalt on the outside has nothing to do with what passes by on the window). A detailed review of explicitly Baroque themes has to be made in minimal art and then, too, in constructivism. See the remarkable analysis of the Baroque by Strzeminski and Kobro, in *L'espace uniste, écrits du constructivisme polonais* (Lausanne: L'Age d'Homme, 1977). And also, in *Artstudio* (no. 6, Fall 1987), the articles by Criqui on Tony Smith; Assenmaker on Carl Andre; Celant on Donald Judd; Marjorie Welish on Sol Lewitt; Gintz on Robert Morris: that move to a constant confrontation with the Baroque (we can especially refer to Robert

Morris's folds of felt, 121, 131). A special study would also have to be written on Christo's "performances," on his giant wrappings and the folds of their envelopments.

5. See not only the pyramid of the *Théodicée,* which covers all possible worlds, but also the cone of the *Nouveaux essais* (IV, chap. 16, § 12), which prevails for the totality of our world: "Things ascend upwards in degrees of perfection. 'Tis an hard matter to say where the sensible and the rational begin. . . . It is like the way quantity augments or lessens in a 'regular' cone" [Remnant/Bennett, 471].

6. On the formation of an infinite universe that has lost its center, and of the role that Giordano Bruno plays in its articulation, see Alexandre Koyré *From the Closed World to the Infinite Universe* (New York: Harper, 1958). Michel Serres demonstrates that a new unity becomes manifest when the summit of a cone is placed at the center of a sphere (*Le système de Leibniz,* II, 653–57). Yves Bonnefoy has studied the complex position of the theater in the theme of the Baroque: neither illusion nor renewed awareness, but using illusion in order to produce one's being, to construct a site of hallucinatory Presence, or "reconverting nothingness glimpsed in presence," since God surely made the world out of nothing. Such is what Bonnefoy calls "the movement of interiority," in *Rome 1630* (Paris: Flammarion, 1970).

7. Benjamin, "Allegory and Trauerspiel," in *The Origins of German Baroque Drama,* trans. John Osborne (London: Verso, 1985). See also Hocquenghem and Scherer, "Pourquoi nous sommes allégoriques," and "Pourquoi nous restons baroques," in *L'âme atomique* (Paris: Albin Michel, 1986).

8. Many seventeenth-century authors (notably Tesauro) attempt to distinguish devices ("imprese") from emblems. The former would refer to an individual, while the latter would express a moral truth and gain the privilege of being developed in cycles. But we all know that the distinction is abstract, and that personal reference does not disappear. Even if it is blurred, a pertinence is evident. See especially Cornelia Kemp, "Cycles d'emblèmes dans les églises de l'Allemagne du Sud au XVIIIe siècle," and Friedhelm Kemp, "Figuration et inscription," in *Figures du Baroque* (Paris: PUF, 1983). Cornelia Kemp cites an especially interesting example in the Saint Leonard cycle in Apfeltrach: the proper name contains a double propositional concept ("leo" + "nardus") that inspires the two parts of the cycles of images.

9. Vanuxem, "Le Baroque au Piémont," in *Renaissance, Maniérisme, Baroque* (Paris: Vrin, 1972), 295.

10. "To reinforce the distinction between essence and definition, bear in mind that although a thing has only one essence, this can be expressed by several definitions, just as the same structure or the same town can be represented by different drawings in perspective depending on the direction from which it is viewed," in the *Nouveaux essais,* III, chap. 3, § 15 [Remnant/Bennett, 294]. We should recall that if the point of view is said to vary with each scenography, it does so only by convenience of expression. In truth, point of view is the condition in which "scenographies" or drawings in perspective form a series.

11. "The ichnographic chart of the Universe, the relation of all-to-one and one-to-all is the systematic theme of Leibnizianism and of this work," Serres, II, 620.

12. Cf. *Théodicée,* § 416. Christiane Frémont has shown in what way the story of Sextus is a "founding narrative" of the Roman empire, in "Trois fictions sur le problème du mal," in *René Girard et le problème du mal* (Paris: Grasset, 1982).

13. *Principes de la Nature et de la Grâce,* § 17 [Parkinson, 203–4].

14. *Eléments de la piété véritable* (Grua, 12). Yvon Belaval, it must be noted, does not believe that Leibnizian harmony attests to a particularly musical inspiration, in *Etudes Leibniziennes* (Paris: Gallimard, 1976), 86. And when he confronts Leibniz with musical forces, he thinks of a modern "algorithmic music" (381), and not of Baroque music of Leibniz's time.

15. *Eléments de philosophie cachée,* J, 35–36. (The text of the *Eléments de la piété* offers

an analogous movement.) Nicolas de Cusa's writing is the *Dialogue sur la pensée,* chap. 6: "There can be only one infinite principle, and that one alone is infinitely simple," in *Oeuvres choisies,* ed. Maurice de Gandillac (Paris: Aubier-Montaigne, 1941), 274–76.

16. For Nicolas of Cusa, the irrational number is the "most simple" because it must itself be odd and even, instead of being composed of an odd and an even. But, according to Leibniz, it happens that the irrational envelops an infinite series of rational finite numbers, in the form of inverse numbers:

$$\frac{1}{1} - \frac{1}{3} + \frac{1}{5} - \frac{1}{7} \cdot \ldots$$

In *Nouveaux essais,* IV, chap. 3, § 6 [Remnant/Bennett, 376–77]; and also *De la vraie proportion du cercle au carré circonscrit* (GM, V, 118–22). Harmony refers to this type of series.

17. On the harmonic triangle of number, see the *Histoire et origine du calcul différentiel* (GM, V, 396–406), and the *Nouvelle avancée de l'algèbre* (VII, 175): the base of the triangle is no longer the succession of natural numbers, but the series of inverse numbers

$$\frac{1}{1}, \frac{1}{2}, \frac{1}{3}, \ldots$$

Serres has studied the characters and laws of the harmonic triangle, and has demonstrated the extent of its importance in theory of harmony (I, 186–92 and II, 448–77, on the relations with music). For the harmonic circulation of the planets, and the law of the proposition inverse to squares, by which Leibniz integrates Newtonian gravitation, see the *Essai sur les causes des mouvements célestes* (GM, VI); and Koyré, *Etudes newtoniennes* (Paris: Gallimard, 1968), 166–79.

18. "This mutual relationship of different substances . . . is one of the strongest proofs of God's existence, or of a common cause that every effect must always express according to its point of view and its ability," in his letter to Arnauld (September 1687), GPh, II, 115 [Mason, 147–48 (9 October 1687)].

19. *Considérations sur la doctrine d'un Esprit universel unique,* GPh, VI, 535. [In French the relation of spirit, breath, or breeze is clearly marked in the presence of the Latin *spiritus* (breath) in *esprit* (spirit, wit, mental capacity, etc. —Trans.]

20. Abraham Robinson, *Non-Standard Analysis,* Amsterdam: North Holland, 1966.

21. Letter to Arnauld (April 1687) [Mason, 113].

22. [The text plays on *accord* as linkage, entente, agreement, but also on its meaning, in music, as chord. As in *Logique du sens,* amphiboly plays throughout the logic of the discussion. —Trans.]

23. On the conciliation of the little elements of disquiet with the bonds of felicity, and the infinite progression that follows, see the *Nouveaux essais,* II, chap. 21, § 36 [Remnant/Bennett, 188–90]; *Profession de foi du philosophe,* ed. Belaval (Paris: Vrin, 1961), 87. For the "harmonic" character of felicity, see 31–33.

24. The minute solicitations of disquiet are not already located in pain or in suffering, but they can be integrated in pain. See the *Nouveaux essais,* II, chap. 20, § 6. Dissonance of pain must be prepared: chap. 21, end of § 36 ("So it is all a matter of 'Think about it carefully' and 'Remember' " [Remnant/Bennett, 189–90]. On the example of the dog, cf. *L'éclaircissement des difficultés que M. Bayle a trouvées dans le système nouveau de l'âme et du corps* (GPh, IV, 532).

25. On the active resolution of dissonance, see the *Profession de foi,* 45, 89, 93.

26. On the situation of the damned, and the way that they are inversely symmetrical to the "blessed," see the *Profession de foi,* 85.

27. *Eclaircissement des difficultés* (GPh, IV, 549). We should note how Raymond Ruyer emphasizes the vertical position of the monads or authentic forms.

28. Correspondence with Clarke, fifth writing, § 91. And in the letter to Wagner, March 1698 (Grua, 395): "sunt monades, non monachae." Cf. André Robinet, *Architectonique* (Paris: Vrin, 1986), 361.

29. Dynamics "do not at all imply something more than a simple coordination of inner spontaneities, that is, preestablished harmony," notes Gueroult, *Dynamique et métaphysique leibniziennes* (Paris: Belles Lettres, 1934), 176.

30. Letter to Arnauld (April 1687) [Mason, 119].

31. On the examples of the boat, of pain, and voluntary movement, see the draft, and then the letter to Arnauld (November 1686) [Mason, 84–85]. Following the case, "distinct expression" of a substance will be said to "be increased" (action) or to "be diminished" (passion). See the *Discours de métaphysique*, § 15.

32. "My hand moves not because I will it to do so . . . but because I could not will it with success: except at the precise moment that the elasticity is about to slacken in the requisite way to achieve this result. . . . They go with one another, by virtue of the relationship established above, but each has its immediate cause in itself," in a letter to Arnauld (September 1687) [Mason, 149 (October 9, 1687)]. "And a soul effects no change in the course of thoughts of another soul. And in general one particular substance has no physical influence over another," in the draft of a letter to Arnauld (November 1686) [Mason, 87].

33. See Manfred Bukofzer, *Histoire de la musique baroque, 1600–1750* (Paris: Lattès, 1982), 242–44, 390–391. On the appearance of a continuous bass, its relation with harmony, tonality, and a new counterpoint, see Leo Schrade's *Monteverdi* (Lattès), and Pascale Criton's forthcoming study.

34. Uexküll has made a great, highly Leibnizian review of Nature as a melody: "Théorie de la signification," in *Mondes animaux et monde humain* (Paris: Gonthier). For "living tonalities" see 103; and for melodies and motifs: "The flower acts on the bee like a sum of counterpoints because its melodies of development—so rich in motifs—have influenced the morphogenesis of the bee, and inversely. . . . I could affirm that all of nature participates like a motif in the formation of my physical and spiritual personality, for if such were not the case, I would not possess organs in order to familiarize myself with nature" (145–46).

35. *Eléments de philosophie cachée*: "The mark of [harmonic] existence is the fact that the senses conform to each other." The quotation from Uexküll above resembles the commentary of this formula.

36. On most of these points, see Bukofzer, especially chap. 1, and the comparative review of the Renaissance and the Baroque (24). Rameau's *Observation sur notre instinct pour la musique et sur son principe* of 1754 (recently reprinted by Slatkine) might be considered as the manifesto of the Baroque and—with its emphasis on the expressive value of accords—the primacy of harmony. Jean-Jacques Rousseau's position, which is frequently misunderstood, is quite interesting because it is resolutely and willfully retrograde. For Rousseau decadence does not begin with harmony of accords and their pretension of being "expressive," but already with polyphony and counterpoint. Rousseau feels that we must return to monody as pure melody alone, that is, a pure line of vocal *inflection* that rightfully precedes polyphony and harmony. The only natural harmony is unison. Decadence begins when, under the influence of the barbaric North, voices become "inflexible," when they lose their inflections for the sake of firm articulations. See Rousseau, *Essai sur l'origine des langues* (Paris: Bibliothèque du graphe, 1979), chaps. 14 and 19. It can be noted that for Leibniz too (and probably for Rameau), harmony and melody always presuppose a line of infinite inflection; yet harmony and melody convey it adequately, and the line cannot exist without them, the line being in itself "virtual."

37. On the evolution of the relation of harmony and melody, and on the formation of a "diagonal," see Pierre Boulez, *Relevés d'apprenti* (Paris: Seuil, 1967), 281–93. And for point of view over the city, *Par volonté et par hasard* (Paris: Seuil, 1975), 106–7. Among the critics of Boulez's *Pli selon pli* (London: Universal Editions, 1982), Ivanka Stoïanova is especially attached to the way that Mallarmé's texts are folded, in accord with new relations of text and music, in *Geste texte musique* (Paris: Union générale d'éditions 10/18, 1978). See also Jehanne Dautrey, *La voix dans la musique contemporaine* (Wyres: Van den Velde, 1987). The expression "fold-in" is borrowed from Gysin and Burroughs, who designate thus a method of textual folding, in extension with the "cut-up." (In the same way Carl Andre defines his sculptures as cuttings or folds in space.)

Index

Compiled by Hassan Melehy